Principles and Practices for Effective Teacher Evaluation

Jerry W. Valentine
University of Missouri—Columbia

Allyn and Bacon
Boston London Toronto Sydney Tokyo Singapore

Copyright © 1992 by Allyn and Bacon
A Division of Simon & Schuster, Inc.
160 Gould Street
Needham Heights, Massachusetts 02194

Library of Congress Cataloging-in-Publication Data

Valentine, Jerry.
   Principles and practices for effective teacher evaluation / Jerry
W. Valentine.
     p. cm.
   Includes bibliographical references and index.
   ISBN 0-205-13138-7
   1. Teachers—United States—Rating of. I. Title.
LB2838.V25   1992
371.1'44—dc20
                                   91–17258
                                       CIP

Printed in the United States of America

10 9 8 7 6 5 4 3 2 1 95 94 93 92 91

This book is dedicated to my parents and the thousands of other parents like them who gave so much of themselves so their children might appreciate the value of education.

Contents

Preface

IN THE SPRING OF 1990 I completed a study of teacher evaluation practices in each of the fifty states. At that time, formal evaluation of teachers was required in 82 percent of the states. Specific evaluative practices were required in 48 percent of the states and recommended in another 10 percent. Few states, and few school systems, left teacher evaluation to chance.

The trend in recent years has been to require not only that evaluation take place, but that specific evaluative procedures be used. In my twenty years as an assistant principal, professor, and consultant, I have seen a shift in emphasis from the traditional "summative-judgmental evaluation for employment decision making" to a "formative-developmental emphasis on personnel growth." School district leaders are realizing the value of a formative approach to evaluation over a summative approach. At the same time, they recognize the need to have the data to make and defend difficult summative decisions. Of the varied strategies for evaluation that I have studied and worked with, the one that I believe has the greatest promise for promoting development of teachers without sacrificing the necessary data for employment decisions is an approach I have labeled *performance-based developmental evaluation.*

This book is about the specific practices used in performance-based developmental evaluation of teachers and the evaluative principles on which that approach and other effective evaluative approaches are based. With the help of teachers, principals, superintendents, graduate students, other professors, and personnel from state departments of education and teacher and administrator professional associations, I have studied the principles and strategies presented in the performance-based developmental teacher evaluation approach. After analyzing these practices in school systems across the country, I am confident that they represent a step in the right direction for evaluation. We must move our thinking from summative to formative evaluation in a manner that promotes trust and confidence, not mistrust and resentment.

The book was written for graduate students and practicing educators studying teacher evaluation. For practicing teachers, principals, or superintendents, the broad discussion of the culture and climate for evaluation, as well as the specific strategies for developing and implementing a system, can serve as a guide to the development or refinement of an evaluation system in their school district.

For those same teachers, principals, or superintendents serving as graduate students in administrator preparation programs, the book can provide the necessary background for understanding various evaluative strategies and the responsibilities of principals to implement those strategies. It can serve as a primary resource for specific graduate coursework in teacher evaluation or as a supplemental resource for courses on the principalship or supervision. Given the increasing demand for principals to spend time in the classroom working with teachers to improve instruction, chapters 3 through 7 should be of particular value in the teaching of specific administrative skills designed to improve instruction.

ACKNOWLEDGMENTS

The study and development of effective evaluation practices require the efforts of many people. Numerous graduate students have given of their time and effort to work with me in the study of teacher evaluation. Of particular importance were studies by Charles Brown, James Davis, Gary Drummond, Nicholas Ginos, Lynne Moore, and Deborah Pulliam. Also important were the efforts of Turner Tyson of the Missouri Department of Education and Brenda Glover of the Kentucky Department of Education. Their leadership in evaluation in those states and their efforts to ensure effective inservice programs for all administrators in their states provided us with fertile ground from which to study effective practices.

To the hundreds of educators who have served on evaluation committees from the scores of districts with which I have worked, I am especially grateful. Of particular assistance were the teachers and administrators from the Missouri school districts of Blue Springs (Kansas City), Carthage, Center (Kansas City), Excelsior Springs Ferguson-Florissant (St. Louis), Hannibal, Jefferson City, Joplin, Liberty (Kansas City), Ritenour (St. Louis), Rolla, Sedalia, Springfield, and St. Joseph. Outside Missouri, the thoughts and efforts of educators in Columbus, Nebraska; Jackson, Mississippi; Lansdale, Pennsylvania; and Beloit, Wisconsin, were also particularly helpful. Personnel from those districts took basic evaluative principles and transformed them into effective practices for teachers and administrators.

For the chapters on evaluation of coaches and sponsors, personnel from the Missouri High School Activities Association and the school districts of Columbia, Parkway (St. Louis), Clayton (St. Louis), and Independence (Kansas City), Missouri, and Fort Collins, Colorado, provided valuable information. For the section on special education teachers, Dennis Buhr of the Special School District of St. Louis County and Arthur Allen of the Jefferson City, Missouri, schools were especially helpful.

The reference notes provided throughout this book do not adequately express the value of certain scholars who are well known for their contributions to education. Of particular value to me were the writings of George Redfern, Dale Bolton, Richard Manatt, James Sweeney, Ben Harris, Kenneth McIntyre, Tom McGreal, Tom Sergiovanni, and Carl Glickman. All have made significant contributions to the field and to my personal thinking about evaluation as a developmental process. Also shaping my thinking was Al Seagren, a professor and administrator at the University of Nebraska. He has been a mentor, a friend, and a role model—always challenging yet understanding, demanding yet compassionate.

Several persons who did not contribute directly to the book helped make my study of evaluation and the preparation of this book possible. I appreciate the patience and understanding of my colleagues at the University of Missouri, our office staff, our graduate students, and the educators across the state and country who were often inconvenienced because I was out of the office developing or studying evaluation programs. Particular appreciation is expressed to Roger Harting, chair of the Department of Educational Administration, and to Wilbur Miller, Dean of the College of Education. Both invested their time and effort to give me the time necessary to analyze evaluation practices and prepare this book. I also want to thank Michael Bowman and James Sweeney for reviewing the manuscript.

Finally, special appreciation goes to my wife, Diane, and our sons, Matthew, Scott, and Daniel, for their understanding and encouragement when my hours on the book were long and our time together as a family was short.

Jerry W. Valentine

CHAPTER 1

A Perspective

Treat people as if they were what they ought to be and you help them become what they are capable of being.
—Johann W. von Goethe

THE ULTIMATE GOAL in education should be to provide the best quality educational experiences for all students. Each process implemented in a school district should contribute toward accomplishing that goal. For an evaluation system to contribute to that goal, it must promote the professional improvement of each staff member and, when necessary, provide data to remove a teacher whose presence in the profession is detrimental to students.

Implementing an evaluation system that improves personnel performance and removes incompetent teachers without creating a climate of mistrust and malcontent is one of the most elusive tasks in education. Teachers generally resent the need to be reviewed through a process they view as punitive. Principals become frustrated with evaluative procedures that have a negative impact on school climate. Superintendents are frustrated with efforts to demonstrate accountability through ineffective procedures. School district trustees anxiously assure the community of the competence of all staff, even though their involvement with the evaluation process is infrequent.

Compounding the frustrations are state legislative mandates requiring evaluation and often stipulating specific procedures. In the aftermath of the numerous educational reform studies of the early and mid-1980s, educators and policymakers across the United States established procedures for assessing and refining educational programs. Systemwide focus on school effectiveness and teacher effectiveness became commonplace, with teacher evaluation programs a frequent target for review and change.

By 1990, educators in 41 states were required to evaluate teachers.

1

Of those states, educators in 34 were required to do so because of state legislation, 30 because of state department of education policy, and 5 because of litigation. Of the 41 states, 24 "mandated" that specific evaluative procedures and/or forms be used, 7 "suggested" specific procedures and/or forms, and 10 neither required nor suggested specific procedures or forms (Valentine, 1990; see Appendix A).

The negative attitudes and frustrations so often associated with teacher evaluation, especially mandated evaluation, are more prevalent than need be. As with many issues, the knowledge base necessary to implement effective evaluative systems exceeds the practices employed in most school districts. Given the "educational knowledge explosion" of the 1970s and 1980s about effective teaching, schooling, and instructional leadership, this "implementation lag" is understandable.

This book presents evaluation principles and practices that contribute to the ultimate goal of enriching the educational experiences of students. There is no panacea, no magic formula, and no definitive evaluation system or model. There are, however, some basic principles and essential practices for implementing those principles that make a difference in most schools. Each principle is enumerated and highlighted as it appears in the appropriate sections of the book. All of the principles are listed and reviewed briefly in the final chapter.

The practices suggested in this book have been used effectively for many years in schools across the country. Those practices have been combined into an evaluative process labeled *performance-based developmental evaluation* (PBDE). In essence, this book is about performance-based developmental evaluation and the manner in which the process incorporates each of the evaluative principles discussed into practical strategies for effective evaluation.

DEVELOPMENTAL PHILOSOPHY

The evaluation principles presented in this book are based on the belief that effective teacher evaluation includes procedures that emphasize personnel development and deemphasize personnel employment decisions. The importance of this developmental philosophy is supported by several authors, including Wise, Darling-Hammond, McLaughlin, and Bernstein (1984), Harris (1986), and McLaughlin and Pfeifer (1988). The developmental philosophy is also supported by findings of evaluative studies presented throughout this book and by experiences in hundreds of school districts in the development, refinement, and assessment of performance-based developmental evaluation practices.

A schema depicting the basic philosophy of performance evaluation as a developmental process is presented in Figure 1.1. PBDE is a function of the principal's role as instructional leader and the teacher's role as instructor. The primary purpose of the process is to improve the teacher's performance. The secondary purpose, and a natural out-

FIGURE 1.1   Developmental evaluation schema.

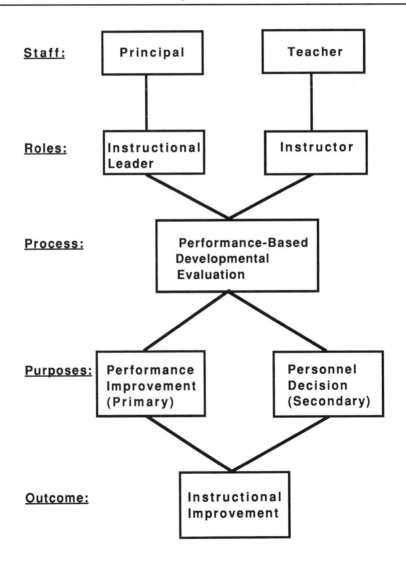

growth of the procedures associated with the primary purpose, is to help in making decisions about employment, promotion, and incentives. The desired outcome of the evaluation process is educational improvement for students, especially instructional improvement.

Personnel evaluation is an integral part of the operational procedures of nearly every school district in the country (Educational Research Services, 1978; Valentine, 1990). Building a detailed rationale for teacher evaluation is not necessary. In recent years, writers have effectively described the "problems" of evaluation (McLaughlin & Pfeifer, 1988), the "need" for evaluation (Harris, 1986), and the most common purposes of evaluation (Bolton, 1973). McGreal (1983) began his book *Successful Teacher Evaluation* by stating, "There seems little need to offer an extensive justification for the existence of teacher evaluation. Among educators it is, in fact, one of the few areas in which there is some agreement." Clearly, then, educators agree that evaluation must take place. And just as clearly, reasons for teacher evaluation cluster in two areas: improvement of teacher performance and effective personnel decision making. Both of these reasons support the overriding purpose of evaluation—enhancement of the learning experiences for students.

DEFINING PERFORMANCE-BASED DEVELOPMENTAL EVALUATION

An operational definition of PBDE provides an important reference for understanding the principles and practices described in this book. Following is a definition of performance-based developmental teacher evaluation and a brief discussion of the elements in the definition. An outline of the definition is provided in Figure 1.2.

Performance-based developmental evaluation (PBDE) is a process for professional improvement that includes identifying performance expectations, documenting performance, conferencing about performance, developing plans to improve performance, and making personnel decisions based on performance.

The outline of this definition presented in Figure 1.2 distinguishes the *formative evaluation phase* from the more traditional *summative evaluation phase.* The first four components represent formative, or developmental, evaluation. These components should account for approximately 95 percent of the time and energy invested in performance evaluation. The fifth component, decision making, is the portion of the definition historically associated with evaluation. In too many school districts, it is the only component of the process. Even in districts that require formative procedures such as classroom observations and postobservation conferencing, if a summative evaluation is completed after each observation, the philosophy that evaluation is summative and judgmental is reinforced in the minds of teachers. The decision-making, summative component should use as little time and energy as possible. The more obviously an evaluation system focuses on the summative phase, the more negative will be the teachers' perceptions of evaluation and the less impact the process will have on the overall goal of instructional improvement.

The statement that PBDE is "a process for professional improve-

FIGURE 1.2   Performance-based developmental teacher evaluation:
A definition.

Performance-Based   Developmental   Teacher   Evaluation

is a

process for professional improvement

which includes:

Formative Phase (95%)

(1) identifying   performance   expectations;

(2) documenting   performance;

(3) conferencing   about   performance;

(4) developing   plans   to   improve   performance;   and

Summative Phase (5%)

(5) making   personnel   decisions   based   upon   performance.

ment" succinctly describes the philosophy of evaluation as presented in this book. Performance-based developmental evaluation is an ongoing process designed to improve a teacher's professional skills. This professional improvement is accomplished by effectively implementing each of the five components listed in the definition. Initially, the supervisor must identify and clarify the expectations of performance. The expectations are the standards that define effective teaching in the given district. These expectations, typically referred to as *criteria*, are identified during the development of the evaluation system and become the common focus for each step in the evaluation process. Performance criteria and related descriptors are discussed in Chapter 3.

After clarifying expectations, the supervisor must collect data about performance. The data collection process must promote fairness, consistency, objectivity, and accuracy. Data are collected in two distinct ways. Some data are collected purposefully and are described as *planned data*. Other data come to the principal's attention without being purposefully collected; these are categorized as *unplanned data*. Both categories of data can be divided into three types: *observed data*, *nonobserved data*, and *artifact data*. The types of data and suggested procedures for collecting and recording them are detailed in chapters 5 and 6.

The formative conference is the key to improvement. Conducting an effective conference requires an understanding of personnel motivation, the use of effective interpersonal skills, a knowledge of effective teaching behavior, and a data base upon which to structure the conference. Basic conferencing strategies are discussed in Chapter 7.

Providing an opportunity for improvement is essential to the overall philosophy of development, rather than judgment. Each staff member should be cognizant of his or her abilities and work toward becoming as good a teacher as possible. The formal vehicle for promoting this improvement is referred to in this book as a Professional Development Plan. When all staff, regardless of teaching ability, work toward improvement through a formal process, the philosophy of performance evaluation as an ongoing system for professional improvement is reinforced. When only those teachers who are obviously deficient in specific skills work toward improvement through a formal process, the belief that performance evaluation is a process that focuses on negatives and weaknesses in order to support employment decisions is reinforced. The Professional Development Plan is a critical link between the formative and summative evaluation phases. Chapter 8 includes suggestions for writing and implementing Professional Development Plans.

Most evaluation systems conclude with a decision-making, contractual phase. The document completed during the phase is typically referred to as a Summative Evaluation Report. The summative report is a synthesis of all data collected and discussed during the formative phase. Various approaches to summative evaluation are presented in Chapter 9, including a discussion of the important concept of linking the summative phase with the formative phase.

The manner in which each component of PBDE is implemented directly affects the degree to which the evaluation process is perceived as, and thus becomes, developmental or judgmental. In evaluation, the perceptions of the key actors—teachers and administrators—are reality. The best intentions are not adequate if the process used to implement the intentions does not reinforce those intentions. This book was written to stimulate thinking about the most effective procedures for accomplishing the goal of professional improvement. Evaluation is not an us-versus-them process. It is a *we* process. The more the process promotes "we" thinking by everyone, the greater the chances the evaluation system will make a difference for teachers, and thus for students.

TERMINOLOGY

A common language is essential to the understanding of any complex process. This is particularly true in the study of evaluation because each writer may use a different term to describe the same concept. Following are explanations of the most important terms as they are used throughout this book to describe performance-based developmental evaluation.

The **formative phase** includes the most critical processes in PBDE. The formative phase is the ongoing process of documentation, conferencing, and growth. It is the "developmental" phase of the evaluation system.

The **summative phase** is the decision-making process. Completion of the Summative Evaluation Report, the summative conference, and decisions about employment are activities typically associated with this phase.

Criteria are the performance expectations of the teacher. These job-related expectations should be based on studies of effective teaching and effective schooling. The criteria represent the standards of performance for teachers throughout the school district. They are the consistent content for each component of the evaluation process. For example, data are analyzed on the basis of the performance criteria, conferences are conducted using the criteria, development plans are written to improve performance on the criteria, and the summative judgments are made for each criterion.

Descriptors are phrases that help to communicate the meaning of a criterion. The descriptors represent specific behaviors often associated with the expected performance described by the criterion. They are a listing of behaviors, but not an all-inclusive listing. Descriptors do not stand on their own; they are not the basis for any component or any specific form used in the evaluation system. Teachers are not held accountable for performing descriptors. They are held accountable for the more significant performance described by the criterion.

Performance areas are groupings of similar criteria. They do not represent expectations but are simply logical groupings that enable the user to locate criteria quickly. They convey a general area of responsibility but do not serve as a basis for evaluation. For example, all criteria associated with classroom instruction might be grouped under the performance area of "instructional process."

The five terms listed here are basic to understanding performance-based developmental evaluation. Each term is discussed in greater detail in other chapters.

EVALUATIVE CULTURE AND CLIMATE

The terms *culture* and *climate* are used frequently and with varied meanings in educational and organizational literature. Understanding the relationships between these two concepts and developmental evaluation is important to the development and implementation of an effective PBDE system.

Culture is to an organization what *personality* is to a human being. Culture is the personality of the school district reflected through the values and beliefs of the members of the organization. It defines the mission and goals of the organization and establishes the beliefs held in highest esteem within the district. Culture is more than a district's catchy slogan, it is the mind set of the members of the organization when they are asked to describe the basic purpose of the district and the beliefs on which that purpose is built. The culture is an intangible, pervasive presence of being that is felt by members of the organization.

Climate is to an organization what *attitude* is to a human being. Climate is the attitude of the school district reflected through the feelings and perceptions of the members of the organization. It is a description of life in the organization. Climate is an intangible, pervasive presence of mind that is felt by members of the organization. It is, to a large degree, a product of the culture of the organization.

The behaviors of personnel within an organization are products of the culture and climate of the organization. When a school district's culture is characterized by a belief in excellence for all students and in fair treatment of all personnel, and the climate is characterized by feelings of trust and commitment, the behavior of personnel in the organization will generally be congruent with those beliefs and feelings.

A Symbiotic Relationship

Teacher evaluation is affected when the beliefs and attitudes within the organization inhibit the development and implementation of the evaluative system. For example, when the perceived behavioral role of a principal is to manage rather than to be an instructional leader, an accepted pattern of "that's the way we do things around here" prevails. A strictly managerial role for the principal is incongruent with developmental evaluation.

Another example is the master contract between the teacher association and school management. Language in the contract may prevent the implementation of an effective evaluative system by dictating procedures that are inconsistent with developmental evaluation. Still another example may be found in the history of relationships between teachers and management of the school system. Climates with strained relationships, cultivated through years of lack of communication and mistrust, are damning to the success of developmental evaluation.

> **Principle 1**
> **Climate, culture and developmental evaluation are interdependent.**

An evaluation process has an impact on the climate and culture of a school or district, just as the climate and culture have an impact on the evaluation process. A well-conceived and effectively implemented developmental approach establishes a belief in and commitment to personnel improvement because such improvement affects the education of students. The developmental process promotes better communication and builds trust and positive relationships between administrators and teachers. Those results in turn promote a positive climate and culture. They are the products of good symbiotic relationships among culture, climate, and performance-based developmental evaluation.

Leadership Commitment

The superintendent plays a vital role in the success or failure of the evaluative system of a school district. Although the superintendent is seldom involved directly in the process, his or her attitude toward evaluation affects the district's climate for evaluation. Through policies, procedures, and a myriad of behaviors, the superintendent builds an important foundation for all staff members' attitudes toward and perceptions of evaluation.

The culture of the school district is established by previous and present leaders and often reestablished by new leaders. Every school district, every organization, has a culture. As Deal and Kennedy (1982, p. 4) explain, "Sometimes it is fragmented and difficult to read from the outside . . . sometimes it is strong and cohesive. Whether weak or strong, culture has a powerful effect on the organization; it affects practically everything."

If the personality (culture) of the organization is in opposition to the philosophical tenets of developmental evaluation, the process will not be successful. The evaluative system will become another of the many tasks in which personnel merely go through the motions. The culture enables effective evaluation to take place when the focus of the culture is congruent with the purposes of the evaluative system.

The effectiveness of any major change in the organization, particularly the implementation of a new evaluative system, depends directly on the support of the organization's leadership. The superintendent *must* envision the worth of the new evaluative system, articulate that worth to personnel and patrons, and commit the resources necessary to develop and implement the system. Improvement through developmental teacher evaluation will not occur unless the superintendent actively, not passively, supports the concept.

Principle 2
District leadership is committed to developmental evaluation.

The effective leader understands the difference between commitment to developing and implementing a new process, and mandating a particular process. Through words and actions, the superintendent's message to all personnel is that "evaluation will make a positive contribution to the quality of education for the students in our school system." The message makes clear that "all parties affected by the evaluation system will share equally in the development of the system, not rubber stamp a system already selected by the administration. Teachers and principals will work together to achieve the common goal of educational excellence, using developmental evaluation as a major vehicle to accomplish that goal."

As any conscientious sophomore English student could explain, personification is the giving of lifelike characteristics to inanimate objects. In this section culture and climate were, in a literary sense, personified. Ascribed to them were values, beliefs, attitudes, and perceptions. But in a practical, educational sense, culture and climate are very real. They clearly reflect the thinking of those inside and outside the organization. Attentiveness to these issues is imperative if evaluation is to have a positive impact on the instructional program of the district.

READINESS FOR CHANGE

Organizational change is defined by Owens and Steinhoff (1976, p. 32) as "a planned, systematic, controlled effort to alter more than one of the following aspects of the organization: (1) its tasks, (2) its structure, (3) its technology, or (4) its participants in ways thought to be more effective in achieving the organization's goals." They contrast organizational change to organizational drift by noting that change "includes a significant level of deliberateness." The development and implementation of a new evaluation system should be a process of change, not drift. Personnel evaluation affects and is affected by most other aspects of the organization. Its development and implementation should represent a planned, systematic, controlled effort to improve the organization.

The events that lead to a change in an evaluative system are usually the result of (1) new organizational goals, (2) new organizational leadership, (3) problems with the current system, and/or (4) external mandates. The leadership of the district must recognize these causal events and identify the procedures for developing a new or refined evaluation system. Some form of assessment is usually the starting point, except where the need for change has been superseded by mandate.

The readiness of the organization for the change is not always apparent, nor does the district leadership always have the luxury of making change when readiness exists. A needs assessment may help determine readiness as well as need, but it is of minimal use when the change has been mandated or when the problems with the current system are so severe that a change is a must. In a study of four major school districts that implemented sophisticated evaluative systems, McLaughlin and Pfeifer (1988, p. 16) found that "some kind of event jolted actors and policy in each district and began the organizational process of unfreezing the 'environment' in preparation for serious consideration of teacher evaluation." Neither the events that precipitate a change nor the readiness of the organization for a change can always be planned.

The astute leader assesses the organization's readiness and proceeds accordingly. There is no patented answer to the question of how to proceed. With mandated change, there is no choice. When the assessment indicates need and readiness, the decision is easy. When events in the organization precipitate readiness, the decision is easy. But when the assessment indicates need without readiness, the decision is difficult.

Principle 3
Teachers and administrators
demonstrate a readiness for change.

SUMMARY

The basic purposes of any evaluation system should be evident to the people affected by that system. At times, those purposes may appear to be in conflict. Improving instruction, increasing student learning, reinforcing superior performance, validating the selection process, and meeting state standards too often appear incongruent to members of the organization. But these "developmental" and "managerial" purposes need not be at odds. The leadership of the district must understand the current culture and climate and assess readiness for change. If change is needed, the evaluation committee and the leadership of the school district must determine the focus of the evaluation system. That focus must be shared with all teachers through verbal and written explanations of the procedures purposefully built into the evaluation system to address the goals of the system.

Performance-based developmental evaluation is based on the belief that evaluation is primarily a process for personnel improvement, and only secondarily a process for personnel decision making. Readers committed to the concept that evaluation is a personnel management process, not a personnel development process, will find that this book challenges their basic beliefs about evaluation. Readers committed to instructional improvement through personnel development will find their beliefs reinforced by the discussions of these **principles and practices that make a difference.**

REFERENCES

Bolton, D. L. (1973). *Selection and evaluation of teachers.* Berkeley, CA: McCutchan.

Deal, T. E., & Kennedy, A. A. (1982). *Corporate cultures: The rites and rituals of corporate life.* Reading, MA: Addison-Wesley.

Educational Research Services, Inc. (1978). *Evaluating teacher performance.* Arlington, VA: Educational Research Services.

Harris, B. M. (1986). *Developmental teacher evaluation.* Boston: Allyn and Bacon.

McGreal, T. L. (1983). *Successful teacher evaluation.* Alexandria, VA: Association for Supervision and Curriculum Development.

McLaughlin, M. W., & Pfeifer, R. S. (1988). *Teacher evaluation: improvement, accountability, and effective learning.* New York: Teachers College Press.

Owens, R. G., & Steinhoff, C. R. (1976). *Administering change in schools.* Englewood Cliffs, NJ: Prentice-Hall.

Valentine, J. W. (1990). *A national survey of state teacher evaluation policies.* Unpublished report, University of Missouri, Department of Educational Administration, Columbia, Missouri. (See Appendix A.)

Wise, A. E., Darling-Hammond, L., McLaughlin, M. W., & Bernstein, H. T. (1984). *Teacher evaluation: A study of effective practices.* Santa Monica, CA: Rand Corporation.

CHAPTER 2

Developing the Evaluation System

I know of no more encouraging fact than the unquestionable ability of man to elevate his life by a conscious endeavor.
—Henry David Thoreau

THE DECISION WHETHER OR NOT to develop a new evaluation process, refine an existing process, or leave the current process unchanged usually rests with the superintendent. This decision is based on the organization's readiness for change, the commitment of the school district's leadership to change, and an assessment of whether the current evaluation system is effectively meeting the educational goals of the school district.

Once the decision to make a change has been made, the superintendent and central office staff must determine the procedures to be used to make the change. Is the process to be developed by the administrative staff of the district or by committee? If by committee, who is represented, how are they selected, how many members should there be? After a process has been drafted, should all personnel have the opportunity to provide input about the draft before it is sent to the school board for action? Will a consultant be used? If so, in what manner? What should be the time line for completion and implementation? When and how will inservice be provided? What procedures should be considered to make the evaluative system more developmental than judgmental? The remainder of this chapter addresses these and other questions associated with developing an evaluative system.

PARTICIPATORY DEVELOPMENT

For change to be effective and lasting, personnel affected by the change must have input into the development, refinement, and implementation of the change. They must understand and support the philosophical basis of the change and be able to envision the positive effects of the change. Participatory development is crucial. Without participatory development, the change, regardless of how appropriate, will not provide the optimum results over a period of years.

> **Principle 4**
> Those affected are involved in developing, implementing and evaluating the system.

A District Evaluation Committee is the structure commonly recommended for the development of an effective evaluation system (Valentine & Harting, 1988). Following is a typical listing of committee tasks.

1. *Review and discuss current literature on effective teaching, effective schooling, and effective evaluation:* The evaluation process should be constructed on a foundation of valid expectations (criteria). Because the committee defines effective teaching through the criteria, the committee members should know and understand the "effective teaching" and "effective schooling" literature. Because the criteria must be applied through an evaluation system that will produce positive results, the literature on teacher evaluation should also be studied.

> **Principle 5**
> System developers study effective teaching, schooling and evaluation.

2. *Review and discuss evaluation models used in other school systems and states:* Evaluation systems may be designed for varied purposes (Bolton, 1973). The evaluative components the committee incorporates into the system dictate the potential outcomes from the system and thus should match the system's basic purposes. The purposes are usually clarified for the committee by the superintendent. The committee should consider those purposes and design a system to meet them. The opportunity to review evaluation models is beneficial as long as the committee members understand the importance of developing a sys-

tem that meets the unique needs of their school district rather than copying verbatim a model from another district.

3. *During the development of the system, utilize a resource person:* Relatively few districts utilize a resource person in conceptualizing and designing their evaluation systems. Those who do quickly realize that a good resource person provides expertise not available in most school systems. A person who consults regularly with districts can help define the basic purposes of the evaluation process, provide leadership for the committee in developing the system, provide inservice for the administrators responsible for implementing the system, and train teams of administrators and teachers responsible for inservicing all staff in the district. The resource person should be capable of articulating to the evaluation committee the literature on effective teaching, schooling, and evaluation. This person should also be able to project the possible consequences of each strategy the committee considers as a part of the overall evaluation system. The use of a resource person should result in a better product and "can significantly hasten the work of the group" (McGreal, 1983).

4. *Draft a statement of philosophy:* The philosophy statement describes the belief system on which the evaluation system is built. It forms the basis for the many decisions the committee must make. It may coincide with the present culture and climate, or it may reflect a desired culture and climate, which the evaluation system can help create. A statement of evaluative philosophy should (a) state the purposes of the evaluation system, (b) provide an overview of how the system will be implemented, and (c) emphasize the importance of commitment by all groups within the organization. These can be stated in three brief paragraphs. A philosophy statement is provided in Example 2.1.

5. *Draft criteria, descriptors, and performance areas:* Founded in a knowledge base of effective teaching and schooling, the criteria define good teaching in the district. Each criterion should represent a valid expectation, which can be assessed. The development of the criteria and descriptors should be deliberate, with thorough discussion of each statement. Examples of criteria, descriptors, and performance areas for "regular" classroom teachers are presented in Chapter 3. Examples of criteria, descriptors, and performance areas for special-purpose teachers, coaches, and sponsors are presented in chapters 10, 11, and 12.

6. *Draft a set of evaluative procedures:* The procedures provide the structure that allows the belief system described in the philosophy statement and discussed during the development of the criteria and descriptors to work. Because drafting the operational procedures is the

---

EXAMPLE 2.1
Performance-Based Developmental
Evaluation: Philosophy Statement

The . . . School District is committed to providing a quality educational program for the students of the district. An effective performance-based developmental evaluation system is essential to accomplishing that goal. The primary purpose of the developmental evaluation system in the . . . District is to enhance the performance of all personnel. The system will also provide information for appropriate personnel employment decisions.

Performance-based developmental evaluation is a continuous process of formative and summative activities designed to promote professional development. The components of the process are identification of job-related expectations, documentation of performance, conferencing about performance, opportunity for improvement of performance, and employment decision making. The activities of each component promote fairness, objectivity, and a climate of mutual trust and respect.

An effective performance-based developmental evaluation system requires a commitment by district teachers, administrators, and board of education members to provide the time, resources, and training necessary for effective implementation of the system. With this commitment, the evaluation system will make a positive difference for the educational program of the district and for the students the district serves.

---

committee's most difficult task, the procedures should be developed after committee members have had time to work together in developing the philosophy statement, criteria, and descriptors. It takes time for the committee to develop positive working relationships, develop a knowledge and understanding of effective evaluation systems, and make a commitment to work as a team to develop a good system. After they have had some time to work together, committee members will more effectively resolve the controversial issues that will surface during the development of the evaluative procedures. Operational procedures for a performance-based developmental evaluation system are presented in Example 2.2.

(text continues on page 26)

EXAMPLE 2.2
Performance-Based Developmental Teacher
Evaluation Procedures

The following is an explanation of the procedures for performance-based developmental teacher evaluation.* The process begins with orientation for administrators and professional staff, continues with the formative phase, and culminates in the summative evaluation. This evaluation process is intended to be continuous, constructive, and cooperative.

I. ORIENTATION

A. Supervisors

Prior to initiating the evaluative process, each supervisor will receive inservice training. Annual inservice sessions will be conducted by the district to improve the consistency and quality of supervisory skills. Supervisors are all personnel responsible for supervising or evaluating teachers, including principals, assistant principals, and subject-area coordinators or directors. Principals and assistant principals have the primary responsibility for evaluation. Subject-area coordinators are responsible for assisting the teachers and principals or assistant principals during the formative phase.

B. Teachers

New teachers shall receive orientation about performance-based developmental evaluation at the beginning of their employment. Annual inservice for all teachers will also occur. These sessions will be conducted to provide information on the evaluation process and procedures, and to promote an understanding of the roles of the teacher and the supervisor in the evaluative process.

II. EVALUATION CYCLE

A. Scheduling for Tenured Staff

A Summative Evaluation Report will be completed at least once every three years for tenured teachers. The Summative Evaluation

---

*The term *teacher* describes all certificated, professional staff members, including counselors, librarians, media specialists, and special education teachers.

Report will be completed during the final year of the three-year cycle. Additional Summative Evaluation Reports may be completed as deemed necessary by the administration or as requested by the teacher. If a Summative Evaluation Report of a tenured teacher is going to occur more frequently than once every three years, the teacher will be notified as soon as practical. Typical examples of reasons for more frequent Summative Evaluations Reports are transfer requests, reassignments, administrative concerns, and teacher requests.

B. Scheduling for Probationary Teachers

A Summative Evaluation Report will be completed for probationary teachers for each year of probationary status. This report shall be completed prior to March 1.

III. FORMATIVE PHASE

The formative phase is the ongoing process for professional improvement. This phase is crucial to the success of performance evaluation and the improvement of instruction for students. Following are the essential components of the formative phase.

A. Data Collection

Effective supervision includes the collection and sharing of information about teacher performance. The data may be categorized as planned or unplanned. All data used for evaluation must be documented on a Formative Data Form and discussed with the teacher.

1. Planned Data
Planned data include all information purposefully collected by the supervisor—observed data, nonobserved data, and artifact data. The most typical planned observations are scheduled and unscheduled classroom visits. Following is an explanation of each type of planned data appropriate to the evaluative process.

a. Observed data (planned). Effective supervision includes the purposeful observation of a teacher's performance. These observed data may be classified as scheduled or unscheduled, depending on

(continued)

EXAMPLE 2.2 continued

---

whether the teacher was aware the supervisor would be observing and whether the two had the opportunity to visit prior to the observation. The observation may focus on specific criteria or may be comprehensive in scope. A minimum of one scheduled observation will occur during each formative phase. A minimum of one unscheduled observation shall occur during each school year. Typically, additional observations will occur.

Prior to a scheduled observation, the teacher and supervisor will establish the time and date of the observation. The teacher and supervisor will complete a Preobservation Worksheet and discuss the lesson to be observed. Each will retain a copy of the worksheet. If unexpected events necessitate a change in the scheduled observation time, the teacher and supervisor will work together to identify an appropriate time for another observation and the need for another Preobservation Worksheet and discussion.

The duration of a scheduled observation will be an entire lesson or activity. The duration of an unscheduled observation may be less than an entire lesson or activity.

The supervisor will take notes during planned observations and interpret them on a Formative Data Form. An observation is not valid for evaluative purposes unless notes are taken, transferred to the Formative Data Form, and discussed in a postobservation conference.

b. Nonobserved Data (Planned). Nonobserved data are collected by the evaluator from other persons. They represent the perceptions and observations of others about specific criteria. Examples include purposeful discussions with students, peers, and parents about specific performance. These data are seldom gathered without the knowledge and support of the teacher. When the data are collected, the responsibility of the supervisor is to determine if the information is significant, document the information on the Formative Data Form if determined significant, and discuss the issue with the teacher within a realistic time frame, usually a few working days.

c. Artifact Data (Planned). Planned artifact data should enhance the supervisor's understanding of the skill of the teacher for specific criteria. Artifact data are typically identified at the beginning of the evaluative cycle and are collected during the formative phase. The teacher will attempt to obtain the data requested by the supervisor and may provide additional data about performance. Examples of planned artifact data include grade books, lesson plans, attendance records, on-task logs, discipline referrals, and workshop handouts.

2. Unplanned Data

Unplanned data include information that comes to the attention of the supervisor without purposeful intent to collect those data. Unplanned data may be observed by the supervisor or by others and may include artifacts not purposefully collected. The use of unplanned data is at the discretion of the supervisor. Following is an explanation of each type of unplanned data appropriate to the evaluative process.

a. Observed Data (Unplanned). Teachers and their supervisors typically work in the same school. Their frequent contact gives the supervisor the opportunity to observe the teacher's performance at times when the supervisor was not purposefully collecting data for the evaluation process. When the supervisor notes performance that is significant, either of a positive or negative nature, the supervisor may choose to document that performance on the Formative Data Form and include the information as part of the teacher's evaluation process. Whenever information is included in this manner, the teacher and supervisor will discuss the information and the teacher will receive a copy of the Formative Data Form.

b. Nonobserved Data (Unplanned). Unplanned nonobserved data are information brought to the attention of the supervisor by others. These are unsolicited, verbal data, such as information from telephone calls and personal discussions. When nonobserved data are shared with the supervisor, the supervisor's responsibility is to determine if the information is significant, document the information on the Formative Data Form if it is determined to be significant, and discuss the issue with the teacher within a realistic time frame, usually a few working days.

c. Artifact Data (Unplanned). Unplanned artifact data include all information that comes to the attention of the supervisor indirectly. These are data that the supervisor did not solicit—for example, letters, memos, and notes about the teacher's performance. The

(*continued*)

EXAMPLE 2.2 continued

---

responsibility of the supervisor is to determine if the information is significant. If it is determined to be significant, the supervisor will document the information on the Formative Data Form and discuss the issue with the teacher within a realistic time frame, usually a few working days.

B. Data Documentation

The Formative Data Form provides the format for documenting all data collected in the formative process. The role of the supervisor is to record pertinent data on the form. The data on the form then become the basis for discussions between teacher and supervisor about job performance. The teacher and supervisor each retain a copy of the form.

The regular-length Formative Data Form contains all criteria and is used to document planned and unplanned data that apply to more than two criteria. Typically, planned observations involve note-taking during the observation and transfer of performance data to the Formative Data Form prior to conferencing.

The Formative Data Short Form is available to document information for a criterion or two criteria. The short form is provided for efficiency and is commonly used for nonobserved and artifact data. It should not be a substitute for thorough documentation of classroom observations using the regular-length Formative Data Form.

C. Conferencing

After recording data on the Formative Data Form, the teacher and supervisor will discuss the data. For observed data, this conference should occur within two school days if practical. If more than five attendance days (days when the supervisor and teacher are at school) transpire between the observation and the conference, either party has the option to reject the observation and request another.

For nonobserved and artifact data, the conference will occur within a reasonable time after the data have been collected and determined significant.

The teacher and supervisor sign the Formative Data Form, indicating the information on the form has been discussed. Either party will have the opportunity to make written comments on the Formative Data Form at that time. Additional written comments by either party should be shared within five working days, appended to the Formative Data Form, and discussed as soon as practical.

D. Professional Development Plans

Professional Development Plans are used to strengthen performance on specific criteria. A well-written Professional Development Plan includes identifiable, precise objective(s); strategies for achieving those objective(s); and the means for determining when the objectives have been accomplished.

A Professional Development Plan will be developed with each teacher at some time during the formative cycle. The plan may make a transition through more than one cycle, especially for probationary teachers on annual cycles.

If the supervisor believes a teacher meets the expected level of performance on all criteria, the supervisor will work with the teacher to develop and implement an "enrichment" Professional Development Plan. The teacher will work to accomplish the plan during the evaluation cycle and will discuss progress and results as appropriate.

If the supervisor believes a teacher's performance on a criterion is below expectations, the supervisor will work with the teacher to develop and implement an "improvement" Professional Development Plan. A teacher will not be rated "does not meet expectations" on the Summative Evaluation Report unless an improvement plan noting a deficiency on that criterion preceded the Summative Evaluation Report.

The teacher's supervisor will work to assist the teacher in the accomplishment of plans. For example, subject-area coordinators, directors, and others may be asked to help the teacher. Participation in activities that occur outside of or during the school day may need to be facilitated by the supervisor.

IV. SUMMATIVE PHASE

The summative phase is the review and synthesis of formative data pertaining to the teacher's performance. It marks the end of the evaluative cycle and includes the completion of a Summative Evaluation

(continued)

EXAMPLE 2.2 continued

Report by the supervisor and a summative conference about performance and job recommendation.

A. Summative Evaluation Report

The Summative Evaluation Report represents the supervisor's judgment about the teacher's performance during the evaluation cycle. The document is a summary of performance for each criterion. It also includes the supervisor's recommendation to the superintendent and the board of education about continued employment.

B. Summative Conference

After the evaluator has completed the Summative Evaluation Report, the supervisor will conduct a summative conference with the teacher to review the information on the report. The Summative Evaluation Report and the conference will be completed prior to March 1 for probationary teachers and at some time during the final year of the evaluative cycle for tenured teachers. If input was provided for the building administrator by other supervisors, such input shall be clarified on the report.

   The teacher and evaluator will sign the Summative Evaluation Report, indicating that the document has been read and discussed. Both parties will have the opportunity to make written comments on the report at that time. Additional written comments by either party must be shared within five working days and will be appended to the original copy of the Summative Evaluation Report. Copies of the report will be retained by the teacher, the evaluator, and the school district personnel office.

V. REVIEW/APPEAL

A teacher may request a review or an appeal of a professional judgment. This review/appeal is not to be confused with a grievance. A grievance is related to a perceived violation of the evaluation process, whereas a review is related to a professional judgment made by the supervisor during the formative process, and an appeal is related to a professional judgment made by the supervisor during the summative process.

   A teacher has the right to request a *review* of data on a Formative Data Form or a Professional Development Plan by the building principal's immediate supervisor. The request must be made in writing to the principal's supervisor within two working days after receipt of the form or plan. The principal's supervisor will review the request and discuss it with the teacher and principal. The principal's supervisor will append a written statement to the form or plan noting the review and the decision about the review.

A teacher has the right to *appeal* the ratings on the Summative Evaluation Report. The appeal must be in writing to the District Evaluation Review Committee within five working days after receipt of the report. It must identify the reason for the request, including an explanation of the information supporting the appeal. The appeal will be reviewed by the District Evaluation Review Committee. The committee will recommend either that the appeal is justified and the Summative Evaluation Report should be changed or that the appeal is not justified and the report should not be changed. The committee will process the appeal within ten working days of receipt and will forward all information and their recommendation to the principal's supervisor for a decision about the appeal. The appeal will be processed by the principal's supervisor within ten working days of receipt from the committee. The principal's supervisor will respond both in writing and in person to the teacher during that time. The teacher has the right to have a mutually acceptable, nonparticipating observer present during this conference.

In all references to review and appeal in this section, if the initial supervisor was an assistant principal rather than the principal, the first course of review and appeal must be to the principal. If it is not resolved with the principal, the official review and appeal procedures begin.

The District Evaluation Review Committee will include three teachers and three administrators. The teachers will be appointed by the local teacher association and the administrators by the superintendent.

VI. SYSTEM REVIEW

The superintendent will cause an annual review of the evaluation system to promote the maintenance of an effective, fair, and efficient system that is comprehensive and performance-based. This review will be made by a District Evaluation Committee composed of seven teachers and six administrators.

7. *Draft the evaluative forms:* The evaluative forms are the vehicles for implementing the evaluative procedures. They should reinforce the basic philosophy and make the process more efficient, not more cumbersome. Attention to detail, efficiency, and feasibility are important. Examples and detailed discussions of the evaluative forms used to implement a PBDE system are presented in chapters 5, 6, 8, and 9.

8. *Present the proposed evaluation system draft to all teachers and principals for input:* After completing the foregoing steps, the evaluation committee has a draft ready to discuss with all staff members. The draft should include the philosophy statement; the criteria, descriptors, and performance areas; the evaluation procedures; the evaluation forms; and a terminology page that defines performance-based developmental teacher evaluation, the formative phase, the Summative Evaluation Report, performance areas, criteria, descriptors, and Professional Development Plans. Using the set of materials, committee members can present the proposed evaluation system to all district staff. The manner used to share the information with all staff is generally determined by the size of the school system. Typically, the committee divides into presentation teams consisting of at least one teacher and one principal. The teams meet with faculty from each school to present the drafted materials, discuss the rationale behind each decision, and listen to reactions from the staff.

9. *Refine the draft into a proposed evaluation system:* When reconvening to discuss staff reactions to the system draft, committee members must be careful not to reject too hastily the many hours of thinking and discussion that went into the development of the evaluation system. The tendency to be influenced by a vocal minority of staff members who share their feelings during the school presentations is a phenomenon to which the committee should be sensitive. The committee members must listen to all staff comments, but they should analyze these comments carefully and put them in perspective in relation to their basic philosophy statement and the procedures designed to implement that philosophy. Many times, staff comments reflect the frustrations and mistrust of previous evaluation systems more than they represent an objective critique of the proposed new system. The committee members must remember that they have become the most knowledgeable persons in the school district about evaluation strategies. With that knowledge comes the responsibility to develop an effective evaluation system.

10. *Present the proposed evaluation system to the board of education for action:* The final step in the development of the evaluation process is working with the board of education toward approval of the system. In some school districts, this can be the most challenging task of all. It takes time for a group of laypeople who constantly feel pressure for accountability to the public to understand and appreciate an evaluation philosophy and system that emphasizes developmental issues more than judgmental issues. It is difficult to understand that a developmental evaluation system will usually produce decisions of better quality than a system designed specifically to be judgmental. Careful explanations of the terminology and processes are essential. At least one work session with the board is helpful before an action session. The committee, working with the superintendent and central office staff, must be patient and realize that by this stage they have been studying evaluation for several months, whereas the board may have considered the issue for only a few hours.

11. *Develop a process for inservicing all staff in the new evaluation system:* New evaluation systems are best initiated at the beginning of a school year. The committee should take an active role in designing and implementing the inservice activities for the new evaluation system. Although a consultant may be needed to inservice principals, teams of committee members and principals should provide the inservice for the teachers in the district. Teachers and administrators should receive inservice training before the implementation of the new system, with inservice continuing to some degree throughout the first year. Principals should receive initial training until they are articulate in the philosophy and process, have an understanding of and a commitment to that philosophy and process, and possess the basic skills needed to implement the process. Initial training for the teachers should help them understand the expectations as defined through the criteria, the process used to implement the criteria, and their own roles in implementing the process. Additional inservice will be needed to refine the skills of all personnel. Several days are necessary for most principals to develop effective skills in documentation, conferencing, coaching, writing development plans, and working with teachers to create a school climate that accepts and promotes development of professional skills that affect students (Valentine & Harting, 1988). Each school year should begin with discussions about the evaluation system philosophy, process, and expectations. Staff development experiences for teachers and principals can be built around the criteria, particularly those that most directly affect students.

EVALUATION COMMITTEE MEMBERSHIP

The evaluation committee should comprise primarily teachers and principals, who are the persons most directly affected by the process. Central office staff and a school board member should also be included. Although parents, students, and members of the community might also be included, experience indicates that their contributions may not be significant enough to warrant the time they must commit to the process.

The leadership in each school district must consider the unique aspects of the community before determining which groups should be represented and how their representatives should be selected (Valentine, 1987). The following issues should be considered when structuring the committee.

1. *Number of members:* The committee should be large enough in numbers to be representative of the appropriate constituents, but small enough to be efficient and effective. A twelve- to fifteen-member committee is usually adequate for all but extremely large school districts.

2. *Staff representation:* For any type of evaluation system, the majority of representatives on the committee should come from the group being evaluated. In teacher evaluation, that means the majority of the committee members should be teachers.

3. *Identification of staff members:* When identifying members for the committee, consideration should be given to representation by race, gender, school grade level, educational experience, and job responsibility. Members should be competent, articulate, and respected by their peers. They should have the ability to present committee decisions to other persons. Membership on the committee is usually the result of: (a) appointment by the superintendent or the board of education, (b) appointment by the local professional associations, or (c) appointment by the superintendent in consultation with the local professional associations.

4. *Community representation:* Various constituent groups within the community might be represented on the committee. Certainly, one or two board of education members should be on the committee. Then, when the system is being reviewed by the school board for approval, some board members will have had firsthand insight into the process used to develop the system and the issues discussed during that development. Other members of the community may be represented, de-

pending on the typical degree of local involvement and the political climate in the community.

In a school district of ten or more schools, a typical committee might be structured as follows: (1) seven teachers, including two each from the elementary, middle, and high school levels and one from the vocational/technical school or other special-purpose schools in the district; (2) four principals and/or assistant principals, including one from the elementary, middle, and high school levels and any special-purpose schools; (3) one assistant superintendent; (4) one school board member; and (5) one parent, such as a parent advisory board member. Although this may be typical, the composition of the committee in each district must be adapted to be representative of personnel in the district.

In smaller school districts, a teacher or administrator from each school in the district can serve on the committee. The more representative the membership, the easier the task of presenting the proposed draft to the district teachers for input.

TIME FRAME

The development or refinement of an evaluation system is best initiated in the fall of the school year and concluded in the spring of that year. Generally, six or seven day-long committee meetings are required to develop a new system, sometimes fewer to revise an existing system. A typical schedule for a committee follows:

Day One (September): Discuss terminology, evaluation models, and philosophy. Draft a philosophy statement.

Day Two (October): Review the philosophy statement. Draft the criteria.

Day Three (November): Review the criteria. Draft the descriptors.

Day Four (December): Review the criteria and descriptors. Draft the procedures.

Day Five (January): Review the procedures. Draft the forms.

Day Six (February): Review all materials. Prepare a document for presentation to all staff at buildings.

Day Seven (March): Present the document to all staff at buildings.

Day Eight (April): Review staff input. Finalize proposed system for presentation to board of education.

PREPARING TEACHERS FOR THE NEW
OR REFINED SYSTEM

Every teacher in the school district should participate in activities and discussions purposefully designed to educate them about the evaluation system. Explaining how the evaluation system was developed and its basic philosophy and purposes is the starting point for developing acceptance of the system among staff. A discussion of the components will help teachers see how each procedure is designed to emphasize the developmental philosophy. Each teacher must receive instruction designed to promote an understanding of the expectations as defined in the criteria and descriptors.

Some of this preparation may be coordinated by the central office staff of the school district, especially during the initial year, when the system is new to all teachers. However, the principal has the ultimate responsibility to articulate the expectations and procedures through formal and informal discussions. This articulation should begin during inservice activities prior to the opening of the school year in which the new or refined evaluative system will begin, and should continue throughout that first year. To assist teachers new to the school district and to internalize the process further with the other teachers, inservice should be conducted at the beginning of subsequent years.

Understanding the Evaluation System

All faculty members should be given both written and verbal explanations of the evaluation process. The written explanation should coincide with a brief presentation to the teachers reinforcing the evaluative philosophy and detailing the activities that will be used to implement that philosophy.

When a new evaluation system is developed, the members of the district evaluation committee should be the most knowledgeable persons about the system. Grouping members of the committee into teams of teachers and principals and having these teams make the initial inservice presentations is an excellent strategy for promoting acceptance of the new system. As teachers throughout the district realize that the system was developed by their peers, they will more readily accept the system's basic philosophical tenets.

> **Principle 6**
> **Staff are inserviced about process and expectations before implementing system.**

Clarification of the performance expectations of all staff is a complex task. The performance expectations described by each criterion and amplified through the descriptors must be discussed with all faculty. Teachers must understand that some criteria are more important than others. For example, a criterion describing teachers' abilities to "use effective techniques, strategies, and skills during a lesson" would typically be considered more important than a criterion that describes teachers' abilities to "assume responsibilities outside the classroom."

The relative importance of a criterion is also situational with respect to groups of teachers with similar assignments or to all teachers on a faculty who face similar challenges. For example, a criterion that describes teachers' abilities to "manage student behavior in a constructive manner" may require more emphasis in some settings than others because of the students' ages or the social complexities of a particular student body. A school or district goal may be to teach more effectively to the district curriculum. Thus, "demonstrates knowledge of curriculum and subject matter" may become a very important criterion for a given school year. Teachers need to be informed if specific criteria are relatively more important at given times.

Situations and needs may also influence the importance of some criteria for individual teachers. An effective evaluation system permits flexibility of emphasis on the basis of the teacher's assignment. Obvious examples are the teachers who work with students who present unique challenges in classroom management or learning abilities. The expectations for individual teachers that are not common to the entire faculty should be discussed individually or in small groups with the appropriate teachers.

> **Principle 7**
> **On-going inservice is provided to improve knowledge and skill on the criteria.**

The criteria represent the most important content in the evaluation system. An administrator must ensure that teachers understand the common and unique expectations as they are described through the criteria and the evaluation process that will be used to help them meet those expectations.

Inservice Activities

The inservice activities for all teachers should be planned by the District Evaluation Committee in conjunction with the leadership of the school system. Strategies to consider when planning the inservice activities follow:

1. New or changed evaluation systems should be implemented at the beginning of a school year, not during the school year.

2. All teachers should be required to participate in the initial inservice activities.

3. The inservice activities should begin early in the school year and be completed within a few weeks after the start of the year.

4. A general presentation to all district teachers prior to the beginning of the school year to discuss the evaluation philosophy and process is usually helpful in setting the stage for meetings at each school. This awareness discussion may be conducted by the leadership of the district and/or by members of the committee. This large-group presentation should not displace the inservice activities at each school or those described in the following items.

5. The initial presentation at each school site should develop a basic understanding of the process and expectations. A one- or two-hour meeting before the school year begins or in the early fall is appropriate.

6. The members of the committee that developed the evaluation system should be divided into teams to present the inservice activities at each school.

7. When possible, the initial presentations at each school should be made on the same day, or within the same week if there are more schools than the teams can cover in one day. Making the

presentations in a short time frame reduces the number of rumors and the amount of misinformation shared by teachers who have had inservice with those who have not.

8. Each principal should consider the appropriateness of follow-up presentations during the fall. These sessions should be designed to improve understanding of the procedures and content by all teachers and to emphasize the criteria and procedures that are most important in a particular school setting.

9. During inservice sessions in subsequent years, time should be devoted to a discussion of the evaluation process. The opportunity to reinforce the philosophy and the process should not be overlooked.

10. Also in subsequent years, teachers new to the school district should receive basic inservice through the school system's personnel office or other appropriate office. The inservice should follow the same outline as the inservice used during the initial year of the system. Each principal should also work with groups and individuals to promote understanding of the process among teachers new to the school district.

The following are suggestions for the basic one- to two-hour inservice of all teachers during the initial year of implementation:

1. Discuss the process used to develop the system.

2. Discuss the philosophy and purposes for the evaluation system.

3. Discuss the definition of performance-based developmental evaluation.

4. Discuss each major component of the evaluation process, emphasizing how each task reinforces the philosophy of development rather than judgment. The components are:
   a. Data collection
   b. Conferencing
   c. Professional Development Plans
   d. Summative evaluation

5. Discuss the criteria and descriptors.

6. Discuss the forms used to implement the process.

7. Discuss the evaluation cycle and the typical number of observations, conferences, and development plans during the cycle.

8. Use a videotape of a classroom teacher to explain the process the principal will use to take notes and conduct postobservation conferences.

9. Demonstrate the process for writing a Professional Development Plan.

10. Emphasize the links between the formative and summative phases and how these links promote fairness and development.

SUMMARY

For an evaluation system to be effective, regardless of the merits of its purposes, those affected must understand and support the system. Because teachers and principals are the key actors in the evaluative drama, they must be meaningfully involved in the development, refinement, and implementation of the system. Nothing short of high-quality, representative participation will suffice. Without it, the change will be short-lived; with it, the change can positively alter the culture and climate of the district.

Whether the evaluative system is newly developed, recently refined, or unchanged for years, the essentials of the evaluation process should be reviewed with all staff each year. Each staff member must be informed of the evaluative process and expectations prior to implementing the system. Preinforming those affected reinforces the emphasis on fairness and the developmental philosophy. The preinforming process is also an important legal safeguard, ensuring that all teachers are aware of expected performance and of the process for evaluating that performance.

REFERENCES

Bolton, D. L. (1973). *Selection and evaluation of teachers.* Berkeley, CA: McCutchan.

McGreal, T. L. (1983). *Successful teacher evaluation.* Alexandria, VA: Association for Supervision and Curriculum Development.

Valentine, J. W. (1987). *Performance/outcome-based principal evalua-*

tion. Paper presented at the annual meeting of the American Association of School Administrators, New Orleans, February 1987. (ERIC Document Reproduction Service No. ED 281 317)

Valentine, J. W., & Harting, R. D. (1988). *Performance-based teacher evaluation in Missouri: A three-year report.* Study prepared for the Missouri Department of Elementary and Secondary Education, Jefferson City, Missouri. (ERIC Document Reproduction No. ED 311 588)

CHAPTER 3

Performance Criteria and Descriptors

The chief virtue that language can have is clearness, and nothing detracts from it so much as the use of unfamiliar words.
—Hippocrates

AFTER THE DISTRICT EVALUATION COMMITTEE has developed a philosophy statement clarifying the basic beliefs about evaluation, the committee should develop the performance criteria, descriptors, and performance areas. The *criteria* are the job-related performance expectations of the teacher. These expectations should be based on educational research about effective teaching and schooling. Each expectation should represent commonly accepted thinking of scholars about the role of the teacher in the educational process. The majority of the expectations should describe what effective teachers do when they are working with students in the teaching–learning process. Criteria that represent expectations about the role of the teacher in the operation of a high-quality school should also be identified, even though those criteria are not directly related to the teaching–learning process. Some criteria are more important than others for particular teaching positions or in specific school settings. Other criteria are equally important regardless of the teaching assignment or school setting. Although the relative importance of criteria may vary, each teacher is expected to maintain an appropriate level of performance on all criteria at all times.

> **Principle 8**
> **Criteria define**
> **expected performance.**

Performance descriptors are statements of teacher behavior that are more specific than criteria. *Descriptors* are examples of specific behaviors often associated with performance of a criterion. Descriptors are not a comprehensive listing of behaviors for a criterion, but they enhance understanding of a criterion. Some descriptors may be appropriate in certain settings, but not in others.

> **Principle 9**
> **Descriptors provide examples**
> **of behavior for the criteria.**

Performance areas are groupings of criteria that are similar. They serve no procedural function in the evaluation process. They could be omitted from the evaluation process without altering the effectiveness of the system. Teachers cannot be held accountable for such broad areas, and thus teachers should not be evaluated on them. Their only value is in assisting personnel in understanding that the criteria represent major areas of responsibility.

THE CRITERIA SELECTION PROCESS

Although the importance of developing quality criteria cannot be overstated, the process is not as difficult as it might appear. Many resources are available to evaluation committee members. Research studies of effective teaching and effective schooling should be a primary source of information. Books and articles about performance evaluation provide examples of criteria. The references at the end of this chapter are some suggested resources for an evaluation committee developing performance criteria and descriptors.

In addition to studying the literature on effective teaching and schooling, the committee members should review criteria used in other school districts. If other sets of criteria are studied, the committee should devote time to analyzing the criteria and then develop statements appropriate to their own school district rather than simply copying those developed for a different district. Persons with expertise about the research on effective teaching and schooling should be consulted.

Through analysis of the literature and other evaluation systems, the knowledge of the committee members grows until they establish a quality listing of criteria. This listing becomes the basis for defining an effective teacher in the school district. In essence, the committee establishes a local standard for performance. This does not imply that the committee will have developed a definitive list of performance criteria or descriptors—or that such a list exists. Any list described as *the* list of performance expectations should be viewed with skepticism. Neither the art nor the science of teaching has become so completely defined. Therefore, the collective opinion of the evaluation committee, based on serious study and review of research and models, becomes the determiner of the criteria and descriptors for the local school system. As with other concepts in our judicial system, the local standards become the standards of acceptance if they are within reasonable bounds. "Within reasonable bounds" means that they can be defended through research or practice as important expectations of teacher performance; they are not contradictory to generally accepted practice.

The realization that no definitive list exists becomes more obvious as each new body of research sheds more light on the teaching–learning process. Because of the expanding knowledge base, criteria and descriptors should be reviewed every four or five years. The criteria should keep pace with new knowledge, and staff development activities in the district should keep pace with both.

PERFORMANCE CRITERIA

The criteria listed in Example 3.1 are not a definitive list to be copied and used verbatim in an evaluation system. They are examples of criteria that I would have provided for a district evaluation committee at the time this book was written. Like all criteria, they should be reviewed and refined periodically. The criteria are grouped by performance areas.

PERFORMANCE DESCRIPTORS

As mentioned previously, the descriptors provide examples of behaviors commonly associated with each performance criterion. Example 3.2 provides examples of descriptors that might be used to communicate the meaning of the criteria listed in Example 3.1.

(text continues on page 46)

EXAMPLE 3.1
Performance Criteria

I. Instructional process (performance area)
The teacher:
  A. Demonstrates evidence of lesson and unit planning and preparation (criterion).
  B. Demonstrates knowledge of curriculum and subject matter.
  C. Uses effective teaching techniques, strategies, and skills during lesson.
  D. Uses instructional time effectively.
  E. Evaluates student progress effectively.
  F. Provides for individual differences.
  G. Demonstrates ability to motivate students.
  H. Maintains a classroom climate conducive to learning.
  I. Manages student behavior in a constructive manner.

II. Interpersonal relationships
The teacher:
  A. Demonstrates positive interpersonal relationships with students.
  B. Demonstrates positive interpersonal relationships with educational staff.
  C. Demonstrates positive interpersonal relationships with parents and other members of the school community.

III. Professional responsibilities
The teacher:
  A. Follows the policies, regulations, and procedures of the school and district.
  B. Assumes responsibilities outside the classroom.
  C. Demonstrates a commitment to professional growth.

EXAMPLE 3.2
Performance Criteria with Descriptors

I. Instructional process (performance area)
The teacher:
   A. Demonstrates evidence of lesson and unit planning and preparation (criterion).
   —Prepares lessons designed to implement curricular goals and lesson objectives (descriptor).
   —Prepares lessons designed to reflect the belief that all students can attain basic goals and objectives if given adequate time and proper instruction.
   —Prepares lessons designed to challenge and stimulate students who quickly master basic goals and objectives.
   —Utilizes student files and seeks to understand student needs, abilities, and interests to develop educational experiences.
   —Designs lessons in a clear, logical, and appropriately structured format.
   —Incorporates content from previous learnings into lesson plans to build upon students' learning experiences and ensure continuity and sequencing of learning.
   —Demonstrates evidence of short- and long-range planning.
   —Has needed equipment and materials readily available.
   B. Demonstrates knowledge of curriculum and subject matter.
   —Teaches lessons using district curricular goals and objectives.
   —Displays competent knowledge of the subject matter necessary to implement curricular goals and objectives in the classroom.
   —Selects subject matter that is accurate and appropriate for the lesson objectives.
   —Selects subject matter that is accurate and appropriate for the students' abilities and interests.
   C. Uses effective teaching techniques, strategies, and skills during the lesson.
   —Develops a mental and physical readiness among students for the lesson.
   —Discusses learning objectives with students when appropriate to lesson methodology.

—Uses a variety of teaching techniques appropriate to student needs and subject matter (e.g., lecturing, modeling, questioning, experimentation, role-playing).

—Presents content accurately.

—Gives clear, concise, reasonable directions to students.

—Stimulates thinking through a variety of questioning levels and techniques.

—Provides opportunities to learn through exploration and investigation.

—Monitors student understanding during the learning process.

—Assigns a variety of activities that require application of the skills and concepts taught.

—Uses current events and unexpected situations for their educational value.

—Provides opportunities for guided and independent practice.

—Summarizes units and lessons effectively.

—Implements activities that develop good study skills.

—Demonstrates ability to communicate effectively during the lesson using appropriate verbal, nonverbal, and written skills (e.g., vocabulary, grammar, voice, facial expressions, gestures, movement about room, spelling, handwriting).

D. Uses instructional time effectively.

—Begins instruction promptly.

—Avoids unnecessary interruptions of instruction.

—Avoids inappropriate digressions from instructional objectives.

—Provides for appropriate learning activities throughout the scheduled instructional time.

—Monitors student time on task.

—Provides for smooth transition between lessons and/or activities.

—Paces instruction appropriately.

E. Evaluates student progress effectively.

—Uses evaluation techniques that are consistent with school and district philosophy.

—Uses evaluation techniques appropriate to curricular goals and objectives.

—Uses a variety of evaluation techniques (e.g., pre- and

(*continued*)

EXAMPLE 3.2 continued

---

posttesting, teacher-made tests, tests from other sources, oral and written activities, projects).
—Constructs tests directly related to skills and concepts taught.
—Provides evaluative feedback in a timely manner.
—Uses a variety of techniques for communicating progress (e.g., immediate feedback, written and verbal comments, grades, scores, individual and group conferences).

F. Provides for individual differences.
—Groups students for each instructional activity in a manner that best facilitates learning.
—Uses knowledge of various learning styles of students.
—Uses knowledge of students' previously diagnosed strengths and difficulties.
—Uses multisensory approaches (e.g., tactile, visual, auditory).
—Uses levels of questions appropriate to student needs.
—Provides activities and materials coordinated with the learning experience and developmental level of each student.
—Provides activities and/or solicits help for remediation and enrichment activities.
—Provides alternative learning experiences for students whose evaluation results indicate the need for reteaching.
—Adapts practice activities to meet students' needs.
—Understands and applies child development principles in the instructional process.

G. Demonstrates ability to motivate students.
—Communicates challenging expectations to students.
—Provides students with opportunities to succeed.
—Stimulates and encourages creative, critical thinking, and problem-solving skills.
—Gives constructive feedback frequently and promptly.
—Uses activities that promote student involvement.
—Uses activities that stimulate learning about relevant situations inside and outside the school.
—Responds positively to students' requests for assistance.
—Helps students develop positive self-concepts.
—Encourages and involves students who show little or no interest.

—Selects and uses appropriate reinforcers to promote learning.

—Demonstrates enthusiasm.

H. Maintains a classroom climate conducive to learning.

—Establishes efficient classroom routines.

—Provides a physical environment conducive to good health and safety (e.g., lighting, temperature, seating).

—Maintains an attractive, orderly, functional classroom.

—Ensures that information can be read, seen, and heard by students.

—Organizes classroom space to match instructional plans and student needs.

—Anticipates classroom disruptions and plans accordingly.

—Establishes and clearly communicates expectations and parameters for student classroom behavior.

—Creates a learning environment appropriate for the activity.

—Establishes a climate of mutual respect and mutuality of purpose.

I. Manages student behavior in a constructive manner.

—Manages discipline problems in accordance with school and district philosophy and procedures.

—Is courteous and sensitive but firm and professional when handling student behavior problems.

—Anticipates and corrects disruptive behavior in a constructive and timely manner.

—Recognizes inconsequential behavior and responds accordingly.

—Endeavors to identify and resolve causes of undesirable behavior.

—Manages the behavior of individuals, thereby maximizing learning for the group.

—Promotes positive self-image within students while managing their behavior.

—Maintains a positive attitude toward student management.

—Uses effective techniques to promote self-discipline and maintain appropriate behavior so the learning process may continue (e.g., social approval, contingent activities, consequences, verbal and nonverbal cues, positive reinforcement).

(continued)

EXAMPLE 3.2 continued

II. Interpersonal relationships
   The teacher:
   A. Demonstrates positive interpersonal relationships with students.
      —Demonstrates respect, understanding, and acceptance of each student as an individual, regardless of sex, race, ethnic origin, cultural or socioeconomic background, religion, or handicapping condition.
      —Interacts with students in a mutually respectful, empathetic, just manner.
      —Respects the individual's right to hold differing views.
      —Communicates effectively in oral and written form (e.g., grammar, syntax, vocabulary, spelling).
      —Uses effective active listening skills.
      —Encourages students to develop to their full potential.
      —Recognizes that students' emotional well-being affects their learning potential.
      —Gives time willingly to provide for a student's academic and personal needs.
      —Assists students in dealing with success and failure.
      —Gives praise and constructive criticism.
      —Makes an effort to know each student as an individual.
      —Shows sensitivity to physical development and special health needs of students.
      —Uses and appreciates humor in proper perspectives.
   B. Demonstrates positive interpersonal relationships with educational staff.
      —Demonstrates respect, understanding, and acceptance of each staff member as an individual, regardless of sex, race, ethnic origin, cultural or socioeconomic background, religion, or handicapping condition.
      —Interacts with other staff in a mutually respectful, empathetic, just manner.
      —Respects the individual's right to hold differing views.
      —Communicates effectively in oral and written form (e.g., grammar, syntax, vocabulary, spelling).
      —Uses effective active listening skills.
      —Provides positive encouragement to other staff.
      —Works cooperatively with colleagues in planning and im-

plementing educational activities that reflect the best interests of the student.

—Shares ideas, materials, and methods with other staff.

—Works effectively with support and ancillary staff.

C. Demonstrates positive interpersonal relationships with parents and patrons.

—Demonstrates respect, understanding, and acceptance of each parent or patron as an individual, regardless of sex, race, ethnic origin, cultural or socioeconomic background, religion, or handicapping condition.

—Interacts with parents or patrons in a mutually respectful, empathetic, just manner.

—Respects the individual's right to hold differing views.

—Communicates effectively in oral and written form (e.g., grammar, syntax, vocabulary, and spelling).

—Uses effective active listening skills.

—Provides positive encouragement to parents working to resolve student problems.

—Works cooperatively with parents in planning and implementing educational activities that reflect the best interests of the student.

—Supports and participates in parent–staff activities.

—Initiates and maintains communication with parents.

—Promotes a positive image of the school within the community.

III. Professional responsibilities

The teacher:

A. Follows the policies, regulations, and procedures of the school and district.

—Demonstrates awareness of policies, regulations, and procedures of the school and district.

—Works cooperatively with other educators to implement school and district policies, regulations, procedures, and goals.

—Selects appropriate channels and procedures for resolving concerns and problems.

—Complies with school policy on attendance and punctuality.

—Completes duties promptly and accurately.

—Maintains and provides accurate records or data.

(continued)

EXAMPLE 3.2 continued

—Provides lesson plans and materials for substitutes in case of absence.

—Demonstrates effective organizational skills in managing professional responsibilities.

—Handles confidential information ethically and with discretion.

—Keeps personal interests and problems separate from professional responsibilities and duties.

—Recognizes and deals effectively with crisis issues (e.g., substance abuse, child abuse, suicidal behavior, mood changes).

B. Assumes responsibilities outside the classroom.

—Performs noninstructional responsibilities as assigned.

—Volunteers for an appropriate share of noninstructional responsibilities.

—Exercises responsibility for student management on school property and at school activities.

—Participates in district and school projects, programs, and activities as needed.

C. Demonstrates a commitment to professional growth.*

—Participates actively in the supervisory/evaluative process to effect ongoing professional growth.

—Maintains current knowledge in teaching/learning theory and practice.

—Participates in professional organizations and activities as available.

—Participates in school and district inservice activities as appropriate.

—Exhibits personal self-control.

—Gives serious consideration and appropriate action to parental comments and criticism.

---

*The teacher is responsible for providing the supervisor with a listing of pertinent information for the current evaluation cycle.

JOB DESCRIPTIONS

Job descriptions are not synonymous with criteria and descriptors in performance-based developmental evaluation. A job description is often a blending of tasks, responsibilities, and behaviors that attempt to represent the various functions a teacher should perform. For example, a job description might state that the teacher is responsible for maintaining appropriate student behavior in the classroom. The same job description might indicate that the teacher is responsible for administering standardized achievement tests at designated times. The first statement refers to a desired outcome statement, the second to a behavior. Such inconsistencies in job descriptions cloud their intent and make direct linkage to the criteria and descriptors difficult, if not impossible. If a school district has a written job description for teachers, it might provide some insight for evaluation committee members as they develop the evaluative criteria and descriptors. In my experience, however, most job descriptions are best left in the filing cabinet when developing the criteria and descriptors for evaluation. They tend to be more task- than performance-oriented. Attempting to draw a parallel between performance and the specific tasks has a tendency to confuse more than clarify. It is better to stick with the literature on effective teaching and schooling and to provide examples from quality evaluation systems.

SUMMARY

In performance-based developmental evaluation, criteria are statements of expected performance for teachers, which are communicated through examples of behaviors called descriptors. The descriptors are not all-inclusive, but the criteria are. All teaching behaviors fit somewhere within the realm of a good listing of criteria. The criteria should be based on current knowledge of effective teaching and schooling and should be reviewed periodically. Principals and teachers should internalize the expectations the criteria represent. This internalization takes time and necessitates an effective process for applying the criteria. The remaining chapters discuss the implementation procedures for developmental evaluation.

SUGGESTED READINGS

Listed here are some suggested readings for evaluation committee members to use in developing performance criteria and descriptors.

Educational Research Services, Inc. (1978). *Evaluating teacher performance*. Arlington, VA: Educational Research Services.

Good, T. L., & Brophy, J. (1987). *Looking in classrooms* (4th ed.). New York: Harper & Row.

Harris, B. M. (1986). *Developmental teacher evaluation.* Boston: Allyn and Bacon.

Medley, D. M., Coker, H., & Soar, R. S. (1984). *Measurement-based teacher evaluation.* New York: Longman.

McGreal, T. L. (1983) *Successful teacher evaluation.* Alexandria, VA: Association for Supervision and Curriculum Development.

Stanley, S. J., & Popham, W. J. (Eds.). (1988). *Teacher evaluation: Six prescriptions for success.* Alexandria, VA: Association for Supervision and Curriculum Development.

Wittrock, M. C. (Ed.). (1986). *Handbook of research on teaching* (3rd ed.). New York: Macmillan.

CHAPTER 4

Collecting Performance Data

Every man has a right to his opinion, but no man has a right to be wrong in his facts.
—Bernard M. Baruch

THE PROCEDURES WITH which performance data are collected, analyzed, and organized for conferencing are vital to the effectiveness of an evaluation system. In a developmental evaluation process, teachers should not have the feeling that Big Brother (or Sister) is looking over their shoulders and recording everything they do wrong. They must have confidence that the performance data will be collected fairly and accurately and will reflect all performance, not just problems or negative behavior. The teachers must be assured that all data will be shared and discussed with them, adding to their understanding of how to improve as teachers.

The way in which principals conduct classroom observations is a good example of the importance of the data collection process. Too frequently, the only time a teacher sees a principal in the classroom making observational notes is in the spring of the year, when the principal must write an evaluation. Teachers are naturally anxious and resent the presence of the administrator when one or two classroom observations are the sum total of the formal information used to determine competence on a Summative Evaluation Report.

Contrast the one-or-two-classroom-observations approach with the strategies used by many principals who are in classrooms numerous times during a school week. Often the principals are there to be visible to the students and staff and to maintain an awareness of the educational program. At other times, the principals visit classrooms to take detailed notes about the teaching–learning process. The presence of these instructionally oriented principals does not significantly alter teachers' behaviors. The teachers become comfortable teaching in the presence of their principals because the principals are present frequently enough to have a valid understanding of the teachers' skills. The notes the principals take are always shared and discussed with the teachers, promoting nonthreatening, collegial relationships that demystify the note-taking process and permit valuable, candid discussions about instruction.

For many principals, instructional supervision is a high-priority role. For others, the priority is best described as "I know it is important. I'll get to it when I can." Most principals are asked to perform the dual roles of school manager and instructional leader. Principals perform each role to a greater or lesser degree depending on their ability and interest in each role. Most tend to maximize the time they spend on the things they do well and to minimize the time invested in things they are less comfortable doing.

A reasonable balance between the roles of school manager and instructional leader is necessary. Studies of effective schooling support the importance of both roles. "I'll get to it when I can" is simply not adequate. Effective principals take the time for instructional leadership. Time spent in performance-based developmental evaluation can be a significant portion of the time and effort the effective principal must spend on instructional improvement.

```
Principle 10
Planned and unplanned data are
integral to the evaluation process.
```

A TYPOLOGY OF PERFORMANCE DATA

Though commonly associated with teacher evaluation, classroom observation is only one type of data collected in an effective performance-based developmental evaluation system. Classroom observation data are a part of the planned data collection process—data collected for the purpose of developmental evaluation. In contrast, unplanned data become part of the evaluation merely by chance, without intent or calculation. The performance documentation schema in Figure 4.1 provides a logical outline of the types of data collected in a performance-based developmental evaluation process.

Planned Data Collection

Planned data are collected with the intent to use the data as a part of the developmental evaluation process. Planned data are collected pur-

FIGURE 4.1   A performance documentation schema.

PLANNED DATA COLLECTION	UNPLANNED DATA COLLECTION
Scheduled Observation Data Pre-observation Worksheet Pre-observation Conference Observation Notetaking and Analysis Formative Data Form	**Unscheduled Observation Data** Record and Analyze Formative Data Form
Unscheduled Observation Data Observation Notetaking and Analysis Formative Data Form	
Non-observed Data Identify, Collect and Analyze Formative Data Form	**Non-observed Data** Record and Analyze Formative Data Form
Artifact Data Identify, Collect and Analyze Formative Data Form	**Artifact Data** Analyze Formative Data Form

posefully and include scheduled and unscheduled observation data, nonobserved data, and artifact data.

Scheduled Observation Data (Planned)

An observation is scheduled if the principal and teacher discuss the upcoming observation and agree on a time and setting for the observation. Scheduled observations are usually observations of classroom teaching. Scheduled observations may also include nonclassroom responsibilities such as playground duty, cafeteria duty, individual tutoring of a student after school, or a parent–teacher meeting.

For a scheduled classroom observation, the teacher is given the opportunity to select the class or group of students, the teaching–learning strategies, the lesson content, and the time of the observation—in other words, all the factors associated with the teaching–learning process. The intent is for the teacher to be as comfortable and as much in control of the situation as possible. Scheduled observations give teachers the opportunities to put their best foot forward, to demonstrate their best skills.

> **Principle 11**
> **Classroom observation data**
> **are emphasized.**

Preobservation Worksheet. Scheduled classroom observations are frequently associated with the concept of clinical supervision. The principal and teacher agree on the time and setting two or three days prior to the classroom observation. Typically, the teacher completes a Preobservation Worksheet (Example 4.1) clarifying the objectives for the lesson and the teaching activities to be used during the lesson. The teacher might also identify specific data to be collected, such as the different levels of questions asked during the lesson or the number of students who participated in the lesson discussion. Unusual circumstances about the class or individual students can be clarified. The Preobservation Worksheet provides specific information that helps the principal understand the lesson. The content of the Preobservation Worksheet in Example 4.2 typifies the issues discussed during the preobservation conference.

While observing the lesson, the principal takes detailed notes about the teaching–learning process, the teacher's behaviors, the students' behaviors, and so forth. Following the observation, the notes are organized into a format for conferencing and a postobservation conference is conducted.

Unscheduled Observation Data (Planned)

An observation is unscheduled if the principal and teacher have not had a preobservation discussion about the observation and have not established the time and setting for the observation. The unscheduled observation provides a look at a closer approximation of typical teacher behavior than the scheduled observation. Because the teacher is not aware that the principal will be observing, the process may appear to

EXAMPLE 4.1
Preobservation Worksheet (Form)

Teacher   Date   School

Subject Area   Grade/Level   Observation Time

Teacher completes this form and discusses content with principal prior to observation.

1. What are the lesson objectives?

2. What teaching/learning activities will be used?

3. How are you going to check student understanding and mastery of objectives?

4. Are there teaching behaviors you especially want monitored?

5. Are there any special circumstances of which the supervisor should be aware?

NOTES:

Teacher's Signature/Date   Principal's Signature/Date
(Signatures imply the content of this document has been discussed)

EXAMPLE 4.2
Preobservation Worksheet (Completed)

Terry Kilmer	*Oct. 20, 1991*	*Jefferson High School*
Teacher	Date	School

English	*10*	*9:30-10:20*
Subject Area	Grade/Level	Observation Time

Teacher completes this form and discusses content with principal prior to observation.

1. What are the lesson objectives?

   Students will be able to:
   -Distinguish principal parts of verbs.
   -Explain difference between regular and irregular verbs.
   -Conjugate selected verbs.
   -Use correct form of verb in sentences.

2. What teaching/learning activities will be used?

   -Review for five minutes or so.
   -Examples and modeling.
   -Guided practice.
   -Homework assignment.

3. How are you going to check student understanding and mastery of objectives?

   -Monitor responses to questions.
   -Observe competence in guided practice.
   -Review part of homework before they leave class.

4. Are there teaching behaviors you especially want monitored?

   -The degree to which I teach to both sides of the classroom; I have tendency to teach more to left side of room.

5. Are there any special circumstances of which the supervisor should be aware?

   -Vietnamese student having particular problems with verb forms. Her homework assignment will be individualized.
   -Attentiveness of Tim. I'm trying to get him more involved. He's capable but not motivated.

NOTES:

Terry Kilmer 10-20-91	*Lee Castleman 10-20-91*
Teacher's Signature/Date	Principal's Signature/Date

(Signatures imply the content of this document has been discussed) have negative connotations; the teacher may feel spied upon. This is not the case if the principal and teacher both understand the developmental philosophy of performance evaluation, wherein the principal is attempting to observe typical behaviors with the goal of professional improvement in mind, rather than trying to catch the teacher in ineffective teaching or inappropriate behaviors.

The Preobservation Worksheet and preobservation conference are not part of an unscheduled classroom observation. However, the other basic procedural steps of note-taking, organizing of notes into a conferencing format, and conferencing are the same as for a scheduled observation.

Nonobserved Data (Planned)

Nonobserved, planned data consist of information purposefully obtained from other persons about a teacher's performance. Though infrequently used, nonobserved, planned data can help the principal and teacher in better understanding how others perceive a teacher's performance. They consist of secondhand, solicited, verbal information, typically used only with the endorsement of the teacher. The most common examples are interviews with students or parents.

Artifact Data (Planned)

Planned artifact data are the types of information identified at the beginning of the evaluation cycle by the principal and/or teacher and collected during the cycle. The data are typically collected by the teacher. Artifacts are any documents that reflect teacher performance in some manner. The principal and teacher usually discuss appropriate artifacts in the fall, and the teacher collects them during the school year. Typical examples include lesson plans, student examinations, standardized or criterion-referenced test data, and letters sent home to parents.

```
                        Principle  12
        Observed,  non-observed  and  artifact
        data  are  collected  during  the  process.
```

Unplanned Data Collection

Unplanned data represent information observed or brought to the attention of the principal merely by chance. Unplanned data are collected without prior intent. When observed or brought to the attention of the principal, unplanned data that the principal determines to be significant are recorded on a Formative Data Form and discussed with the teacher.

Observed Data (Unplanned)

Unplanned, observed data are circumstances witnessed by the supervisor at times when the supervisor did not plan to collect performance data. A principal has many of these incidental contacts with a teacher during a typical work week. Whether the impressions are formed while having a cup of coffee and discussing a particular student or while talking with a teacher while the principal supervises students in the cafeteria, the principal is constantly forming impressions about a teacher's ability. When these impressions formed through informal observations begin to flavor, either positively or negatively, a principal's assessment of a teacher's competence, the principal has the obligation to discuss those impressions with the teacher. In particular, if the concern about the teacher is negative, the principal is ethically obligated to discuss the concern with the teacher at the time it becomes significant to the principal. For example, if a teacher develops a sour attitude toward a student or group of students and this becomes apparent to the principal through informal, incidental discussions with the principal, then the principal has the obligation to address the issue with the teacher. If the concern is significant enough to cause the principal to feel that the teacher is not meeting expected performance standards for a criterion, then the principal should formalize the concern and begin to work with the teacher to improve the behavior. That is a typical example of a negative impression caused by unplanned, incidental contact with the teacher. Positive impressions are just as frequently created through unplanned situations. The skilled leader takes the opportunity to reinforce those positive behaviors, not just point out the negative ones. The skilled leader also knows the difference between significant behaviors, which should be formally documented and discussed, and insignificant behaviors, which might simply be discussed or overlooked.

Nonobserved Data (Unplanned)

Most principals have had the late-night phone call from a parent who was thoroughly disgusted with a teacher's behavior. Such phone calls are examples of unplanned, nonobserved, data—secondhand, unsolicited, verbal information that is brought to the attention of the

principal by another person. As with all forms of data, particularly negative data, the principal must determine the significance of the information. If it is determined to be significant, the principal has the obligation to discuss the concern with the teacher, obtaining the teacher's
perception of the situation and objectively documenting the information. If, at the time of the occurrence, the principal determines that the
information is insignificant, the incident should not be ignored at that
time only to be resurrected during the writing of the final evaluation.
Remember the old evaluative cliché, "If you didn't write it down and
discuss it, it didn't happen." If it is significant, it should be recorded
and discussed.

Like all forms of data, unplanned, nonobserved data can be positive
as well as negative. Supportive phone calls and positive personal comments from parents or students are examples. Like negative data, significant positive data should be documented and discussed. These positive strokes form an excellent psychological basis for approaching
professional development from a foundation of trust rather than mistrust.

Artifact Data (Unplanned)

Unplanned artifact data are unsolicited documents given to the supervisor by other persons. Examples include letters of commendation
or condemnation from parents or other community members. A professional manuscript written by a teacher and shared with the principal
may be a very positive artifact. Unplanned artifacts are the documents
that are not a part of the purposeful data collection process but help
form a supervisor's professional impression about a teacher.

RECORDING DATA

Strategies for recording observation data, particularly classroom observation data, appear as numerous as the educators who study and
write about the issue. In recent years, however, many commonalities
are evident. And although an extensive analysis of data-recording
strategies is inappropriate to the purposes and length of this book, a
general overview is essential to the understanding of effective performance-based developmental evaluation.

Planned observation data may be categorized as *comprehensive* or
focused, depending on the purpose of the data collection. As mentioned

before, planned observations can be either scheduled or unscheduled, depending on the degree of planning prior to the observation. Figure 4.2 shows four quadrants representing the categories of planned observations.

Comprehensive Observations

Comprehensive observations are more common to evaluation procedures than focused observations. Harris (1986) describes observations as comprehensive when the purpose of the observation is to survey and develop an overall view of the teaching practices. A comprehensive observation, whether scheduled or unscheduled, implies that the observer will document most performance behaviors occurring during the observation. In a classroom observation, this usually means the principal will take copious, detailed notes, giving particular attention to recording what the teacher and students are saying and doing during the lesson. These "scripting" notes have become commonplace in educational observation, with variations ranging from attempts to write down every word and behavior to very general descriptions of what is said and done.

> **Principle 13**
> **Comprehensive and focused**
> **data collection strategies are used.**

FIGURE 4.2   Planned observation processes.

| | PURPOSES: | |
	Comprehensive Observations	Focused Observations
TYPES: Scheduled Observations	Comprehensive Scheduled	Focused Scheduled
Unscheduled Observations	Comprehensive Unscheduled	Focused Unscheduled

Focused Observations

Focused observations are planned with the intent of observing and recording only specific behaviors associated with specific criteria. For example, if the teacher is interested in knowing which students participate in a class discussion, the principal may use a seating chart and place a mark by each student's name each time he or she participates. Or perhaps the teacher would like to know the details of the students' comments. Then the principal would record the name of the student, the student's comment, and the context in which it was made. Perhaps the teacher would like detail about the types of questions asked during a lesson. The principal would record each question and each response, noting the different levels of questions used by the teacher. Focused observations are particularly useful as part of the data collection process when working with a teacher to improve instructional skills through a professional development plan.

Comprehensive Note-taking

The ability to script every word and detail when observing a teacher requires significant training and a commitment to develop and maintain this impressive skill. Relatively few principals have the opportunity to develop their observation skills to such a high level. At the other note-taking extreme are notes with too little specificity, lacking the information necessary for an effective postobservation conference. Somewhere between writing down everything, and writing only generalities and impressions, is the concept I have labeled *comprehensive note-taking*. Comprehensive notes include specific statements and behaviors of the teacher and students, or whomever the teacher is working with, without attempting to record every word and detail. The observer becomes a selective recorder, writing down specific words and behaviors based on what the principal knows about effective teaching performance.

The criteria and descriptors become the important knowledge base that determines the behaviors recorded. At times the notes need to reflect nearly every word and behavior; at other times, insignificant statements or behaviors are omitted to be sure the more significant ones are recorded. When in doubt about whether to write down a statement or behavior, the good note-taker relies on the observational adage, "When in doubt, write it down."

For the newcomer to the note-taking process, the rule of "write down as much as you can until you have an adequate knowledge base to know what to leave out" is a safe axiom. Knowing what to write and what not to write takes months of practice, combined with training in note-taking and a knowledge of effective teaching behaviors. Quality note-taking is one of the vitally important skills of the instructional leader. Scripting every word may be unnecessary and unattainable for many, but taking comprehensive notes is necessary and is within the capacity of all supervisors who make an effort to understand the teaching–learning process.

As an example of comprehensive note-taking, a transcript of the first few minutes of a sophomore English lesson and the notes the principal took during the lesson are presented. Example 4.3 is the transcript of the lesson. The principal's observation notes are presented in Example 4.4.

The comprehensive notes in Example 4.4 are presented to resemble a page of paper, including the top and left side margins. The marginal notations and the items written in the body of the notes provide a clear picture of the lesson as it evolved. The notes describe accurately, and with appropriate detail, the important behaviors of the teacher and the students.

The principal who took the comprehensive notes in Example 4.4 has obviously conducted many classroom observations and taken many pages of comprehensive notes in recent years. Important characteristics of comprehensive classroom observation notes are discussed in the following sections.

Detail

The body of the notes should include exact statements, paraphrased statements, and accurate descriptions of behavior. The detail in Example 4.4 is excellent, with a blending of quotations, paraphrasing, and descriptive behaviors.

Observers should be careful not to get into the habit of using generalities rather than specifics. Consider the following examples in which one use of a generality might be acceptable, but the other is not. The acceptable example from the observation of Example 4.3 might read, "took roll and then rapped with kids about band contest." This description is reasonably accurate and does not omit significant teaching–learning behaviors, primarily because it describes general classroom behavior prior to the lesson. Contrast that use of generality with the following: "Began lesson about verbs, discussed lesson objectives, then reviewed previous work." In the latter example, the recorder sum-

---

EXAMPLE 4.3
Sophomore English Class Transcript, First Three Minutes

T: Teacher Statements   S: Student Statements

T: O.K. I think it is time to start class. I'm so glad to see the band students back. You did a good job in the band contest, didn't you? Just a good job? You don't have anything else to say about it?

S: We were great! We got ones on all our ratings!

T: You got ones--that's great! Keep up the fine tradition.

S: Even the freshmen got ones.

T: Even the freshmen. That is a miracle! Now, if we can just win the game tonight it will be a clean sweep for the week.

T: Now it's time to start our lesson. Today's lesson is about verbs. We've been in grammar this entire quarter, so you are beginning to develop a foundation for what I consider to be probably the most difficult lesson we've had thus far. Studies have shown that something like fifty percent of all the mistakes in grammar come from the usage of verbs. And that's what we are going to focus on today. Based on what you have done so far in this grammar unit, I am confident you can handle this. But it is complex, it is difficult and I need you to pay close attention.

T: By the end of the hour today, you are going to know the principal parts of a verb. You are going to know the difference between regular and irregular verbs. You are going to know how to conjugate verbs--let that word roll off your tongue--con-ju-gate. Not as hard as it sounds. And you're going to know how to use verb forms correctly in sentences.

T: Now, we are going to accomplish this by a little bit of review, to see what you already know about verbs. We've studied the parts of speech and we know that the verb is probably the most important of the parts of speech. You know that it fills the second slot in a diagram and you know that we have action verbs and what other kind? What other kind, Jeff?

S: State of being.

T: State of being. We have a name for the state of being verbs. What is that?

S: Linking.

T: Linking verbs. Very good. You also know that we classify verbs into two major classifications. What are those two classifications? Betsy.

S: Transitive and intransitive.

T: Transitive and intransitive. Don't forget that. What is the difference between a transitive verb and an intransitive verb? Anyone remember? Marty.

S: In transitive verbs, the action passes from the doer to the receiver.

T: That's right. What about intransitive?

EXAMPLE 4.4
Comprehensive Observation Notes, First Three Minutes
of Class

	Terry Kilmer English 10 10/20/91 9:30
9:30	*Checks attendance as students enter. Bell rings. Places attendance*
Roll	*in clip at door.*
Rapport	*"O.K. Time to start." Band back. Did a good job?*
	S: Did great
	Do you know ratings?
	S: Ones
PR	*Smiling...Keep up tradition, even freshmen, miracle. If can win*
	game.
9:31	*"Time to start lesson." Lesson about verbs. Grammar this quarter.*
(SET)	*We've developed foundation. 50% errors from verb usage.*
Expectations	*"Confident you can handle." Complex. Difficult. Pay attention.*
Objectives	*"By the end of hour today you will know principal parts of verb."*
	Difference-regular and irreg. Conjugate. How to use in sentences.
Review	*Going to review--verb important part of speech. 2nd slot diagram*
9:33 CQ	*Action verbs and what other-Jeff?*
	Jeff: State of being
CQ	*What is name for state of being verbs? Many hands up.*
	S: Linking
PR CQ	*Very good. Two classif. of verbs? Betsy*
	Betsy: Tran. and intran.
CQ	*Tran and intran--"Don't forget that" What's difference? Marty*
Board	*"Tran.-intran"*
	M: Tran. action passes from doer to receiver.
PR CQ	*"That's right" And intran?*

marizes several minutes of teaching in one sentence of generalities. The specific statements and behaviors necessary to objectively complete a postobservation form or effectively conduct a postobservation conference are missing.

Objectivity

Most observers begin a classroom observation with a preconceived impression of the teacher's competence. Consider the potential difference in notes taken by the same principal when observing a teacher whom the principal considers one of the best in the building and a teacher whom the principal considers one of the worst the principal has ever supervised. On a given day, both teachers may do a comparable, and excellent, job with their respective lessons. Yet the note-taking comments for the "best" teacher are inflated through bias, whereas the comments for the "worst" teacher are deflated through bias. An outsider reading the two sets of notes would have difficulty realizing that the two teachers were, for the observed lessons, comparable. Biases are part of human nature. They are difficult to remove, but they must be controlled. Objectively recording detail in the notes is the best safeguard against observer bias.

Understanding the value of objectivity is important; learning to record objectively is the challenge for the supervisor. Consider the following examples describing the same scene, in which a teacher is having classroom management problems. The objective description might be: "As teacher turns back to class and writes on board, two students in back left of room pass a note, three students in front of room whisper to each other, one student tosses an eraser to another student. Noise level in class rises as others begin to talk." The less objective description might be: "When you turn your back, students misbehave." The first example will help the teacher understand what is occurring that the teacher does not see. The second will often be perceived by the teacher as something the teacher already knew, or perhaps something the teacher does not consider fair because the principal is "just looking for problems to rate me down on."

Accuracy

Valid data are essential to a fair evaluation process. Like objectivity, accuracy is intertwined with detail. Detail eliminates the underlying cause of most observational inaccuracies—omission of the information necessary for effectively understanding performance. In addition, accuracy implies correctness of the notes that are taken. The recording of specific language and descriptive statements of behavior should equate to accuracy of data collection. All are a function of the skill of the note-taker.

Value Judgments

Value judgments are impressions we have in our minds as we watch a teacher teach that easily, and inappropriately, creep into written form on our notes. The statements may represent either positive or negative impressions, but both are detrimental. An example of a positive statement might be, "You did a nice job of settling the class after they became so loud when Sara blurted out her stupid answer." This statement represents a stroke of positive reinforcement for the teacher and would be taken as such. But once a note-taker begins a pattern of value judgments, teachers expect such judgments in the notes and become more interested in what the observer thought of each aspect of the lesson than in discussing their (the teacher's) thoughts about the lesson. The postobservation conference becomes a feedback conference rather than a collegial dialogue emphasizing self-assessment.

The note-taker who writes value judgments rather than objective descriptions may purposefully, or inadvertently, insert negative judgments. Negative statements have a devastating effect on the potential for a good postobservation conference. Consider the reaction of a teacher who reads the following statement on the observation notes:

> Discipline is obviously a problem. During deskwork time Mary talked repeatedly and Tom ignored you. You need to get control of the class.

Think of the time that will need to be invested in explaining and justifying those value statements and addressing the defensiveness that will probably characterize the teacher's attitude during the postconference. The same situation should have been written as follows:

> Students completing worksheet. Mary whispered to Sue three times in a five-minute period. Teacher motioned for Tom to stop talking. He continued to talk to student on his left. Teacher went to Tom's desk and spoke to him. He resumed working on his worksheet.

The second description of behaviors is both more accurate and less value-laden. It contains ample information for the principal to use in talking with the teacher about student discipline if the principal has that concern.

Marginal Notes

In Example 4.4, key words or phrases were placed in the left margin. The marginal notes represent a summary of a significant behavior described in the body of the notes. For example, the word *objectives* was recorded next to the statement of lesson objectives in the body of the notes. Likewise, PR was placed next to the examples of positive reinforcement, and CQ was used for content-level questions. The words chosen for the margins are logical notations and reflect the vocabulary and knowledge base of the observer. During the conference, the principal can interpret less obvious terms for the teacher.

The recording of marginal notes during the observation serves three purposes. First, it expedites the transfer of information from the classroom observation notes to the Formative Data Form used for conferencing. Second, the marginal notes enhance the ability of the supervisor to follow the flow of the lesson and see the larger picture as the lesson progresses. When taking detailed notes during a classroom observation, it is easy for the supervisor to become so engrossed in writing the notes that he or she does not reflect on the sequencing of events in the lesson or follow the basic concepts discussed. The marginal notes force the supervisor to reflect, to pause for a moment and understand what has transpired or is transpiring in the class. The third value of the marginal notes is apparent during the postobservation conference. As the supervisor works with the teacher during the postobservation conference, they will be discussing information about the criteria on the Formative Data Form. Consider the impression made on a teacher when the supervisor indicates that most of the questions asked during a lesson were content/recall-level questions, and, to underscore that point, the supervisor simply points to the marginal notes, identifying each CQ and quickly reading some of the examples of content questions. Having such data at one's fingertips adds to the impression that the supervisor is a skilled observer. The more skilled the observer, the more confidence the teacher will place in the notes and in suggestions made by the observer. If these suggestions make a positive difference in teaching skill, the teacher will be receptive to more data. This positive cycle is enhanced by the recording of quality marginal notes and the ability to use them effectively in a conference.

Time Sequence

Referencing time during an observation is a common practice. In contrast to educational research, where behaviors are often analyzed by minutes and seconds, the recording of time in a comprehensive observation need not be so precise. However, a notation of time is particularly valuable when a different teaching strategy or activity begins. In Example 4.4, the principal recorded the time the class began, the time the teacher began the lesson, and the time the review began. The principal and teacher could then determine if class began promptly, how much time was given to what the principal called "rapport," how much time was devoted to establishing set, and how much time was spent in the review portion of establishing set. Being a constant clock-watcher is seldom productive in a comprehensive observation, but recognizing when to record time in the margin will be very helpful for understanding the lesson.

Observation Frequency

As an instructional leader, the effective principal has an awareness of the competencies of all teachers. This knowledge is developed through many unplanned, incidental observations and an adequate number of planned observations. How many planned observations are an adequate number? How many scheduled classroom observations are appropriate? How many unscheduled classroom observations are appropriate? There is obviously no definitive answer to these questions. The number of planned observations necessary to understand the skill and be of assistance to one teacher may be very different than for another teacher. The number depends on many variables, including, but not limited to, the teacher's previously demonstrated competence, the level of sophistication of the supervisor in recognizing teaching competence, the setting in which the teacher teaches, the variety of teaching activities observed, the typicality of the lessons observed, and the length of the evaluation cycle.

The basic question for the supervisor to consider when determining if enough planned observations of classroom performance have been conducted is one of fairness and ethics. Have I observed and visited with the teacher enough times to understand the teacher's competence on each instructional criterion, to provide instructional assistance, and to make accurate, objective judgments about the teacher's competence on each instructional criterion on the Summative Evaluation Form? For some teachers, an affirmative answer may require a scheduled observation and two or three unscheduled classroom observations during the school year. For other teachers it may mean twice that many observations; for still others, many more.

Observation Length

The length of a classroom observation is determined by the type and purpose of the observation. For example, a comprehensive, scheduled classroom observation should be for the duration of the lesson discussed in the preobservation conference. The teacher has prepared for the lesson with the expectation of receiving notes and conferencing about the lesson. The supervisor should observe and take notes during the entire lesson, whether the lesson is thirty minutes or fifty-five minutes long.

A comprehensive, unscheduled observation provides the opportunity for flexibility. The supervisor need not observe the lesson from beginning to end. A briefer observation may better fit the time available to a principal and the goal of more frequent classroom visits. In fact, more frequent observations of shorter duration can be more valuable than fewer observations of longer duration to attain an understanding of the teacher's competence, provide instructional assistance, and collect adequate data to make accurate, objective judgments on the Summative Evaluation Form.

SUMMARY

The data collected in performance-based developmental evaluation provide the formal documentation of a teacher's performance. Whether the data are the result of planned, purposeful data collection strategies or of unplanned, incidental observations and events, the data collection process forms the foundation for the dialogue that must occur between principal and teacher about the teacher's performance. The procedures with which the data are collected and shared directly affect the attitudes of teachers about evaluation. While the procedures suggested in this chapter have been successful in hundreds of school systems, all procedures are subject to failure if a supervisor does not apply them in an open, ethical manner. As is the case in all aspects of evaluation, the commitment, ability, and attitude of the person collecting and analyzing the data are excellent predictors of the impact the evaluative procedures will have on improving teacher performance (Valentine & Harting, 1988; Davis, 1988; Brown, 1987).

REFERENCES

Brown, C. A. (1987). *Teacher perception of the process, purpose and impact of performance-based teacher evaluation in Missouri.* Doctoral dissertation, University of Missouri–Columbia, 1987. (*Dissertation Abstracts International,* 49/07, 1630-A)

Davis, J. W. (1988). *The relationship between selected performance evaluation procedures and principals' perceptions about performance evaluation.* Doctoral dissertation, University of Missouri–Columbia, 1988. (*Dissertation Abstracts International,* 50/04, 837-A)

Harris, B. M. (1986). *Developmental teacher evaluation.* Boston: Allyn and Bacon.

Valentine, J. W., & Harting, R. D. (1988). *Performance-based teacher evaluation in Missouri: A three-year report.* Study prepared for the Missouri Department of Elementary and Secondary Education, Jefferson City, Missouri. (ERIC Document Reproduction Service No. ED 311 588)

CHAPTER 5

Documenting Performance

Our duty is to believe that for which we have sufficient evidence, and to suspend our judgment when we have not.
—John Lubbock

IN PERFORMANCE-BASED DEVELOPMENTAL evaluation, the criteria define the expected performance of teachers. From the development of the criteria to the completion of a summative evaluation report, the criteria are the common thread of content running through each procedural step in the evaluation system. The criteria cover the entire spectrum of desired performance, from classroom instruction through noninstructional professional responsibilities. All data collected, whether planned or unplanned, must be organized into an appropriate format for discussion. The criteria provide the logical basis for organizing the data and for conducting conferences. Studies of performance evaluation systems indicate positive relationships between the appropriate use of a Formative Data Form for conferencing and the attitudes of teachers and principals about performance evaluation. Studies also indicate positive relationships between the appropriate use of the form and the perceptions of teachers and principals about the impact of the evaluation systems on teacher performance, instructional improvement, and student learning (Brown, 1987; Davis, 1988; Drummond, 1988).

Principle 14
Data are documented on the formative data form under the appropriate criteria.

The Formative Data Form is a listing of the performance criteria with room to record information after each criterion (Example 5.1). The supervisor records specific behaviors and statements next to the appropriate criteria. There are several advantages to using a Formative Data Form:

1. Documentation on a form by the appropriate criterion is more likely to reflect performance than recorder bias.

2. Grouping the data by performance expectation reinforces the importance of the criteria and maintains an intellectual and psychological focus on the stated expectations.

3. The form organizes the data in a logical format for conducting a formative conference.

4. A consistent format is used for formal recording of all performance data. The use of a common form reduces the number of memos and detailed explanations about noninstructional problems, which take clerical and administrative time. Those problems can be described efficiently on the Formative Data Form by the appropriate criterion. If detailed explanations are needed, they can be prepared and appended to the form.

5. The use of one form brings consistency and trust to the evaluation process for all personnel. Principals, teachers, central office administrators, and school board members know that the Formative Data Form contains the supporting data for all judgments made on the Summative Evaluation Report. Teachers can have confidence that throughout the process, any concerns will have been recorded on the form and discussed, so there will be no surprises on the Summative Evaluation Report. Central office administrators and board of education members know that detailed data related to summative judgments made by the supervisor are available and, if necessary, can be reviewed when making employment decisions.

The most notable shortcomings of the use of a Formative Data Form are more a result of misuse of the form than of the concept of the form. This misuse is more prevalent for unplanned than for planned data. Most planned data are gathered as a result of scheduled and unscheduled classroom observations. Following those observations, the supervisor records specific behaviors on the form next to the appropriate criteria. In contrast, unplanned data are recorded on the form at the discretion of the supervisor. For example, when principals use the form only to record concerns or make reprimands, they reinforce the concept

(text continues on page 74)

EXAMPLE 5.1
Formative Data Form: Teacher

Teacher	Date	School

Content	Grade/Level	Observation Time

Data: ____Sched. Obs. ____Unsched. Obs. ____Non-observed ____Artifact

I. **Instructional Process**
   A. **Demonstrates evidence of lesson and unit planning and preparation.**

   B. **Demonstrates knowledge of curriculum and subject matter.**

   C. **Uses effective techniques, strategies, and skills during lesson.**

   D. **Uses instructional time effectively.**

   E. **Evaluates student progress effectively.**

(continued)

EXAMPLE 5.1 continued

F. Provides for individual differences.

G. Demonstrates ability to motivate students.

H. Maintains a classroom climate conducive to learning.

I. Manages student behavior in a constructive manner.

II. Interpersonal Relationships
A. Demonstrates positive interpersonal relationships with students.

B. Demonstrates positive interpersonal relationships with educational staff.

C. Demonstrates positive interpersonal relationships with parents and other members of the school community.

III. Professional Responsibilities
A. Follows the policies, regulations, and procedures of the school and district.

B. Assumes responsibilities outside the classroom.

C. Demonstrates a commitment to professional growth.*

Comments:

_____   _____
Teacher's Signature/Date   Supervisor's Signature/Date
(Signatures indicate the data have been read and discussed. Copies to teacher and supervisor.)
*The teacher is responsible for providing the supervisor with a listing of pertinent information for the current evaluation cycle.

that evaluation is a judgmental, punitive system, thus causing teachers to view the use of the form with contempt. The form should be used to record significant performance, whether positive or negative.

Another problem can come from overzealous use of the form to record unplanned data. The supervisor should not feel the need to "grab a form" every time a particularly positive or negative behavior is observed. For positive behaviors, a periodic discussion will suffice. The positive behaviors can often wait until after a classroom observation, when the principal must complete the form for the observation. At that time, additional positive data can be added and clarified with respect to time and situation. There is no urgency about sharing the positive data except insofar as such sharing might constitute positive reinforcement for the teacher.

By contrast, the supervisor should record and share all significant concerns with the teacher as soon as possible. An explanation of the concern should be noted on the form and discussed with the teacher, and a copy of the form given to the teacher. But such serious concerns are rare. More common are the little things a principal might notice and want to help the teacher improve. Usually, a brief discussion, a reassuring statement, or a suggestion for change is more valuable than written documentation on a form. The Formative Data Form was not developed to displace such interaction but, rather, to document a concern formally if that concern is significant. The supervisor must determine significance and use good judgment about which concerns need to be recorded on the form and which are so minor they are best resolved less formally.

To simplify the amount of paperwork and expedite the completion of Formative Data Forms, supervisors and teachers like to use a short form when the data to be documented are for only one or two criteria. The manner for documenting data on the Formative Data Short Form is the same as on the regular Formative Data Form. A copy of the short form is provided in Example 5.2.

Documenting of information on a Formative Data Form varies with the type of data that have been collected. To clarify the differences, documenting procedures for planned and unplanned data are discussed separately.

DOCUMENTING PLANNED DATA

Planned data sources include scheduled observations, unscheduled observations, nonobserved information from others, and artifacts. Sched-

---

EXAMPLE 5.2
Formative Data Short Form

| Teacher | Date | School |

| Content | Grade/Level |

Data: ____Sched. Obs. ____Unsched. Obs. ____Non-observed ____Artifact

This form is used in lieu of the longer form when only one or two criteria are being documented, typically non-classroom data.

Criterion:

Data:

Criterion:

Data:

| Teacher's Signature/Date | Supervisor's Signature/Date |

(Signatures indicate the data have been read and discussed. Copies to teacher and supervisor.)

---

uled and unscheduled observations can be further classified as classroom observations and nonclassroom observations. To explain the procedures for documenting these varied types of data, the discussion and examples that follow are grouped by classroom observation data, non-classroom observation data, nonobserved data, and artifact data.

Planned Classroom Observations
(Scheduled and Unscheduled)

When a principal observes a teacher in the classroom setting, the principal typically takes comprehensive notes, recording specific statements and behaviors of the teacher and students. Those data are recorded as they occur in the classroom. The principal then transfers the data to a Formative Data Form, grouping the data by the appropriate criteria. In Example 5.3, two criteria typically included on a Formative Data Form and the documentation of the observation as it might have been transferred to a Formative Data Form are presented.

When transferring classroom observation data to a Formative Data Form, particular attention should be given to the objectivity of

---

EXAMPLE 5.3
Formative Data Form (Unscheduled Observation)

Casey Fisher	1/18/91	North Middle
Teacher	Date	School

Math 7	7 (Remedial)	8:05-8:55
Content	Grade/Level	Observation Time

Data: _____Sched. Obs. __X__Unsched. Obs. _____Non-observed ____Artifact

I. Instructional Process

    A. Demonstrates evidence of lesson and unit planning and preparation.
       -Handouts, overheads and chalkboard prepared.
       -Lesson sequence included roll, set, extensive review, new content,
       practice activity, and homework assignment.
       -"For the past two weeks we have worked on addition and subtraction of
       fractions. After we briefly review a few key points about working
       with fractions, we will study the process for multiplying fractions.
       By the close of class you will be able to..."

    B. Demonstrates knowledge of curriculum and subject matter.
       -When stating unit objectives, paraphrased those in curriculum guide.
       Covering multiplication in curriculum sequence.
       -"When multiplying fractions you..." explained the process succinctly
       and with clarity. After receiving questions, reexplained it using
       different examples to stress the concepts students misunderstood.

---

the notes. Value or qualitative judgments should be avoided when transferring the notes to the Formative Data Form, just as they should have been avoided when taking the comprehensive notes during the classroom observation. In Example 5.3, specific behaviors are described and specific statements are quoted without placing value or qualitative judgments on the form at this time. Notice the absence of statements such as "Nice job," or "I really liked the way you began class," or "Why didn't you try . . . ?" Accuracy, objectivity, specific examples, and no editorializing are characteristics of good-quality data transfer to a Formative Data Form.

Principle 15
Specific behaviors, not value judgments about the behaviors, are documented.

The principal may wish to make additions to the form during the postobservation conference. For example, during the conference more insight may be gained into the manner in which Casey Fisher, the teacher in Example 5.3, prepared for the class. Additional notations may be made on the form at that time, with a notation indicating they were from the conference. The principal might add the following information to the first criterion on the Formative Data Form after discussing lesson preparation with the teacher during the conference.

As per conference: four resource books used to obtain examples, two worksheets prepared but not used because students not ready.

The addition indicates that, as a result of the conference discussion, the principal learned that the teacher used specific resources and had other worksheets prepared. Adding this information reinforces the intent to record the data as honestly and accurately as possible. It makes a positive impression on the teacher and builds trust and confidence.

Perhaps the principal notices a concern during the observation. Writing the concern on the observation notes or the Formative Data Form prior to the conference might bother the teacher so much that many minutes of conference time would have to be spent dealing with the teacher's emotions rather than the content of the concern. If the principal verbally discusses the concern in the proper context rather than sharing it initially in writing, the teacher will better understand the degree of the concern and more readily adapt to the issue. The concern, and any suggestions made by the principal to resolve the concern, can be added to the form during the conference. For example, the following might be appropriate for Casey Fisher.

> As per conference: Discussed the lack of alternative activities for those students who demonstrated mastery of the objectives before the majority of the class. The teacher will be more attentive to this problem and begin preparing materials to stimulate those who master the objectives more quickly than others.

The addition of data to the Formative Data Form as a result of the dialogue during the conference applies to each of the different types of data collection discussed in the following sections. The goal is to have accurate, fair data on the form. Any information obtained during the conference that adds to that goal should be included.

Each criterion is seldom documented on a single Formative Data Form. For example, a classroom observation will typically not provide data about the nonclassroom criteria. When the form is completed, those criteria for which there are no data are left blank, or N/O (for "not observed") is written under criterion.

**Planned Nonclassroom Observations
(Scheduled and Unscheduled)**

Planned observation of a teacher during nonclassroom activities is rare, but sometimes appropriate. For example, a principal may be concerned about a teacher's ability to work effectively with parents. The principal may be aware that the teacher has a parent conference later in the week and may choose to observe the conference to obtain firsthand information about the teacher's skill in working with parents. During the observation the principal should take comprehensive notes about the teacher's behavior and, when appropriate, record specific statements made by the teacher and the parents. Following the observation, the principal should complete a Formative Data Form, responding to the criteria that define performance expectations for parent relationships. Example 5.4 represents the information the principal might record on the form under the appropriate criterion.

Again, note the absence of value or qualitative statements and the presence of objective, specific statements. Quotations are used, opinions are absent. The data are a fair reflection of the teacher's behavior.

EXAMPLE 5.4
Formative Data Form (Scheduled Observation)

Casey Fisher	1/25/91	North Middle
Teacher	Date	School

Parent Conference	7	3:10-3:30 p.m.
Content	Grade/Level	Observation Time

Data: __X__Sched. Obs. ____Unsched. Obs. ____Non-observed ___Artifact

---

II. Interpersonal Relationships

   C. Demonstrates positive interpersonal relationships with parents/patrons.
   -*Observed data: conference with Mr./Mrs. Acheson re Tom's semester grade*
   -*"Mr./Mrs. A, I'm pleased we have this opportunity to talk. I tried to call you yesterday to discuss..."*
   -*"The real concern I have for Tom is his inability to concentrate for more..."*
   -*"It would help Tom if you would work with him at home on...I will send practice problems each day for the next...Then we can talk by phone."*
   -*"I appreciate your support. We'll make progress if..."*

Planned Nonobserved Data

On occasion a supervisor decides that nonobserved data that could add to the principal's understanding of a teacher's competence should be solicited. For example, a principal might purposefully visit with members of the student council to obtain students' perceptions about their teachers. Such discussion may provide data that the principal feels must be shared with a given teacher. The documentation of planned, nonobserved data follows the format described for other planned data. The data are recorded under the appropriate criteria and discussed with the teacher. Example 5.5 shows how a principal might complete the Formative Data Form after a student council discussion. Specific statements are included, but the principal will probably choose not to identify the specific students.

Planned Artifact Data

Artifact data are typically identified at the beginning of the school year and collected by the teacher during the year. The Formative Data

---

EXAMPLE 5.5
Formative Data Form (Nonobserved Data)

Casey Fisher	3/15/91	North Middle
Teacher	Date	School

Student Council	7	12:15-12:45 p.m.
Content	Grade/Level	Observation Time

Data: ____Sched. Obs. ____Unsched. Obs. __X__Non-observed ___Artifact

II. Interpersonal Relationships

    A. Demonstrates positive interpersonal relationships with students.
        -*Students indicated the following concerns during a discussion of seventh grade teachers.*
        -*"Fisher never knows our names--in class or out of class."*
        -*"...yells frequently during class. Seems very mean and unhappy."*
        -*"Knows math really well. Expects a lot out of students."*
        -*"I do like Fisher as a teacher." "Me too." "Needs to be more friendly."*
        -*All comments listed above were shared or supported by most of the students present. These were individual comments, confirmed by the group.*

Form is an excellent document for summarizing artifact data. The summary statements are placed under the appropriate criteria, and more detailed data are appended. The portion of the Formative Data Form included in Example 5.6 presents documentation for a survey of students about teacher performance.

DOCUMENTING UNPLANNED DATA

Unplanned data are those that come to the attention of the principal without purposeful intent to gather such data. Unplanned data may be observed by the principal or observed by others and shared with the principal. As with planned data, there are three basic classifications—observed, nonobserved, and artifact data.

Unplanned Observation Data

Principals are in frequent contact with teachers at times when they are not purposefully observing the teacher to collect observation data.

EXAMPLE 5.6
Formative Data Form (Artifact Data)

Casey Fisher	5/16/91	North Middle
Teacher	Date	School

Student Survey	7	n/a
Content	Grade/Level	Observation Time

Data: ___Sched. Obs. ___Unsched. Obs. ___Non-observed _X_Artifact

II. Interpersonal Relationships

   A. Demonstrates positive interpersonal relationships with students.
       Student identified the following concerns on the annual teacher survey
       form.
       Scale was 1-5 with 3 as typical.
       -Treats students with respect and dignity--2.1
       -Works with students before and after school-1.3
       -Knows each student by name--1.4
       -Likes students--1.7
       -Is friendly to students--2.0

When significant issues arise, the principal may determine that documentation of the performance is appropriate. The manner in which the data are entered on the form is similar to that used in examples 5.3 and 5.4, which describe planned observation data. The noticeable difference will be the lack of specificity. More general statements are a necessity because the principal did not enter into the situation with the intent to record data and must therefore make entries on the form on the basis of sketchy notes or memory. A description of the situation and the behavior observed is made under the appropriate criteria on the Formative Data Form.

Unplanned Nonobserved Data

Unsolicited verbal information shared with the principal by another person must be documented fairly. When the information is shared, the principal should attempt to take notes about the situation and determine the accuracy of the information. The principal must then attempt to be as specific as possible when making entries on the Formative Data Form. The recording of the information on the Formative Data

Form is similar to the documentation of planned nonobserved data presented in Example 5.5.

Unplanned Artifact Data

Artifact data from unsolicited sources are common in public service. The supervisor must attempt to determine the accuracy of the information in the artifact document and then represent that information on the Formative Data Form. The recording of unplanned artifact data on the Formative Data Form is similar to the documentation of planned artifact data depicted in Example 5.6.

SUMMARY

The consistent manner with which data are recorded and shared with teachers directly affects the teacher's attitude toward performance evaluation. Specificity and objectivity are critical characteristics of an appropriately completed Formative Data Form. The form is a basic tool for an effective performance-based developmental evaluation system. When used properly, it becomes the road map that provides direction for the principal and teacher during formative conferencing.

REFERENCES

Brown, C. A. (1987). *Teacher perception of the process, purpose and impact of performance-based teacher evaluation in Missouri.* Doctoral dissertation, University of Missouri–Columbia, 1987. (*Dissertation Abstracts International,* 49/07, 1630-A)

Davis, J. W. (1988). *The relationship between selected performance evaluation procedures and principals' perceptions about performance evaluation.* Doctoral dissertation, University of Missouri–Columbia, 1988. (*Dissertation Abstracts International,* 50/04, 837-A)

Drummond, G. L. (1988). *Perceptions of Missouri secondary school principals about performance-based principal evaluation.* Doctoral dissertation, University of Missouri–Columbia, 1988. (*Dissertation Abstracts International,* 50/04, 838-A)

CHAPTER 6

Formative Conferencing

To be persuasive, we must be believable. To be believable, we must be credible. To be credible, we must be truthful.
—Edward R. Murrow

THE FORMATIVE CONFERENCE in performance-based developmental evaluation is a discussion between the supervisor and the teacher about performance on one or more criteria. When formative conferencing is an integral part of the evaluative process, the teacher becomes confident that all criteria will be discussed on a regular basis and, if the supervisor has a concern about performance, the teacher will be apprised of the concern as soon as feasible. This promotes the opportunity to address a concern during the formative process and thus try to resolve the concern before the supervisor must complete a Summative Evaluation Report.

Conducting an effective formative conference is one of the most challenging tasks for a supervisor. Whether it is set up to discuss observed data, nonobserved data, artifact data, or any combination thereof, the formative conference demands the supervisor's best analytical and interpersonal skills. Using these skills in a culture and climate where positive working relationships between supervisor and teachers have been built through developmental evaluation can be very rewarding for both supervisor and teacher. Conducting the conference in a culture or climate that lacks such positive relationships and trust can be frustrating to both parties. In such cases, the principal must use the conference and the evaluative process to promote a trusting, collegial relationship and an understanding of the nature of performance-based developmental evaluation. Teachers and principals indicate that over a period of two or three years, skillful conferencing can improve performance and attitudes about evaluation systems (Davis, 1988; Moore, 1986).

A RATIONALE

For decades, teacher evaluation was synonymous with the completion of a final rating form each spring. The principal and teacher discussed the ratings on the evaluation form, signed it on the appropriate line, and concluded the evaluation conference. These "summative conferences" reinforced among teachers the concept that evaluation was something done *to* them, not with them.

In purpose and process, formative and summative conferences are different. The basic purpose of formative conferences is to *promote professional growth* through discussion of performance. The purpose of a summative conference is to share with the teacher the supervisor's overall *judgments about performance* on each criterion. Formative conferences are *developmental;* the summative conference is *judgmental.* Formative conferences are ongoing interactions throughout the evaluation cycle, the summative conference denotes finality because it concludes the evaluation cycle. Formative Data Forms are the bases of formative conferences; they are working documents between supervisor and teacher. The Summative Evaluation Report is the basis of the summative conference and is the final rating form that becomes the permanent record of the teacher's competence. Formative conferences are plural during the evaluation cycle, the summative conference is singular.

Formative conferences meet numerous needs in an effective performance-based developmental evaluation system. The conferences provide a forum for communication about effective performance between teacher and supervisor. The conferences provide a focus on, and reinforcement of, the performance criteria. They give the supervisor the opportunity to listen to and understand the reasons behind specific behaviors by the teacher. The conferences provide the opportunity for the supervisor to share perceptions about performance and to discuss competence in a nonthreatening, nonjudgmental manner. The conferences give the teacher and the supervisor an opportunity to discuss performance on an ongoing basis. Finally, the conferences give the teacher the opportunity to self-assess performance by obtaining data relevant to performance and dialoguing with the supervisor about the data.

GUIDELINES FOR WHEN TO CONFERENCE

A logical concern for both teacher and principal is the frequency with which formative conferences should be conducted. Neither principals nor teachers have the time and patience to visit every time a principal observes a positive or negative behavior of a teacher. Therefore, the evaluation process must include guidelines that assure teachers that significant positive and negative performance will be discussed in a timely manner during the formative process. Principals must have assurances that the conferences can blend feasibly with their myriad of responsibilities. A list of recommended guidelines for formative conference frequency is provided in Figure 6.1.

For supervisors not accustomed to formative conferences, these guidelines may appear to mandate an unrealistic number of conferences during the school year. However, adherence to these guidelines can promote positive teacher attitudes toward the evaluative process. And the more positive the teachers' attitudes toward developmental evaluation, the more likely the process will make a difference for the teachers, the school program, and, most important, the students.

In a planned observation, the supervisor takes observation notes about the teacher's performance and transfers those notes to a Formative Data Form. The first guideline recommends that a formative conference be conducted within two days after each planned, scheduled, or

FIGURE 6.1   Guidelines for conferencing frequency.

Formative conferences should occur

...within two working days after any planned, scheduled or unscheduled observation of teaching performance.

...within two working days after any unplanned behaviors are observed about which the principal has a significant concern.

...within two working days after any non-observed data are shared with the principal about which the principal has a significant concern.

...at least once during each evaluation cycle to discuss artifact data being collected during the cycle.

...at least once during each evaluation cycle to discuss criteria not otherwise discussed during the cycle, particularly criteria not related to classroom performance.

...within two working days after any data are recorded on a Formative Data Form.

unscheduled observation of a teacher. Planned observations are usually classroom observations. As a result of interviews with teachers and supervisors, Ginos (1985) found a noticeable difference in teachers' attitudes toward evaluation when the conference was conducted more than two days after the observation. In contrasting conferences occurring within two days after the observation with those occurring after two days, Ginos indicated that teachers in conferences after two days made more excuses for their poor performance, "forgot" some of the basics of how class was conducted, and resented the fact that the conference was not conducted in a timely manner. They viewed the conference as important, and the message the principals were giving the teachers by delaying the conference was that it was not important.

Principle 16
Conferences are held as soon as possible after data collection.

An unplanned observation occurs when the supervisor notes significant behavior at a time when the supervisor was not purposefully observing the teacher with the intent to record observation data and confer. The phrase *significant behavior* is important. To describe an observed behavior as significant means that the behavior is representative of performance that will affect the supervisor's judgment when the supervisor completes a Summative Evaluation Report. If the significant behavior is a concern, prompt conferencing is crucial to the integrity of the developmental evaluation process. The supervisor has the obligation to share the concern with the teacher and does so by describing the behavior on the Formative Data Form and discussing the behavior with the teacher within two days.

Some data do not represent a significant concern when they first occur, but become significant when other similar occurrences create a *cumulative effect*. In such instances, the supervisor has the obligation to share the concern with the teacher at that point in time when enough data have accumulated to be of concern.

Planned and unplanned nonobserved data and unplanned artifact data should be shared using the same guidelines as for unplanned observation data. If the information creates a significant concern, the supervisor should document the information on a Formative Data Form and discuss it with the teacher within two days.

When planned artifact data are identified, a time frame is usually established for reviewing the data. At the time of review, the data are summarized on the Formative Data Form and discussed. If a supervisor conducts a planned observation at approximately the time the artifact data are to be reviewed, the artifact data could be discussed during the postobservation conference, eliminating the need for a separate conference.

> **Principle 17**
> **Non-classroom data and artifact data conferences are held at least once a cycle.**

Some criteria represent performance not associated with classroom instruction. Supervisors can easily forget to discuss those criteria with teachers until they are completing the Summative Evaluation Report. At that time the supervisor may realize that a concern exists about a criterion. But, when a summative report is being completed, it is too late to give the teacher a fair opportunity to resolve the problem. To alleviate such errors and to promote an ongoing focus on all criteria, school districts using performance-based developmental evaluation have instituted operational procedures to ensure timely discussion of all criteria. In some districts, principals are required to complete the Formative Data Form for each nonclassroom criterion and to conduct a special conference about those criteria at least once a year, usually by midyear. Another common procedure is to require that principals monitor the frequency with which they discuss all criteria and be certain that at least once a year they discuss all criteria during a formative conference following a classroom observation.

The final guideline in Figure 6.1 is really a catch-all to eliminate any ambiguity about whether or not a conference needs to be conducted. Knowing when a conference is unnecessary is just as important as knowing when to conference. The most common confusion results from brief classroom visits that were made for reasons other than collecting performance data. Effective principals are highly visible throughout the school building, particularly in the classrooms. Therefore, the frequency with which they go to the classroom to collect observation data that necessitate a conference may be only a small percentage of the overall time they are in classes. Teachers and principals should be aware of the importance of visibility throughout the building and realize that postobservation conferences will be held if the principal was conducting a planned observation or noted significant performance during an unplanned observation. A conference must be conducted if the principal recorded information on the Formative Data Form. Careful consideration of this guideline will reduce teachers' anxiety about conferences and give the principal a clear understanding of when to conference. Evaluative consultants have an axiom for this guideline: "If you didn't write it down, it didn't happen. If you didn't discuss it, it didn't happen. If you do one, you must do both."

STRATEGIES FOR CONFERENCING

A basic psychological premise for effective conferencing is that professional development of adults occurs more rapidly and with greater effectiveness when the adult is receptive to professional development. There is a greater chance that this receptivity will be present if teachers are treated as professionals and given the opportunity to assess and understand their abilities rather than having their strengths and weaknesses itemized for them by the supervisor during a conference. Internalizing the attitude of openness and the skill of self-analysis are important goals of the formative conference.

Educators commonly refer to formative conferences as feedback conferences. Consider the meaning of the word *feedback* and the conferencing process typically used in school districts. The term implies (and common practice supports the notion) that a feedback conference is one-way communication from the supervisor to the teacher about performance. In the literal sense, feedback is appropriate in particular situations, but it should not become the commonplace methodology for conferencing, particularly formative conferencing. Although all conferences are situational, a skilled supervisor attempts to emphasize the self-assessing, collegial aspects of the conference and deemphasize the feedback, authoritative approach.

The educational literature and administrative workshops are replete with suggested strategies for conducting teacher conferences. Most of these suggestions evolve from writings about clinical supervision. Often the authors deliberately disassociate clinical supervision from evaluation. However, the principal who confronts the realities of teacher evaluation on a daily basis must develop conferencing skills, and many of those skills have evolved from the field of clinical supervision. Yet, evaluative conferencing is more complex than clinical supervision conferencing because of the need to discuss both classroom and nonclassroom performance and to assess performance on specific criteria. For the principal skilled in clinical supervision conferencing, integration of those skills with the following suggestions should increase effectiveness in developmental evaluation conferencing. For the principal developing initial skills in conferencing, the suggestions can provide a foundation for developmental conferencing. Instruction, practice, self-assessment, and feedback, followed by more instruction, practice, and self-assessment, are key ingredients to developing effective conferencing skills. Educators who regularly provide workshops on conferencing skills indicate that several days of training and many weeks of practice on the job are necessary to develop high-quality conferencing skills.

Classroom Observation Conferences

Postobservation conferences are the most common type of formative conference. Conducting an effective formative conference necessitates the use of many general administrative skill areas, particularly analysis, judgment, sensitivity, and communication. The principal must analyze the teaching performance, use good judgment about the effectiveness of both the lesson and the strategies to work with the teacher, be sensitive to the teacher's personal and professional needs, and communicate effectively with the teacher during and after the conference. An effective conference is the result of proper planning and the understanding and application of effective interpersonal communication skills, both principal–teacher verbal behavior (Valentine, Tate, Seagren, & Lammel, 1975) and nonverbal behavior (Stephens & Valentine, 1986).

Numerous manuscripts (Hyman, 1975; Acheson & Gall, 1980; Cogan, 1973; McGreal, 1983; Glatthorn, 1984) have been published describing the specific skills necessary for conducting effective postobservation conferences. Skills more specific to postobservation conferences in performance-based developmental evaluation systems were listed by Tyson and Valentine (1984). They described four skill areas: (1) promoting self-assessment, (2) sharing notes, (3) discussing each criterion, and (4) creating participative dialogue. Pulliam and Valentine (1987) refined the skill areas with the development of the Assessment of Post-Observation Conference Skills instrument (APOCS). The APOCS instrument grouped conferencing behaviors in seven skill areas: (1) Preparation, (2) Establishing Set, (3) Diagnosis, (4) Focus for Growth, (5) Commitment to Growth, (6) Closure, and (7) Interpersonal Communication (Appendix B). Pulliam (1988) further refined the instrumentation to the skill areas of (1) Diagnosis, (2) Focus, (3) Communication, (4) Orientation, (5) Utilization of Notes, and (6) Environment.

The terms used to describe the skill areas are descriptive of the issues principals should consider when conducting postobservation conferences. The following sections provide specific suggestions for conducting effective postobservation conferences in performance-based developmental evaluation.

```
┌─────────────────────────────────────────────────┐
│                  Principle 18                     │
│        Effective  preparation  precedes           │
│            effective   conferences.               │
└─────────────────────────────────────────────────┘
```

Preparing for the Conference

A principal who is preparing for a postobservation conference must complete several physical and mental tasks. These include (1) preparing the observation notes and Formative Data Form, (2) determining the time and location of the conference, (3) arranging the conference setting for effective communication, (4) determining the teacher's receptivity to the process, and (5) maintaining a focus on improved outcomes.

Notes and Forms.   A good-quality set of observation notes is the foundation of a good conference. When feasible, the teacher should be given a copy before the conference. Specific examples of behavior and appropriate information from the observation notes should be transferred to the Formative Data Form prior to the conference. The observation notes and the Formative Data Form should be ready for use during the conference, and the teacher should leave the conference with a copy of the observation notes and the form.

Time.   The principal should work with the teacher to schedule the conference within two school days after the observation. Enough time should be set aside to complete the conference so that neither party feels rushed. As a rule of thumb, principals seem to complete postobservation conferences within a time frame comparable to the length of the classroom observation. For example, if the principal took notes for thirty minutes, thirty minutes should be allowed for the conference.

Location.   A location that affords privacy is a must for conferencing. Conducting the conference in the teacher's classroom is unwise. A student or another teacher may inadvertently hear a comment out of context, and soon the rumor mill will be overflowing with the teacher's problems. No teacher deserves to have others think the principal is concerned about his or her behavior. The principal's office is usually the most appropriate place. The secretary should be asked to hold all nonemergency calls. Behind closed doors, the principal and teacher can relax and enjoy a few uninterrupted minutes talking about effective teaching.

Setting. Postobservation communication is usually most effective when the principal and teacher are seated at the corner of a table or desk with the observation notes and Formative Data Form between them so that both can view the material they are discussing. Furniture may need to be rearranged to promote this setting.

To underscore the importance of working at the corner of a table or desk, consider two other typical settings. First, think about the teacher's perception of the conference when the principal sits behind a desk, with the teacher seated on the opposite side of the desk. This "power position" is seldom appropriate for postobservation conferences because it is not conducive to a collaborative discussion. Second, consider the perceptions of a teacher when the principal sits beside the teacher at a table or on a couch. To view the same notes, the two must sit rather close. No matter how innocent, an inadvertent touch or an arm around the back of the chair can cause discomfort or intimidation without the slightest intent to do so. Administrative behavior should promote trust and security, not anxiety. The physical setting should promote the best chance of an effective collegial conference. Most principals who have tried the "corner setting" like it.

Receptivity. Assessing the teacher's receptivity to observations, conferencing, and suggestions for improvement is a task most principals complete subconsciously. Because of the obvious relationship between conference effectiveness and teacher receptivity, this assessment should be conscious. Understanding the teacher's attitude toward the evaluation process or the teacher's mental readiness for growth may affect the goals the principal establishes for the conference and the manner in which the principal conducts the conference. If teacher receptivity is low, extended time may be needed to underscore the value of the process and reinforce a collegial, developmental philosophy. Detailed dialogue about the purposes of performance-based developmental evaluation and the roles of the principal and teacher in the process may be appropriate. At that time, building a trusting relationship may be a higher priority than detailed analysis of teaching behavior.

In extreme cases, a teacher's attitude may be so negative that the concept of collegial conferencing must be set aside in favor of a more authoritative conference. A principal should make the decision to move from a collegial to an authoritative conference on the basis of observed behavior of the teacher, not an assumption about attitude before the conference begins. The teacher deserves the benefit of the doubt until his or her behavior proves that there is a problem. In other words, the principal should try to proceed with the conference in a collegial manner until such time as a change in strategy is forced by the teacher's behavior.

Outcomes. Use of the classroom observation notes to complete the Formative Data Form promotes analysis of the instructional process and the teacher's performance. At that time the principal should begin to conceptualize desired outcomes for the conference. A desired outcome may be at the knowledge, understanding, application, internalization, process, or attitude level. The intent of the outcome need not reflect a perceived deficiency in performance. Too often principals feel the need to identify a problem in performance even when there is none. Looking for problems often results in a focus on trivial behavior rather than on skills that make a difference for students. This type of principal behavior creates attitude and credibility problems with the teacher. The criteria, not the descriptors, are the basis for assessing performance problems. Maintaining a focus on the criteria helps alleviate "trivial pursuit" and promotes a focus on worthwhile goals for the conference.

Establishing Set for the Conference

The first few minutes of a formative conference set the stage for the conference. During that time, the principal wants to develop in the mind of the teacher a mental readiness for the conference. Consider the importance of the following issues in the establishment of that positive set.

Purpose and Perspective. A brief discussion of the value of the conference and its relationship to the PBDE process clarifies the significance of the conference for the teacher. The discussion should reassure the teacher that the objective of the conference is instructional improvement, not employment decision making. A description of the activities that will make up the conference may be reassuring to the teacher and help him or her to understand why the criteria are the content of the conference. Referencing previous conferences or explaining how this conference fits with the other components of performance-based developmental evaluation may promote an appreciation of the value of the conference and the entire evaluation process. The purpose of the conference is to discuss effective teaching, and the teacher needs to hear that stated as such.

Clarify Roles. The principal should discuss the importance of the teacher taking an active role in the conference. The teacher needs to understand that this is a collegial and collaborative activity and that his or her perception is as important as, or more important than, the principal's. The principal should discuss the value of self-assessment and point out that the conference is designed to promote self-assessment. He or she should indicate that both the principal and the teacher should discuss each criterion and that, for the conference to be worthwhile to the teacher, discussing the data and stimulating thinking must be shared roles.

General to Specific. Understanding the effectiveness of a lesson requires the assimilation of many factors. By the end of a conference, the teacher and the principal should be able to discuss the degree to which the lesson did or did not make a difference for the students. To arrive at that point, the principal facilitates self-assessment on the criteria, the critical aspects of effective teaching. To initiate the self-assessment, the principal might ask the teacher to move from the general to the specific—in other words, to "consider the overall impact of the lesson in the context of the desired learner outcomes, the lesson objectives." Then specific criteria can be discussed. When approached effectively, this opening discussion can establish a pattern of involvement and self-assessment for the remainder of the conference.

Example 6.1 is an opening statement as a principal begins a conference with a teacher named Loren Stewart. Critique this opening statement on the basis of the issues discussed in this section on establishing set.

Promoting Self-Directed Learning

The conference is a learning experience for principal and teacher alike. Each should teach and each should learn. For effective learning to occur, the level of thinking must rise above superficial analysis of

---

EXAMPLE 6.1
Postobservation Conference with Loren Stewart:
Opening Comments

Loren, as you recall from our previous meetings, this conference provides us with the opportunity to discuss the lesson I observed. As you know, while I was in the classroom I took detailed notes of what you and the students were saying and doing. Those notes provide the basis for our discussion.

After the observation, I took a few minutes and grouped the notes according to the criteria on our Formative Data Form. Our task now is to consider what we can learn from that information about the effectiveness of the lesson.

Thinking through those issues is a responsibility for both of us. I would like us to talk through the notes together. In fact, I would like for you to do as much or more talking than I because you have the best handle on the lesson--the objectives and activities you chose to reach the objectives. Conferencing is much more valuable for you, the teacher, if it involves self-assessment.

As you know, my role is to stimulate our thinking, not to have all the answers. I would like us to think through the lesson together, using the criteria on the Formative Data Form to focus our discussion. We'll look at the data on the Form, the notes I took in class and I'll make additional notes as you help me better understand your thinking during the lesson. To begin with, I would like for us to first consider the bigger picture of the lesson. You had some objectives you wanted to accomplish with the lesson. If you would, share with me what those objectives were and how you felt about your ability to accomplish the objectives.

---

teaching behaviors. The focus of the conversation must continually return to the impact of the lesson on the students. Teaching is more than merely performing skills for the principal to observe and record. It is a relationship with students that stimulates their intellectual and emotional capacities because the teacher makes appropriate decisions. Teaching is decision making exhibited through performance. The principal and teacher should discuss both the performance and the decision making—in other words, the behavior and the thinking that precipitated the behavior. They should begin the discussion with a focus on desired learner outcomes, continue that focus with discussions of the criteria, and conclude the conference with student interests in mind.

```
                        Principle  19
        Conferencing  is  teaching  self-assessment
               and  self-directed  learning.
```

As the principal assesses the lesson and works with the teacher to promote self-assessment, the principal's role is in fact that of a teacher. The principal's goal for the teacher is self-directed learning. In other words, the principal desires to develop within the teacher the ability to self-assess the lesson and the teacher's performance and, theoretically, to conduct the postobservation conference without assistance. Unfortunately, few teachers achieve the goal of self-directed learning. Assistance is necessary, and the conference provides the opportunity for that assistance.

Focusing on Observed Data and Criteria

The criteria define the competencies expected of teachers in a given school system. They should be the framework for the conference. Notice the statement by the principal from Example 6.1: "I would like us to think through the lesson together, using the criteria on the Formative Data Form to focus our discussion." The principal plans to discuss each instructional criterion with the teacher. Proceeding in that manner, the principal brings attention to the defined issues of teaching. The dialogue can revolve around observed data and lead to a productive learning experience about the importance of each criterion and the skills typically associated with the criterion.

```
                        Principle  20
        The  criteria  on  the  Formative  Data  Form
        are  the  content  basis  for  the  conference.
```

Using the criteria as the procedural basis for the conference also eliminates a sometimes conscious, sometimes unconscious psychological nemesis. Too often principals spend the first thirty minutes or so of a conference discussing all the good skill areas and save the bad areas for the last few minutes. When teachers learn to expect this as standard operating procedure in a conference, they will be inattentive during the "strokes" because of their anxiety while awaiting the "zingers." Such conferencing strategies can lead to feelings of being manipulated, feelings not conducive to an effective conference. If the principal follows the criteria in the order they appear on the Formative Data Form, the "strokes" and "zingers" are not patterned. This approach promotes greater attentiveness and better communication and trust during the conference (Valentine, 1988).

Good judgment is needed when deciding whether or not to deviate from discussing the criteria in the exact order they appear on the Formative Data Form. For example, a teacher might initiate a discussion about the fifth criterion while the principal and teacher are discussing the second criterion. To fail to take advantage of the comments and move to a discussion of the fifth criterion might mean losing the moment of interest and receptivity. As in teaching, flexibility and decision making are important skills in supervision. When the teacher is mentally ready to discuss the fifth criterion, why delay the discussion ten minutes just to maintain sequence? However, those who hop around during the discussion of the criteria, should check off each criterion as it is discussed so they are certain each has been covered. It is discomfiting to the principal when a teacher indicates two months later that the principal did not discuss a particular criterion. Being systematic in the conference assures the principal that all the issues were discussed.

The criteria form the basis for diagnostic thinking. Specific diagnostic behaviors include probing and analytical questions, stimulating comments, challenging suppositions, affective questions, encouragement, and reinforcement. Collegial assessment and problem-solving skills that focus on each criterion are essential to effective diagnosis during a developmental conference. Example 6.2 is a continuation of the postconference with Loren Stewart. The comments are those of the principal after Loren and the principal discussed the lesson objectives and their feelings about accomplishing the objectives established through the comments in Example 6.1. Consider how the principal brings the discussion with Loren to the criteria on the Formative Data Form.

Promoting Self-Assessment

Understanding the importance of self-assessment is much easier than implementing the concept during a postobservation conference. The questions asked of teachers during the conference are essential to effective self-assessment. Recall-level questions usually elicit responses that describe behavior. Higher order questions, which require

---

**EXAMPLE 6.2
Postobservation Conference with Loren Stewart:
Criterion Diagnosis**

Loren, let's look next at the criteria on the Formative Data Form. As you can see, the first criterion is demonstrates appropriate preparation for classroom instruction. Let's consider that criterion on two levels. First, the cognitive level. What information did you consider using as you conceptualized your lesson plan? Second, what tasks or activities did you complete to physically and intellectually prepare for the lesson?

---

analysis, decision making, and expression of feelings and perceptions, usually stimulate higher order thinking and self-assessment (Valentine, 1973). The use of probing questions to follow up a response promotes self-assessment. Indirect verbal behaviors such as paraphrasing, restating, or reinforcing a teacher's comments also promote self-assessment (Denney, 1983). The use of active listening skills such as facial expressions of interest, body posture, smiles, eye contact, and attentive comments encourages communication and self-assessment during a conference. Principals should use eliciting, rather than constraining, communication behaviors (Valentine, 1973; Kettler, 1982; Denney, 1983).

An interesting barometer of self-assessment is the amount of talking done by the principal and the teacher, respectively, during a conference. Although there is a lack of causal data relating the amount of talk directly to the effectiveness of the conference, some implications can be made from the research and from field observations (Valentine, 1973; Kettler, 1982; Denney, 1983). A ratio of 1:1—in other words, 50 percent principal talk and 50 percent teacher talk during a conference—is a logical expectation. The conference is collaborative, and that implies that both parties participate significantly. Increasing teacher talk to 60 or 70 percent might be appropriate when trying to promote self-assessment. However, too many variables affect those ratios to permit the establishment of definitive percentages. The experience of the teacher, their understanding of the process, the intellectual level of the teacher or the principal, the sophistication of the lesson, and the teacher's receptivity are some of the more typical compounding variables.

Extremes near either end of this verbal percentage continuum should send warning signals to the principal. It is very common in postobservation conferences for nearly all talk to be by the principal. The principal has invested time in observing the lesson, transferring the notes, and planning and conducting the conference. Therefore, the principal should have a good knowledge of the teacher's skills during the lesson. Given the time invested and the knowledge developed, there is a tendency for the principal to *tell* the teacher all that he or she has learned rather than to ask the teacher to share what the latter was doing, feeling, and thinking during the lesson. When principals are in the mode of telling rather than listening, they place themselves in the difficult position of having to have all the answers to all the problems. The conference should be an exercise in collaborative, not unilateral, problem solving.

At the other end of the continuum is the conference at which the teacher does all or almost all of the talking. The principal elicits comments and the teacher carries the entire conversation. If the teacher has internalized the self-assessment skills and moved to the higher levels of thinking necessary to be a self-directed learner, the principal can sit back and marvel at the teacher's ability. However, few teachers exhibit that skill. The conference is the principal's classroom, and active teaching requires interaction with the students (i.e., the teachers). A conference totally dominated by either person is seldom as productive as a collaborative effort.

Although the benefits of the self-assessment approach outweigh the negative aspects, problems occasionally arise with some teachers. For example, consider the teacher who refuses to self-assess performance or competence honestly. The principal has patiently asked the teacher to discuss the criteria, and the teacher has consistently responded with obviously erroneous answers. The teacher will not admit to ineptness in the classroom for fear the principal will use that admission against the teacher. Obviously, the real problem is lack of trust in the principal, the process, or both. In such instances, the principal must candidly address the lack of self-assessment. If the teacher persists in making erroneous self-assessments and offering inflated perceptions, the principal may need to become more authoritative than collegial and reclarify the teacher's responsibility in developmental evaluation. If the teacher refuses to cooperate, then consideration should be given to issuing a formal reprimand or to developing a Professional Development Plan designed to modify the teacher's attitude. There is no place in teaching for a person who is not open to a fair process of professional development, especially when that process is consciously designed to help the teacher improve before summative evaluations are prepared.

Two caveats concerning the principal–teacher talk ratio are appropriate for those principals desiring to gauge their own talk ratios. First, each conference is unique. Circumstances dictate strategies, and the

50-50 talk ratio is only a gross measure of self-assessment, to be used with caution. Second, experience from workshops in which principals estimate the amount of time they talk indicates that their self-estimates are unreliable. Observers note that principals generally underestimate the amount of time they talk. In other words, principals who estimate they talk 50 percent of the time during a conference really talk 60 or 70 percent of the time.

Clarifying All Critical Issues

Although self-assessment is a major strategy for most formative postobservation conferences, the principal must be clear when expressing concern about critical issues. For example, if the principal is concerned because the teacher did not establish set for the lesson the principal observed, the principal cannot just casually mention that the teacher should "find ways to better begin classes," and expect the teacher to understand the level of concern or strategies to resolve the concern. The principal must clearly state the concern, discuss why it is a concern in the context of student learning and effective teaching, and discuss strategies for addressing the concern. These clarifying tasks can usually be accomplished without sacrificing the overall strategy of self-assessment; without putting the teacher on the defensive; and without moving from an indirect, collaborative, problem-solving approach to a more direct, authoritative approach.

> **Principle 21**
> **All significant issues are clarified during formative conferences.**

The principal must also clarify the degree of concern. Most concerns about teaching performance are relatively minor and easily resolved by discussing the issue and making suggestions for change. A concern that was noticed and discussed for the first time as a result of a classroom observation is seldom significant enough to proceed directly to a Professional Development Plan denoting a deficiency. Usually, the first step is to make verbal suggestions and to give the teacher the opportunity to resolve the concern. Most issues are best solved at that level. If not resolved through verbal suggestions, the next step might be to document the concern on the Formative Data Form and make written suggestions on the form. If the problem is not resolved within a realistic time frame, the next step might be to formalize the concern as a Professional Development Plan. Good teachers take pride in their work and are sensitive to their skills and to the needs of their students. Every effort should be made to treat them with sensitivity and professional courtesy. Using the sledge hammer to kill the mouse in the basement is seldom the most appropriate strategy. The task may be accomplished, but the damage to the basement will be noticed for years. Performance problems are best resolved at the level of least damage to the professionalism of the individual.

Achieving Closure

In the jargon of teaching and learning, achieving closure means reviewing, reinforcing, and placing in context the main points of the lesson for the learner so the students leave with a clear understanding of what they have learned during the lesson (Valentine, 1984, 1985). In the formative conference, closure is essentially the same process with the same desired outcome. Closure provides the opportunity to reinforce important issues and check for agreement and understanding. It provides the link to future observations or developmental activities. Any suggested strategies for improvement or plans for future meetings to develop growth plans can be reinforced.

As with so many terms in education, the word *closure* is misleading when considered literally, because it implies finality. In reality, closure is more than the conclusion of a conference; it is the planting of seeds for future discussions about teaching performance. It sets the stage for future activities and therefore should be a positive and realistic experience. If change is needed, honesty is imperative. But honesty can be tempered with positiveness about the potential for the teacher and the students if the change is accomplished. The postobservation classroom conference should end on a positive but realistic note.

Nonclassroom Observation Conferences

An effective performance-based developmental evaluation system requires formative conferencing for all types of performance data. In the previous sections, suggestions were made for conferencing following scheduled or unscheduled classroom observations by the principal. Although those are the most common types of conferences, PBDE procedures also require conferences concerning nonclassroom data that are observed, nonclassroom data that are not observed by the principal, and artifact data.

Conferences should be similar regardless of the type of data. Performance data are recorded on the Formative Data Form prior to the conference. The teacher is expected to participate actively in the conference and to self-assess his or her ability. The framework for all conferencing should be the criteria. The focus of a conference should be on what is best for students even though the behaviors discussed are not as directly related to students as is teacher performance in the classroom. Good judgment and common sense applied to the suggested strategies discussed for conferencing following classroom observations are the basis for effective conferencing about nonclassroom performance.

SUMMARY

The principal should be the consummate teacher! This concept is certainly ideal, but is it realistic? Consider the teacher as the pupil, the postobservation conference as the classroom, more effective teaching through internalization of the professional development process as the curricular goal, and the following objectives to accomplish the goal:

1. Develop a competent knowledge base about effective teaching.

2. Develop the ability to translate that knowledge base into instructional performance.

3. Develop a commitment to self-improvement.

4. Develop the ability to evaluate performance.

5. Develop the ability to conceptualize strategies to improve performance.

A cynic might say that such a goal and objectives are unrealistic. But why not be idealistic? High expectations have to be established. Without such expectations, the principalship will never transcend the image of manager to become that of educational leader. The principal as the teacher of teachers is an honorable role, one that is being fulfilled by thousands of principals every day across our nation.

In striving for the goal of internalization of the professional development process, adult learning theories must be considered. Costa, Garmston, and Lambert (1988) present a model of adult learning that categorizes "learning" for entry-level teachers, tenured teachers, and master teachers. Each level proceeds through the developmental phases of knowing, doing, valuing, and thinking. Benchmarks of development are provided for each level and phase of the learning model. The model personifies the effective teacher—the educator who values, develops, and internalizes openness, self-improvement, and conceptual thinking. These are the outcomes to be valued in the dialogue between principal and teacher as they interact throughout the school year about professional performance and the resultant impact on students. Pragmatically speaking, these are desired results of effective formative conferences.

REFERENCES

Acheson, K. A., & Gall, M. D. (1980). *Techniques in the clinical supervision of teachers: Preservice and Inservice Applications.* New York: Longman.

Cogan, M. L. (1973). *Clinical supervision.* Boston: Houghton Mifflin.

Costa, A. L., Garmston, R. J., & Lambert, L. (1988). Evaluation of teaching: The cognitive development view. In S. J. Stanley & W. J. Popham (Eds.), *Teacher evaluation: Six prescriptions for success* (pp. 145-172). Alexandria, VA: Association for Supervision and Curriculum Development.

Davis, J. W. (1988). *The relationship between selected performance evaluation procedures and principals' perceptions about performance evaluation.* Doctoral dissertation, University of Missouri–Columbia, 1988. (*Dissertation Abstracts International,* 50/04, 837-A)

Denney, J. D. (1983). *The relationship of principal verbal behavior to teacher perception of communication and organizational climate in middle level schools.* Doctoral dissertation, University of Missouri–Columbia, 1983. (*Dissertation Abstracts International,* 44/10, 2937-A)

Ginos, N. A. (1985). *The relationship of inservice training to effective evaluation.* Doctoral dissertation, University of Missouri–Columbia, 1985. (*Dissertation Abstracts International,* 47/02, 361-A)

Glatthorn, A. A. (1984). *Differential supervision.* Alexandria, VA: Association for Supervision and Curriculum Development.

Hyman, R. (1975). *School administrator's handbook of teacher supervision and evaluation methods.* Englewood Cliffs, NJ: Prentice-Hall.

Kettler, R. E. (1982). *An analysis of principal verbal behavior.* Doctoral dissertation, University of Missouri–Columbia, 1982. (*Dissertation Abstracts International,* 43/06, 1771-A)

McGreal, T. L. (1983). *Successful teacher evaluation.* Alexandria, VA: Association for Supervision and Curriculum Development.

Moore, L. C. (1986). *The relationship between performance evaluation job targets and teacher attitudes and success.* Doctoral dissertation, University of Missouri–Columbia, 1986. (*Dissertation Abstracts International,* 47/08, 2833-A)

Pulliam, D. J. (1988). *Assessment of principal conferencing skills.* Doctoral dissertation, University of Missouri–Columbia, 1988. (*Dissertation Abstracts International,* 49/11, 3227-A)

Pulliam, D. J., & Valentine, J. W. (1987). Assessment of post-observation conference skills, Form 4-87. In Pulliam (1988).

Stephens, P. S., & Valentine, J. W. (1986). Assessing principal nonverbal communication. *Educational Research Quarterly, 10*(3), 60–68.

Tyson, T., & Valentine, J. W. (1984). PBTE: Tips for organization and implementation. Available from Missouri Leadership Academy, Missouri Department of Elementary and Secondary Education, P.O. Box 480, Jefferson City, MO 65102.

Valentine, J. W. (1973). *A model of administrative verbal behavior for principal-teacher interaction.* Doctoral dissertation, University of Nebraska–Lincoln, 1973. (*Dissertation Abstracts International,* 34/05, 2248-A)

Valentine, J. W. (1984). Instructional strategy. In J. W. Keefe & J. M. Jenkins (Eds.), *Instructional leadership handbook* (Section 73). Reston, VA: National Association of Secondary School Principals.

Valentine, J. W. (1985). Applying the steps in the teaching process. *Missouri Schools, 51*(1), 18–20.

Valentine, J. W. (1988). *Performance/outcome-based principal evaluation.* Paper presented at the annual convention of the National Association of Secondary School Principals, Anaheim, California, March 6, 1988.

Valentine, J. W., Tate, B. L., Seagren, A. T., & Lammel, J. A. (1975). Administrative verbal behavior: What you say does make a difference. *NASSP Bulletin, 59*(395), 67–74.

CHAPTER 7

Professional Development Plans

The greatest revolution of our generation is the discovery that human beings, by changing their inner attitudes of their minds, can change the outer aspects of their lives.
—William James

A PROCESS FOR continual professional development is critical in an effective evaluation system. Consider the definition of performance-based developmental evaluation presented in Chapter 1. *Performance-based developmental teacher evaluation is a process for professional improvement that includes identifying performance expectations, documenting performance, conferencing about performance, developing plans to improve performance, and making personnel decisions based upon performance.* The "opportunity to improve performance" on a continuous basis supports the primary goal of evaluation as a process for promoting teacher development, not for gathering data to make employment decisions. This ongoing process for performance improvement is a vital component in the formative phase of performance-based developmental evaluation.

CONTRASTING APPROACHES TO IMPROVEMENT

The importance of the improvement component as a basic part of an evaluation system is supported in educational literature. Terminology frequently used to describe these processes include Management by Objectives (Odiorne, 1965), Job Improvement Targets (Redfern, 1980; Manatt, 1988), Practical Goal-Setting Approach (McGreal, 1983), Growth Plans (Harris, 1986), and Professional Development Plans (Valentine, 1986). Many school districts refer to their specific improvement plans as a Growth Plan, a Professional Development Plan, a Professional Improvement Plan, a Job Target, a Personal Development Plan, or any of several terms usually formed from the adjectives *professional, personal, improvement,* and *growth* (Valentine, 1987).

While the basic concept of improvement appears similar because of similar terminology, the implementation strategies associated with evaluation models vary significantly. McGreal (1983) grouped the various models into three approaches: (1) the Management by Objectives approach, (2) the Performance Objectives approach, and (3) the Practical Goal-Setting approach. He explained each approach, describing the typical differences and similarities between them. He noted that each approach attempts to bring focus to the teacher–principal activities through a goal-setting process.

The term Professional Development Plan is used to describe the formal process for improvement in performance-based developmental teacher evaluation. Although the Professional Development Plan is a unique approach, it does share some of the basic concepts of the three evaluative approaches described by McGreal (1983). The Performance Objectives approach and the Practical Goal-Setting approach have the most in common with the Professional Development Plan approach described in this book. For example, the Professional Development Plan approach and the Performance Objectives approach use: (1) criteria as the basis for improvement, (2) collaborative discussion of the teacher's performance, and (3) an action plan to accomplish the objectives. For more detailed information about the Performance Objectives approach, George Redfern's (1980) *Evaluating Teachers and Administrators: A Performance Objectives Approach* is recommended.

Concepts common to the Professional Development Plan approach and the Practical Goal-Setting approach include (1) emphasis on the quality rather than the amount of time spent between principal and teacher, (2) clear delineation of the basic purpose of the evaluation system, and (3) an understanding that not all improvement activities are for remediation of deficiencies. *Successful Teacher Evaluation* (McGreal, 1983) is an excellent source for more information about the Practical Goal-Setting approach.

THE PROFESSIONAL DEVELOPMENT
PLAN APPROACH

Implementing the improvement component is one of the most challenging tasks for the principal in the performance-based developmental evaluation process. The principal must understand, be able to articulate, and be committed to a philosophy of improvement. The principal must also possess the skills necessary to implement the process in a manner that promotes among teachers feelings of trust and confidence in the principal and the process.

The obvious rationale for the use of an improvement component is to improve performance. It is based on the premise that all personnel should maintain a focus on improvement during their professional career. That is not to imply that teachers are deficient. To the contrary, few teachers receive deficiency ratings on summative evaluations if the principal works effectively with the teachers during the formative evaluation cycle. However, the statement does imply that every professional educator should be responsive to the continual need for improving professional competence. Not to make a conscious effort to grow as a professional is to lose ground with respect to one's current knowledge and skill in the profession. To choose not to grow is to regress—and that is inexcusable for a professional. For example, the knowledge base about effective teaching is constantly expanding. Without a commitment to growth, a teacher will not be aware of or able to implement current knowledge about teaching. Over time, students will not receive the quality of teaching that might have been possible had the teacher kept abreast of that knowledge base. Educators must be committed to continuous professional maturation.

Principle 22
Professional development plans
are developed collaboratively.

Few teachers consciously reject the opportunity to develop professionally. Unfortunately, however, too few school systems provide an ongoing focus on individual development in the personnel evaluation process. Staff development activities provided in school systems are frequently large-group sessions consisting of presentations and workshops at a school, a district office, a university, or a conference center. The topics are designed to meet the common needs of many, rather than the specific needs of individuals. Certainly, there is a need for the large-group dissemination of information and the opportunity to apply that information. But personalized staff development is just as important, if not more so. The Professional Development Plan provides the format that ensures that a logistically manageable, ongoing, personalized development program will occur on a regular basis for each teacher in the district.

An effectively implemented Professional Development Plan approach to improvement can produce the following outcomes:

1. Promote a belief among staff that improvement is an important professional responsibility.

2. Develop a level of expectation that all staff should strive to grow professionally.

3. Create a climate of receptivity to new ideas and knowledge.

4. Promote dialogue between principal and teacher about professional performance and effective schooling.

5. Promote among principals a commitment to development of all teachers.

6. Develop among principals the ability to articulate and implement developmental activities.

7. Develop among teachers the belief that principals are knowledgeable about instructional improvement.

8. Promote an intellectual focus on specific performance criteria and objectives for growth.

9. Promote growth, not busy-work.

10. Positively reinforce quality teachers.

11. Force principals and teachers to discuss their concerns collegially and develop plans to address these concerns.

12. Facilitate teachers' abilities to internalize the improvement process.

13. Structure the process for improvement to include objectives, activities, responsibilities, time frame, and outcomes.

14. Create a personalized staff development plan for each teacher.

Although all of the outcomes listed here are possible, they are not always achieved when a school or school system implements an improvement plan process. Obviously, the improvement component must be implemented as a part of an entire developmental evaluation process, and specific procedures should be followed to increase the opportunity for success. Omission of key procedural steps, the principal's lack of specific skills, and overriding cultural or climatic problems are three of the more apparent reasons that some school districts reap fewer benefits than others from improvement plans.

Operational Procedures

Making effective use of the professional development plan approach requires that the principal have an understanding of and an ability to articulate the rationale and procedures for professional improvement. The principal must also have the ability to implement the procedures in a manner that promotes trust and confidence. Attention to the operational questions discussed in this section and to the details for developing plans discussed in the next section will increase the likelihood that the process will achieve the outcomes previously listed. The sequence of events for writing a Professional Development Plan (PDP), outlined in Figure 7.1, are discussed in the remainder of this chapter.

1. *Who writes the PDP?* The Professional Development Plan (PDP) is written by the principal in collaboration with the teacher. The principal does the writing to ensure consistent expectations and a high-quality plan that will make a difference for the teacher, not just create busy-work. Although the principal may do the actual writing, the ingredients of the plan should be discussed and developed together with the teacher. Teachers in schools where improvement plans are developed collaboratively believe the evaluation process has a significantly more positive impact on instruction and student achievement than in schools where principals prepare the plans and give them to the teachers or, conversely, where teachers prepare the plans and give them to the principal (Brown, 1987). The improvement plan should be a joint endeavor.

2. *Which teachers have PDPs?* Each teacher should have an improvement plan at some time during the evaluation cycle. When all teachers develop a plan for improvement, the developmental nature of evaluation is reinforced. When *only* those teachers who are marginal or obviously deficient have improvement plans, the summative, judgmental nature of evaluation is reinforced. As with all components of the evaluation process, the operational procedures selected by the District Evaluation Committee when the evaluation system was developed directly affect the attitude of staff toward the evaluative process. Davis (1988) found significantly more positive perceptions of the effective-

FIGURE 7.1   Professional Development Plan approach.

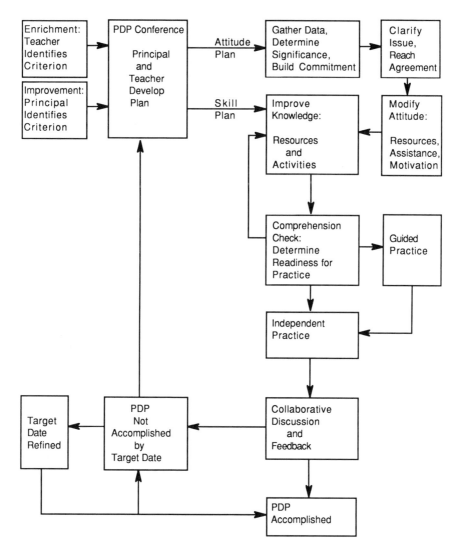

ness of the evaluation system and its impact on instructional improvement if improvement plans were used for all teachers, not just those with deficiencies. Developing plans for all teachers is a key to the overall effectiveness of the PDP approach. Without it, the evaluation system becomes a staff development process for only the weaker teachers, not a developmental process for all staff. The adage, "You don't have to be ill to get better," applies to all teachers.

Principle 23
Professional development plans are for all staff at some time in the formative phase.

---

3. *How frequently are PDPs developed?* The principal should work with each teacher to develop at least one PDP during each evaluation cycle. Some teachers may need to work on more than one. Because all staff members will work with the principal to prepare the PDP, the frequency with which plans are developed for each teacher must take practical considerations into account. While few would question the importance of investing time in instructional leadership, or the key role developmental evaluation can play in accomplishing the goal of instructional leadership, all aspects of the evaluation process must be "time-realistic." If the principal is expected to spend an inordinate amount of time in a given process, he or she may have no choice but to omit a procedure or rush through the task. Too often, when a principal rushes the process, the task is poorly accomplished, or the principal and teacher may simply go through the motions to finish the task. Teachers will express reluctance to develop improvement plans when they feel the principal is not effective in working with them to develop a quality plan (Moore, 1986).

Two suggestions can make the process of implementing PDPs more palatable. Place most veteran or tenured teachers on an evaluation cycle of two or three years, and develop a PDP at some time during that two- or three-year period. For teachers new to the profession and for nontenured teachers, use an evaluation cycle every year. Because these teachers are still developing their abilities and usually need more assistance, a Professional Development Plan each year during the early stages of a career is appropriate.

4. *Is the PDP enrichment or improvement?* When establishing the time and location for the PDP conference, the principal must clearly indicate whether the purpose of the conference is to write an enrichment or an improvement plan. An *enrichment* plan signifies that the principal has no concerns at this time about the teacher's competence or performance on any criteria. An *improvement* plan means the

principal has a concern about the teacher's performance on some criterion and that this concern will be formalized in the PDP. The improvement plan means the teacher's performance is viewed as deficient and needs to be improved.

Principle 24
Professional development plans are for enrichment and improvement.

If the plan will be for enrichment, the principal should involve the teacher in identifying the criterion for enrichment. The teacher should be asked to review the performance criteria and descriptors prior to the conference and to identify a criterion for which he or she would be interested in preparing a plan. The principal must reassure teachers that they will be writing an enrichment plan, explaining the rationale for the process and describing the basic procedures. If the principal takes the time to articulate the purpose and process, the teacher will usually view this conference without anxiety or resentment. If the principal is skillful in working with teachers to develop meaningful plans, teachers will welcome this conference as an important step in their professional development.

If the plan will be for improvement, the principal must be prepared to explain why there is a concern about a particular criterion. Observed data, nonobserved data, and/or artifact data should be presented to support the concern. Identifying the criterion for an improvement plan is the responsibility of the principal. An improvement plan indicates that the principal believes the teacher's performance on that criterion is not at an acceptable level; if the principal had to complete a Summative Evaluation Report at that time, the teacher would be rated as below expectations on that criterion.

As soon as the principal realizes a concern about performance on a criterion, the principal must visit with the teacher and begin developing the improvement plan for the deficient criterion. If a teacher has a deficiency on more than one criterion, a separate plan must be written for each. Seldom will a teacher have more than two or three deficiencies. If two or more PDPs for improvement need to be developed, the principal should state all concerns and institute a logical process to develop the plans within a reasonable time. Usually, the principal will work with the teacher to develop the first plan, then develop the second a week or so later and the others in a similar sequence. All plans should be identified and developed so the teacher understands the concerns and can begin to resolve them.

5. *Does an improvement PDP always result in a "does not meet expected performance" rating?*   An improvement PDP does not always result in a summative rating below expected performance. Understanding this is important to the philosophy of performance-based developmental evaluation. An improvement plan means there is a concern at the time the plan is developed. But a Summative Evaluation Report to conclude the evaluation cycle may not be written for months or years. During that time, the teacher may have adequately resolved the concern, demonstrated internalization of the skill, and shown no signs of regressing to previously deficient performance levels. In such cases, the principal would be justified in rating the teacher at a "meets expected performance" level on the Summative Evaluation Report. The expected-level rating may be appropriate even though the PDP has not yet been completed. However, if the principal gives a "does not meet expected performance" rating on the next Summative Evaluation Report, a PDP should have been in place to formalize the concern with the teacher and to provide the teacher with strategies, and as much time as feasible, to resolve the concern. Chapter 8 provides more information about the guidelines for preparing summative reports.

6. *Is the focus of the PDP knowledge, skill, or attitude?*   A Professional Development Plan improves effectiveness because the teacher and principal work together to identify and accomplish specific objectives. Plans can be categorized as one of three types: (a) improvement of a knowledge and/or understanding necessary for effective performance, (b) improvement of skill necessary to demonstrate effective performance, and (c) improvement of an attitude that affects effective performance. Plans focusing on knowledge and/or understanding are seldom developed because they assume translation of the knowledge and understanding into performance. The typical PDP combines the improvement of knowledge and/or understanding with the improvement of skill necessary for effective performance. Plans designed to improve attitudes are developed infrequently. They are difficult to conceptualize, defend, and assess, and the success rate is relatively low when compared with skill plans.

7. *What are the options when the PDP has not been accomplished by the completion date?*   Each Professional Development Plan includes a target date for completion of the plan. Whether the PDP was

an enrichment or an improvement plan, the principal must determine if the activities have been completed and appropriate professional growth has been accomplished by the target date.

To conclude an improvement plan, the improvement must have moved the teacher's performance to an acceptable level. If "significant" improvement was accomplished, and the skill level now meets performance expectations, the plan has been completed, and it is signed and filed.

If the performance level for an improvement plan is not acceptable by the completion date, the principal and teacher must discuss the plan and determine the next step. If the improvement activities were accomplished but significant progress was not made, new activities should be developed. If the activities were not completed, more time and perhaps additional resources, activities, or strategies are appropriate. In either case, an improvement plan should not be signed and filed unless it has been completed. The third possibility for an improvement plan is that the plan was written for the wrong criterion and a completely new plan must be written.

If the activities for an enrichment plan have not been accomplished by the completion date, the principal and teacher should consider the same alternatives of refining the activities, extending the time frame, or developing a different plan. If an enrichment plan was not completed because of purposeful neglect of responsibility, an improvement plan for "demonstrating commitment to professional growth" should be discussed and considered.

Strategies for Writing Professional Development Plans

The items listed on a PDP are similar to those found in growth plans in most evaluation systems. The plans typically include a statement of objectives, a list of the activities designed to accomplish the objectives, a description of the assessment method, and a place for signatures (Example 7.1). The manner in which the segments are written distinguishes plans that will make a difference in teacher effectiveness from those that will not. The remainder of this chapter provides suggestions and examples for completing each segment of a PDP in a performance-based developmental evaluation system.

Identification of the Criterion

Identification of the performance criterion is the first step in the development of a Professional Development Plan. A PDP is written to

---

EXAMPLE 7.1
Professional Development Plan (Form)

Teacher:_____ School: _____ Date:_____

CRITERION:

OBJECTIVE(S):

PROCEDURES FOR ACHIEVING OBJECTIVE(S):

ASSESSMENT METHOD AND DATES:

COMMENTS:

This Professional Development Plan is developed to: (check one)
_____Enrich Effective Performance   _____Improve Below Expected Performance
Plan Developed:_____   _____
                        Teacher's Signature/Date   Principal's Signature/Date
If Plan Revised (Date/Initials):_____
If Alternate Plan Developed (Date/Initials): _____
Plan Achieved:_____   _____
                        Teacher's Signature/Date   Principal's Signature/Date
One PDP is used for one criterion. This form is completed by principal during discussion with teacher. Any additional comments will be permanently appended to this form and initialed by teacher and principal. Signatures/initials imply this Plan has been discussed.

---

improve performance on a criterion. Once the criterion is identified, it is written verbatim on the form, not abbreviated or referenced by number. Using the exact wording reinforces the importance of the criterion in the process.

Improvement Objectives

The improvement objective is the desired outcome for the plan. It is a statement of the specific skill or behavior for development. The descriptors listed with each criterion can be very helpful when writing objectives because they often provide the concept and the wording for specific performance objectives. More than one objective may be appropriate to accomplish the desired development for a particular criterion, but only one criterion is addressed on an individual PDP.

Procedures for Achieving Objectives

This procedural segment is the game plan for accomplishing the objective. This segment should provide an explanation of the activities designed to accomplish the objective. The responsibilities of the teacher, the principal, and other parties assisting with the plan are clarified in this segment. When writing PDPs for knowledge or skill objectives, the procedures should include, but not be limited to (1) appropriate learning resources and activities, (2) strategies for checking comprehension, (3) opportunity for practice and implementation, and (4) plans for discussion and feedback. For PDPs attempting to improve an attitude problem, the plan should also include activities to: (1) determine the significance of the attitude issue and develop commitment to the change, (2) clarify the attitude issue and reach agreement to proceed with modification strategies, and (3) develop and implement strategies to modify the attitude.

Many educational resources are available to the principal and teacher as they work to complete a PDP. Figure 7.2 provides examples of the types of resources frequently used in PDPs. Many principals find it helpful to create a file folder for each criterion. In the folder they place copies of articles or other reading materials that might be a valuable resource for a teacher working on a plan for that criterion. When the principal and teacher are developing the plan, they can review the resources in the folder and select those that might be appropriate. Many districts appoint a central office administrator to serve as a clearinghouse for pertinent resources and ask that person to disseminate the resources to all principals in the district.

After listing appropriate resources and tasks to improve knowledge about the desired performance, the principal should include some strategy for checking the teacher's understanding of the skills associated with the knowledge. Opportunity to practice these skills should then be provided. The practice may be independent if the teacher appears to have a good understanding and the principal believes the

---

FIGURE 7.2   Examples of educational resources.

Articles	Audio-visuals
Conferences	Peer Observations
Books	Peer Assistance
Courses	Activity Logs
Workshops	Visitations
Modeling	Curriculum Guides

teacher is prepared to implement a skill effectively. The practice may be guided if the principal believes the teacher needs additional assistance in implementing the skill. Or, if the teacher does not have an adequate understanding of the skill, the principal may suggest or require additional tasks before encouraging the teacher to implement the skill with students. The preparation of an effective procedural game plan is one of the most challenging intellectual tasks for the principal in performance-based developmental evaluation.

Assessment Method and Dates

The means by which the PDP objectives will be evaluated are listed in the assessment method section of the plan: "How will the principal and teacher know when the objective has been accomplished?" Referencing the specific tasks listed in the procedural game plan is usually the most efficient way to express the assessment method.

Two types of target dates should be described for each PDP for improvement. The first is a short-term date, the date by which accomplishment of the objective should be evident. This date, the time when the behavioral change is first implemented, is particularly important if the improvement plan was written to resolve a skill deficiency in the teaching–learning process. The short-term time frame is typically expressed in days or weeks.

The second time frame is a long-term date, the point in time by which the teacher should have mastered the objectives and the performance or attitude change should have been internalized. The long-term time frame is usually expressed in months or years. Reviews of ineffective improvement plans frequently indicate that adequate time to internalize the improvement plan was not provided. In such cases, a temporary change may have been made but not maintained. When skill or attitude improvement is desired, it is frustrating to have to rewrite the plan and begin the process again. Improvement plans are not a quick fix; they are an investment over time. Patience through long-term dates is important to the change and internalization of a skill.

An improvement plan should also include a statement establishing the principal as the determiner of "significant progress." This is necessary because a teacher may complete the activities but never really accomplish the objectives or internalize the skill or attitude. The teacher might assume the plan was completed because the tasks were accomplished. The principal must make it clear to the teacher that the principal will be the determiner of successful completion of the plan.

Comments

The teacher should be given the opportunity to write comments on the form when the PDP is developed and again after it is completed. If the teacher disagrees with the plan, the written comments may attack the plan or the principal. The principal should be judicious in reply. A debate in writing about the appropriateness of the plan should usually be avoided. If the principal must respond, specific data that support the need for the plan should be cited. The principal should avoid making unprofessional, emotional, and unsubstantiated comments.

Signatures

The Professional Development Plan is a joint effort by principal and teacher. Seldom is the teacher concerned to the point of refusing to sign the PDP form once the plan has been developed. If the teacher decides not to sign the form, the principal should simply obtain an adult witness and ask the teacher to sign the form again. If the teacher again refuses, the refusal should be noted on the form along with the name of the witness. If possible, the witness should sign next to the notation. This should be done in a matter-of-fact, professional manner with minimal emotion and attention. Obtaining the signature is not crucial to the accomplishment of the improvement plan, but ensuring that the teacher and principal have discussed the plan *is* crucial to appropriate due process for the teacher.

A more significant problem arises if the teacher refuses to participate in the PDP conference or work toward accomplishing the plan after it has been developed. This is seldom a problem unless the plan is for improvement and the teacher does not accept the fact that a problem exists. When this occurs, patience, perseverance, and many discussions about the value of the plan may resolve the problem. If the teacher persists, involvement of the school district's legal counsel would be appropriate. Depending on state regulations, district policy, and established evaluative procedures, the next step may be a written directive to participate, development of another improvement plan to address the teacher's attitude problem in not cooperating, or initiation of procedures for dismissal on the grounds of insubordination or lack of compliance with district policy. When the procedures recommended for development and implementation of performance-based developmental evaluation have been followed, such problems are rare.

Professional Development Plan Examples

PDPs are the vehicle for professional growth in the performance-based developmental evaluation process. The plan may be for enrichment or for improvement and may focus on knowledge and understanding, skill, or attitude. The plan is written by the principal in collaboration with the teacher during a Professional Development Plan conference. Four examples of PDPs are provided in this section. The plan in Example 7.2 was written to enrich the skill of a science teacher who wanted to improve teaching techniques. Example 7.3 was written to enrich the skill of a physical education teacher who was ready to make a commitment to professional renewal. Example 7.4 was written to improve a math teacher's deficient use of instructional time. Example 7.5 was written for improvement because of a concern about an English teacher's ability to work with parents. The first two examples are enrichment activities, one for a criterion directly affecting classroom instruction, the other for a noninstructional criterion. The third and fourth examples are improvement plans designed to improve performance determined to be below expectations. As in the first two examples, one is directly related to instruction, the other is not. The fourth example is also an attitudinal problem that must be resolved before the skill of working effectively with parents can be improved.

The four plans are typical examples of how to implement the questions and suggestions discussed in the previous sections of this chapter. Other subtleties of writing improvement plans can also be observed in these four PDPs. For example, the segments of the procedural game plan in Example 7.3 are enumerated to correlate the activities with the objectives. Also, beginning each procedural statement with the name

(text continues on page 123)

EXAMPLE 7.2
Professional Development Plan
(Completed for Enrichment)

Teacher: __B.J. Hatfield__   School: __Wadsworth Junior High__   Date: __2-15-91__

CRITERION: Implements effective teaching techniques.
OBJECTIVE(S):
1. Establish lesson set effectively.
2. Provide for summary/closure of each lesson and unit.
3. Increase the variety of teaching strategies used regularly.

PROCEDURES FOR ACHIEVING OBJECTIVE(S):
The following activities apply to all objectives:

1. The teacher will read "Successful Teaching Strategies," by Brophy, *Kappan*, April, 1982.
2. The teacher will view *Effective Teaching for Higher Achievement*, ASCD Videotape, 1984.
3. The teacher will read "Instructional Strategy," by Valentine, NASSP *Instructional Leadership Handbook*, Section 73, 1984.
4. The teacher will read "Closure, The Fine Art of Making Learning Stick," by Phillips, *Instructor*, October, 1987.
5. The teacher will read "Putting Learning Strategies to Work," by Derry, *Educational Leadership*, January, 1989.
6. The teacher will observe Robin Hudson's class three times during next school year. The teacher will take notes during the observations, with attention to the strategies used in the lessons. The teachers will discuss the lessons after each observation.
7. The principal will provide copies of the above materials and discuss the observations with Robin Hudson.
8. The principal and teacher will discuss the readings/tape/observations as time permits next school year.
9. The teacher will independently implement various strategies discussed.
10. The principal will observe at least four lessons during the next two years and discuss observed performance.

ASSESSMENT METHOD AND DATES: Classroom observations and discussion will be the assessment method. Procedures 1, 2, 3, 4, 5, 7 will be completed by December, 1991. Procedures 6, 8, 9, 10 will be completed by May, 1992. Consistent, effective integration of the objectives should be evident by May, 1992. If so, the Plan will be completed at that time.

COMMENTS:

This Professional Development Plan is developed to: (check one)
__X__ Enrich Effective Performance   ____ Improve Below Expected Performance
Plan Developed: __B.J. Hatfield 2-15-91__   __Leslie Thompson 2/15/91__
                    Teacher's Signature/Date   Principal's Signature/Date
If Plan Revised (Date/Initials): _____
If Alternate Plan Developed (Date/Initials): _____
Plan Achieved: _____   _____
                    Teacher's Signature/Date   Principal's Signature/Date
One PDP is used for one criterion. This form is completed by principal during discussion with teacher. Any additional comments will be permanently appended to this form and initialed by teacher and principal. Signatures/initials imply this Plan has been discussed.

EXAMPLE 7.3
Professional Development Plan
(Completed for Enrichment)

Teacher: Whitney Atkins   School: Fairveiw H.S.   Date: 9-18-91

CRITERION: Demonstrates commitment to professional growth.
OBJECTIVE(S):
    1.   Participate in inservice activities and professional organizations appropriate to the area of teaching responsibility.
    2.   Serve as a mentor for the new P.E. teacher.
PROCEDURES FOR ACHIEVING OBJECTIVE(S):
    1.1 The teacher will join the state P.E. organization.
    1.2 The teacher will attend the state P.E. meeting in the capital city next year.
    1.3 The principal will provide for a substitute.
    1.4 The teacher will debrief the principal about the meeting and make recommendations about appropriateness for other staff.
    2.1 The teacher will read "Synthesis of Research on Staff Development for Effective Teaching," by Sparks, *Educational Leadership*, November, 1983.
    2.2 The teacher will read "What We're Learning about Teaching and Learning," by Bloom, *Principal*, November, 1986.
    2.3 The teacher will model selected teaching strategies for the new teacher.
    2.4 The principal and teacher will discuss the readings and identify others over the next year.
    2.5 The teacher will meet with the new teacher every other week for the first semester and monthly for the second semester. An agenda will be developed to discuss with the new teacher strategies for pupil management and classroom instruction. A copy of the agenda will be given to the principal.
    2.6 The teacher will visit with the principal at the end of the school year to discuss progress toward the objectives.
ASSESSMENT METHOD AND DATES:
    The assessment method will include a two-page report prepared in May, 1993 by the teacher describing professional benefits derived from the plan. All procedural items will be completed by that time. The principal and teacher will meet in May, 1993 to discuss the report and determine if the Plan has been completed and was effective for the teacher.
COMMENTS:

This Professional Development Plan is developed to: (check one)
  _X_ Enrich Effective Performance   _____Improve Below Expected Performance
Plan Developed: Whitney Atkins 9-18-91   Chris Sumner 9-18-91
                    Teacher's Signature/Date   Principal's Signature/Date
If Plan Revised (Date/Initials): _____
If Alternate Plan Developed (Date/Initials): _____
Plan Achieved: _____   _____
                    Teacher's Signature/Date   Principal's Signature/Date
One PDP is used for one criterion. This form is completed by principal during discussion with teacher. Any additional comments will be permanently appended to this form and initialed by teacher and principal. Signatures/initials imply this Plan has been discussed.

EXAMPLE 7.4
Professional Development Plan
(Completed for Improvement)

Teacher:_ Shannon Seward _   School: _Hinson Middle School_ Date: _10-18-91_

CRITERION: Uses instructional time effectively.

OBJECTIVE(S): 1. Begins activities promptly. 2. Continues learning activities for the duration of the scheduled instructional time. 3. Monitors students' time on task.

PROCEDURES FOR ACHIEVING OBJECTIVE(S):

The following procedures apply to all objectives.

1. The teacher will read "Instructional Time: How Can Teachers Manage It Better?" by Berliner, *Instructor*, October, 1984.

2. The teacher will read "Learning Time and Educational Effectiveness," NASSP *Curriculum Report*, December, 1980.

3. The teacher will read "What Research Says to the Practitioner about Classroom Time," by Johnston and Markle, *Middle School Journal*, August, 1980.

4. The teacher will read "Time Use and Activities in Junior High Classes," by Sanford and Evertson, *Journal of Educational Research*, January, 1983.

5. The teacher will read "Time on Task: Implications for Middle Level Instruction," by Shockley and Johnston, NASSP *Schools in the Middle*, December, 1983.

6. The teacher will read "Time on Task Reconsidered: A Synthesis of Research on Time and Learning," by Karweit, *Educational Leadership*, May, 1984.

7. The principal will provide the above readings.

8. The principal and teacher will discuss the readings after they have been read.

9. The teacher will keep an "engaged time on task" log during the first week of each month and give a copy of the log to the principal at the end of each week.

10. The principal will observe the teacher at least three times this school year and next school year and provide observation notes and conferencing.

ASSESSMENT METHOD AND DATES: The assessment method will include completion of the procedural activities, analysis of the time log, discussion of the impact of time on learning and classroom observations. Procedural items 1 thorough 8 will occur during this semester. Items 9 and 10 will occur throughout this school year. By November 6 the teacher will be using instructional time effectively. The objectives will be monitored by the principal throughout this school year and next school year. In May, 1993, the principal and teacher will review the performance data and the Plan and the principal will determine if significant progress has been made in the effective use of instructional time.

COMMENTS:

This Professional Development Plan is developed to: (check one)

____Enrich Effective Performance   _X_Improve Below Expected Performance

Plan Developed:_Shannon Seward 10/18/91_   _Lynn Marcie 10/18/91_____

                    Teacher's Signature/Date   Principal's Signature/Date

If Plan Revised (Date/Initials): _____

If Alternate Plan Developed (Date/Initials): _____

Plan Achieved: _____   _____

                    Teacher's Signature/Date   Principal's Signature/Date

One PDP is used for one criterion. This form is completed by principal during discussion with teacher. Any additional comments will be permanently appended to this form and initialed by teacher and principal. Signatures/initials imply this Plan has been discussed.

EXAMPLE 7.5
Professional Development Plan
(Completed for Improvement)

Teacher:__Carey Kersch___ School: _Wade School_____ Date:_11/7/91_

CRITERION: Demonstrates positive interpersonal relations with parents.

OBJECTIVE(S): 1. Demonstrate cooperative efforts and positive attitudes when working with parents. 2. Initiate communication with parents when appropriate. 3. Interact with parents in a respectful and friendly manner.

PROCEDURES FOR ACHIEVING OBJECTIVE(S):

1. The teacher will critique in writing 3 recent parent contacts, including the initiator, the reason, the outcome and specific examples of behavior; the principal will summarize parent comments.

2. The principal and teacher will discuss the behaviors and comments and determine the significance of the problem.

3. The teacher will write a self-assessment of personal feelings about students' parents, indicating specific reasons for resentment and lack of tolerance.

4. The principal and teacher will identify several specific readings and a workshop which might be of assistance to the teacher in understanding and modifying attitude.

5. Once the teacher has a better grasp of the attitude problem and can begin to modify feelings, the principal and teacher will develop a list of behaviors which they will monitor when the teacher is working with parents.

6. The teacher will interview three selected teachers to obtain suggestions for developing better relations with parents.

7. The teacher will develop and implement a plan for initiating parent contacts that will be beneficial to the students.

8. The teacher will independently monitor parental contacts, consciously recognizing successful and unsuccessful interactions, and prepare a written progress report at the end of each semester.

9. The principal will observe the teacher interacting with parents during staffings and share the observation data through conferencing.

ASSESSMENT METHOD AND DATES:

Procedural items 1 through 3 will be completed prior to the upcoming Christmas vacation. Items 4 through 6 will be completed by the end of February, 1992. Items 7 through 9 will be completed by the end of this school year. Assessment of the Plan will include discussions with the teacher, comments from parents, written progress reports by the teacher and observed performance. A noticeable change in attitude is expected by the end of this school year. The concern will be monitored until the end of the 1992-93 school year. At that time, the principal will determine if significant progress has been made to conclude the Plan.

COMMENTS:

This Professional Development Plan is developed to: (check one)
_____Improve Effective Performance __X__Improve Below Expected Performance
Plan Developed:__Carey Kersch 11/7/91___   ___Lou Collias   11/7/91_____
                    Teacher's Signature/Date   Principal's Signature/Date
If Plan Revised (Date/Initials): _____
If Alternate Plan Developed (Date/Initials): _____
Plan Achieved: _____ _____
                    Teacher's Signature/Date   Principal's Signature/Date

One PDP is used for one criterion. This form is completed by principal during discussion with teacher. Any additional comments will be permanently appended to this form and initialed by teacher and principal. Signatures/initials imply this Plan has been discussed.

of the person responsible for that activity, followed by an action verb and the task to be accomplished, adds clarity and makes writing the plans much easier.

SUMMARY

The importance of the professional development plan component in an effective evaluation system can not be overstated. If an evaluation system is to make a difference, the opportunity for each teacher to improve and try to become a better teacher over a reasonable time frame must be provided. Most teachers will make the commitment to try to improve professionally if they are treated as professionals. The basic ingredients in the professional development plan approach are (1) quality data collection and conferencing procedures that provide the content for realistic development plans for all staff, (2) an understood and established improvement process that places a premium on teacher involvement in the development and implementation of plans, and (3) a principal sensitive to teachers' needs to be treated as professionals and skillful enough to work with them in that context.

REFERENCES

Brown, C. A. (1987). *Teacher perception of the process, purpose and impact of performance-based teacher evaluation in Missouri.* Doctoral dissertation, University of Missouri–Columbia, 1987. (*Dissertation Abstracts International,* 49/07, 1630-A)

Davis, J. W. (1988). *The relationship between selected performance evaluation procedures and principals' perceptions about performance evaluation.* Doctoral dissertation, University of Missouri–Columbia, 1988. (*Dissertation Abstracts International,* 50/04, 837-A)

Harris, B. M. (1986). *Developmental teacher evaluation.* Boston: Allyn and Bacon.

Manatt, R. P. (1988). Teacher performance evaluation: A total systems approach. In S. J. Stanley & W. J. Popham (Eds.), *Teacher evaluation: Six prescriptions for success* (pp. 79–108). Alexandria, VA: Association for Supervision and Curriculum Development.

McGreal, T. L. (1983). *Successful teacher evaluation.* Alexandria, VA: Association for Supervision and Curriculum Development.

Moore, L. C. (1986). *The relationship between performance evaluation job targets and teacher attitudes and success.* Doctoral dissertation, University of Missouri–Columbia, 1986. (*Dissertation Abstracts International,* 47/08, 2833-A)

Odiorne, G. S. (1965). *Management by objectives.* New York: Pitman.

Redfern, G. (1980). *Evaluating teachers and administrators: A performance objectives approach.* Boulder, CO: Westview Press.

Valentine, J. W. (1986). *Performance/outcome-based principal evaluation: A summary of procedural considerations.* Paper presented at the annual meeting of the National Middle School Association, Atlanta, October. (ERIC Document Reproduction Service No. ED 281 318)

Valentine, J. W. (1987). *Performance/outcome-based principal evaluation.* Paper presented at the annual meeting of the American Association of School Administrators, New Orleans, February. (ERIC Document Reproduction Service No. ED 281 317)

CHAPTER 8

Summative Evaluation

Each time a man stands up for an ideal, or acts to improve the lot of others, or strikes out against injustice, he sends forth a ripple of hope . . . and crossing each other from a million different centers of energy and daring those ripples build a current that can sweep down the mightiest walls of oppression and resistance.
—Robert F. Kennedy

THE FORMATIVE EVALUATION PHASE is an ongoing process of data collection, conferencing, and development plans. The purpose of the formative phase is professional improvement through application of the procedures described in previous chapters. It is the developmental phase of the evaluation system.

In contrast, the summative evaluation phase is a brief, infrequently used process which requires the completion of a Summative Evaluation Report and a conference to discuss the report. The purpose of the summative phase is to recommend appropriate employment decisions. It is the personnel decision-making phase of the evaluation system. The differences between the formative and summative phases are deliberate. The leadership of most school districts desires evaluation systems that provide both personnel development and employment decision making.

SUMMATIVE APPROACHES

In recent years, school systems have tried, with varying degrees of success, several approaches to meet the needs of personnel development and/or personnel decision making. These approaches can be categorized into four types: (1) separate formative and summative systems, (2) only a formative system, (3) only a summative system, and (4) a linked formative–summative system.

Separate Systems

Some school systems attempt to accomplish personnel development and personnel decision-making goals by establishing two distinct evaluation systems. At times, the principal wears the hat of colleague and supervisor, conducting classroom observations that have no relationship to personnel matters. At other times, the principal wears the hat of evaluator, visiting the same classrooms but doing so with the intent of collecting data on which to base personnel decisions. Such procedures can be confusing to teachers and principals. Both groups have difficulty separating the two roles in their minds because all the data and all of the interactions a principal has with a teacher affect the principal's perceptions of the teacher. And how does the principal find the time to complete two separate processes that require many of the same tasks? If the same person has to perform these separate functions effectively, the chances for success are minimal.

Popham (1988) proposes three options for staffing the separate systems approach. He suggests the following:

1. Assigning the formative process to one administrator and the summative to another if the school is large enough to have two administrators

2. Assigning the formative process to capable teachers and the summative to the principal if the school has only one administrator

3. Assigning the formative process to the principal and the summative process to central office administrators if the school has one administrator

Shortcomings of these suggestions include staffing costs and operational incongruence. Two people are completing many of the same tasks, but they should not discuss what they are learning or doing. As Popham (1988) indicates, data gathered by the formative evaluator must never be shared with the summative evaluator. Because of these limitations, achieving success within the "separate system" approach would be difficult in most school districts.

Formative System Only

Some school systems establish evaluation systems that do not include summative evaluations. The contention is that supervision of classroom performance is adequate. Procedures commonly referred to as clinical supervision are used to meet the important goal of improving performance, usually in the classroom. Such systems do not address the need to make personnel decisions about performance, particularly comprehensive judgments about the teacher's total professional competence. Performance in the classroom may be the most important role for teachers, but it is not the only role. Although the majority of performance criteria should be directly related to classroom performance, criteria must also cover responsibilities outside the classroom that affect school effectiveness. Because a teacher's professional responsibilities transcend performance in the teaching–learning setting of the classroom, and because most states require some form of summative judgments (Valentine, 1990), an evaluation system without a summative phase falls short of meeting the needs of most school districts.

Summative System Only

Another approach to evaluation is the use of only summative procedures. This approach does not include a formative process of ongoing data collection, formative conferences, and professional development plans. Although such systems appear to be diminishing in use, some school districts continue to use only summative processes to meet state or local evaluation mandates. The summative-only system, which typically involves conducting a classroom observation and then preparing an evaluation report, is the quick and simple way to accomplish evaluation in the traditional sense. But such strategies are antiquated and accomplish little more than creating climates of mistrust among teachers, principals, and school district leadership.

The shortcomings of summative-only systems are obvious. The evaluation process is seldom based on adequate performance data and seldom leads to instructional improvement. The professional improvement of teachers and the impact for students is marginal. To have no evaluation system at all may be better than to have a system that is solely summative.

Linked Formative–Summative System

If the developers of a school district's evaluation system decide to use a single evaluation system to accomplish the goals of personnel development and personnel decision making, procedures must be established that effectively *link* the formative and summative phases. The linkage provides the opportunity for the two phases to complement each other, thus promoting rather than inhibiting the success of each phase. In the performance-based developmental evaluation approach described throughout this book, the criteria and the professional development plans provide the content and procedural linkages that enable the formative and summative phases to function independently *and* cooperatively. Without this linkage, the evaluation system is impaired because the principal must perform two very different but interrelated roles. Teachers will not readily accept performance of the two roles by the same person unless they understand that the interrelatedness creates positive results. The results are positive because the links promote fairness for the teacher. When the formative and summative systems are articulated properly, the teacher knows that every effort has been made to understand the teacher's ability and work with that ability before the summative evaluation report is prepared.

> **Principle 25**
> **Effective linkages between formative and summative phases are essential.**

Content Linkage

In each component of the performance-based developmental evaluation process, the criteria are the crucial content. They are the content linkage between the formative phase and the summative phase, which ensure consistent expectations throughout the evaluation process. The role of the principal is to synthesize the information about each criterion from the formative process into a judgment of competence for the summative process.

Procedural Linkage

The Professional Development Plan serves as a buffer between the formative and summative phases. The PDP becomes a procedural safeguard for fairness, reassuring staff that the summative report will contain no surprises. The assurance is possible because of one simple rule that must be followed: *A rating of "does not meet expected performance" does not occur on the Summative Evaluation Report unless a Professional Development Plan for improvement was developed during the formative phase.* This simple guideline is the glue that procedurally links the formative and summative phases. This procedural linkage enables teachers to view the formative phase as a developmental process without anxiety about formative data mysteriously affecting their final evaluations. The teachers realize that if a concern about performance exists, the concern will be clarified and opportunity to address it will be provided prior to the summative report.

The key to accomplishing the goals of personnel development and personnel decision making is not to have two separate systems, but to link two systems into a single system with a primary and a secondary emphasis. Personnel in the district perceive the primary emphasis as the goal that receives the greatest amount of time and energy. Thus, it is important to place much more time and energy in the formative process than in the summative process.

THE SUMMATIVE EVALUATION REPORT

The formative–summative linkages, and especially the safeguard for fairness rule, make completing the Summative Evaluation Report relatively easy for the principal. In fact, completing the report is one of the least time-consuming tasks in the PBDE process. To complete the report, the principal reads each criterion and places a mark in the small box that designates the level of performance most descriptive of the teacher's performance. The principal makes the judgment on the basis of all the information collected and discussed with the teacher during the formative phase. All performance criteria must be rated at expected levels of performance unless an "improvement" Professional Development Plan was written.

A Summative Evaluation Report is presented in Example 8.1. This example and other similar examples are discussed below.

(text continues on page 133)

EXAMPLE 8.1
Summative Evaluation Form—Teachers

Teacher:_____School:_____

Performance Area: Instructional Process

The teacher:

A. Demonstrates evidence of lesson and unit planning and preparation.

☐ Meets expectations ☐ Does not meet expectations

B. Demonstrates knowledge of curriculum and subject matter.

☐ Meets expectations ☐ Does not meet expectations

C. Uses effective teaching techniques, strategies, and skills during lesson.

☐ Meets expectations ☐ Does not meet expectations

D. Uses instructional time effectively.

☐ Meets expectations ☐ Does not meet expectations

E. Evaluates student progress effectively.

☐ Meets expectations ☐ Does not meet expectations

F. Provides for individual differences.

☐ Meets expectations ☐ Does not meet expectations

G. Demonstrates ability to motivate students.

☐ Meets expectations ☐ Does not meet expectations

H. Maintains a classroom climate conducive to learning.

☐ Meets expectations ☐ Does not meet expectations

I. Manages student behavior in a constructive manner.

☐ Meets expectations ☐ Does not meet expectations

COMMENTS:

Performance Area: Interpersonal Relationships
The teacher:
A. Demonstrates positive interpersonal relationships with students.

   ☐ Meets expectations   ☐ Does not meet expectations

B. Demonstrates positive interpersonal relationships with educational staff.

   ☐ Meets expectations   ☐ Does not meet expectations

C. Demonstrates positive interpersonal relationships with parents and other members of the school community.

   ☐ Meets expectations   ☐ Does not meet expectations

COMMENTS:

Performance Area: Professional Responsibilities
The teacher:
A. Follows the policies, regulations, and procedures of the school and district.

   ☐ Meets expectations   ☐ Does not meet expectations

B. Assumes responsibilities outside the classroom.

   ☐ Meets expectations   ☐ Does not meet expectations

C. Demonstrates a commitment to professional growth.

   ☐ Meets expectations   ☐ Does not meet expectations

COMMENTS:

(continued)

EXAMPLE 8.1 continued

Administrator's Recommendation:

☐ Reemployment recommended.

☐ Reemployment not recommended.

☐ No recommendation made at this time.

Teacher's Comments:

Administrator's Comments:

_____   _____
Teacher's Signature/Date   Administrator's Signature/Date
(Signatures imply the content of this document has been discussed.
Explanatory comments required for all ratings not meeting expected
performance.)

Meets Expected Performance

In Example 8.1, the principal selects from one of two performance levels. Either the teacher is or is not demonstrating competence at the expected level of performance. A rating marked "meets expectations" means "the teacher is doing a good, solid job for that criterion." It means there are no concerns about the teacher's performance at the time of the rating. This is not a rating of "average." There is no average, or below or above average. The process does not disperse teachers across a normal curve or compare one teacher's performance with another's. The question the principal must ask himself or herself to determine the rating is simple: "Does the teacher demonstrate performance that meets the expectation as stated by the criterion and amplified through the descriptors?" A teacher who meets that expectation is obviously performing at a high level of quality. This is obviously the desired rating for all teachers on all criteria. An "expected performance rating" on the Summative Evaluation Report reassures the teacher that there is no concern about the teacher's performance for the criterion.

Principle 26
Expected, not comparative, performance is rated on the summative report form.

Does Not Meet Expected Performance

A rating of "does not meet expectations" simply means that "the teacher is not consistently doing a good, solid job for that criterion." The teacher is not demonstrating competence on the performance standards for the district. A rating in this column will have been preceded by a Professional Development Plan for improvement designating a deficiency for the criterion.

Generally, a good-quality teacher would not have a rating in this column. A marginal teacher might have a couple of ratings in this column, and a weak teacher might have several. But these are only typical numbers and should not be taken literally. The number of ratings below expected performance is not as significant as which criteria are rated below. Some criteria are more important in all situations, and others may be more important in specific situations. There is no definitive number of ratings of "below expected performance" that should designate nonrenewal or dismissal. The principal must apply good judgment when making the employment recommendation.

Professional Development Plan

The rule that a teacher will not receive a rating of "does not meet expected performance" without a Professional Development Plan for improvement makes the decision-making process much easier. The most difficult decisions are made during the formative phase, when there is time to work with the teacher and try to improve performance before and after a PDP was developed. However, if a PDP was developed, the principal must decide if the teacher has made enough improvement by the time the summative report is prepared to be rated at "meets expected performance." As discussed in Chapter 7, the PDP should have both short-term goals for performance change and long-term goals for performance internalization. The decision to rate the teacher at or below performance expectation should not be made on the basis of the short-term goals of behavior modification or skill implementation. Those goals are usually accomplished shortly after writing the plan. The real issue is the degree to which the teacher has internalized the improvement. Is the performance a natural part of the teacher's repertoire, and does the principal expect it to remain so? If there is any doubt about the internalization, a rating of "does not meet expectations" should be made on the report. A rating of "meets expected performance" should be made on the next Summative Evaluation Report if internalization was demonstrated by that time.

Principle 27
A professional development plan must be in use before a "does not meet" rating.

Above Expected Performance

Many teachers desire, and deserve, plaudits for their abilities and performance. Several strategies have been used in PBDE systems to provide positive strokes. Three of the more practical strategies are described next.

Above Expectations Rating

A rating of "above expected performance" is one of the most common methods for reinforcing outstanding performance. However, developing an accurate description of what constitutes performance beyond expectations becomes a challenge for the evaluation committee. Succinctly describing the performance is one of the shortcomings for this strategy. A second is the relationship between the use of an "above expected performance" rating and teachers' perceptions of the effectiveness of the evaluation process. Feedback from districts using an "above expected performance" rating are more frequently negative than positive about the overall evaluation process. Principals and teachers report that after a year or two using the "above" rating, teachers begin to resent not receiving frequent "above" ratings. Then principals are caught in a dilemma. Overuse of the "above" rating means losing focus on the real issue of effective performance and potentially inflating all ratings by one level or relegating the "meets expectation" rating to the concept of "average." The "does not meet expectations" rating can also lose impact as a means of communicating concern about performance. School districts that carefully consider these concepts are more likely to develop systems without the "above" rating.

Above Expectations Rating with Memo

Using an open-ended strategy is often a better alternative than just marking an "above expectations" rating on the report. If the evaluation form has a place for an "above" rating, the principal marks the rating and is then required by the process to write a one- to two-page memo explicating the information that justifies the rating. This simple requirement reduces the frequency with which principals use the "above" rating and thus may prevent overuse of the rating as described previously.

Comment Sections

Using a report format that does not have an "above" rating but does have a place for written comments by the principal at the end of each performance area or at the bottom of each page is an effective method of "stroking" teachers. The written compliments can be discussed during the summative conference and appear permanently on the form. This is the format presented in Example 8.1 and the one that most districts that consider the issues tend to prefer.

THE SUMMATIVE CYCLE

School district evaluation committees must determine an appropriate length of time from one summative phase to the next. Davis (1988) concluded that the more frequently a summative is conducted, the less positive are the teacher's attitudes about performance evaluation. Although cause-and-effect data are not available, a theoretical explanation is depicted in Figure 8.1. The attitudinal line for the effectively linked system shows a positive gain from September to February as the teacher and principal work together in the formative phase. As the month of March and the usual time to complete the Summative Evaluation Report approach, the anxiety level rises and the positive attitudes begin to subside for less secure teachers. Some positive attitudinal gains are lost and have to be recovered during the next formative phase, from April to the following March. If the slope of the line seems gradual, consider the attitudinal line for a formative process not effectively linked to the summative process. Or worse, consider the line if only a summative process were used. It would begin on a downward trend and would probably not move upward.

Probationary Teachers

In most states, teachers are probationary for a specified number of years, then move to tenure status if they are reemployed after the probationary period. For probationary teachers in 1990, summative evaluations were required at least once a year by state statute or regulation

FIGURE 8.1   Relationship between summative frequency and teacher attitude about evaluation.

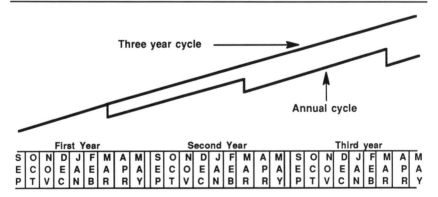

in over half of the states. Unfortunately, some states required summative evaluations more frequently than once a year (Valentine, 1990), thus increasing the likelihood that the teacher would view the evaluation process as judgmental rather than developmental. Even in states where summative evaluations were not required by the state, school systems frequently established local summative evaluation requirements.

The recommended evaluation cycle for probationary teachers in districts using PBDE is a formative process followed by a Summative Evaluation Report each year. For the teacher's first year in the system, the formative phase starts at the beginning of employment and continues until the summative report is written, usually in March. The formative phase resumes after the summative report and continues into the next school year, when the next summative report is written. The cycle continues in that manner until tenure is granted or the teacher is not reemployed.

Tenured Teachers

In 1990, approximately one-third of the United States required, either by statute or by regulation, summative evaluations for teachers with tenured status (Valentine, 1990). As with probationary teachers, however, it was a common practice in school systems across the country to complete summative evaluations of tenured teachers annually. In PBDE, the recommended evaluation cycle for tenured teachers is a three-year formative process, with a Summative Evaluation Report culminating the formative phase and simultaneously initiating the next formative phase.

```
┌─────────────────────────────────────────┐
│            Principle  28                  │
│    Summative  reports  are  used  as      │
│       infrequently  as  possible.         │
└─────────────────────────────────────────┘
```

Summative Reports When Needed

While the typical cycle in a PBDE school district may be every year for probationary teachers and every three years for tenured teachers, the principal should have the ability to initiate a summative evaluation at any point in the cycle when the principal believes the summative report is in the best interest of the students, the teacher or the school. Completing the summative report out of cycle would be considered unusual and should cause the teacher to realize that significant concerns are being communicated to which the teacher should be attentive. The operational guideline that a Professional Development Plan be completed before a "does not meet expectations" rating is given should apply regardless of when the summative report is completed. In a situation where a teacher "falls apart" without warning or commits a heinous act that is detrimental to students, staff, or the school, most districts and states make provisions in policy and statutes for immediate removal of the teacher from the school setting, with established guidelines of due process for addressing the problem.

THE SUMMATIVE CONFERENCE

The summative conference is different from the formative conference in intent and process. Its purpose is to discuss the summative judgments made for each criterion. Although a teacher may gain some knowledge and understanding of effectiveness as a result of this conference, the role of the conference as a teaching–learning setting is not as crucial as that of the formative conference. If the formative process has been completed effectively, the summative conference should be routine.

Preparation for the conference includes review of all formative data and completion of the Summative Evaluation Report. The setting should ensure privacy and be arranged for effective communication. Adequate time should be scheduled. The teacher's attitude, which can usually be predicted from previous interactions, will obviously affect the degree to which the conference is collaborative or authoritative. In contrast to the formative conference, where the emphasis is on joint discussion and analysis of performance, the decisions for the summative conference are made by the principal prior to the conference. This necessitates less dialogue and more direct principal talk. Unless the teacher has a concern about a rating, the conference is usually brief, seldom lasting more than thirty minutes.

Although the brevity and routineness of the conference can be expected, the act of making judgments about performance creates some anxiety and can result in complications during the conference. For example, a teacher may be upset because the teacher believes he or she deserved a rating of "meets" rather than "does not meet" expected performance. The teacher contends that he or she met all requirements listed in the procedural section of the Professional Development Plan. However, the principal is not yet confident the skills have been internalized. As with any conference, effective verbal and nonverbal communication skills are important. Patience in explaining the process and the principal's reason for the judgment are also important. Discussions with the teacher prior to completing the summative report may provide additional insight helpful to the principal in determining the degree to which the teacher's performance has been internalized.

Reaching closure for the conference includes emphasizing criteria to which the teacher might give particular attention in the future. Seeds may be planted for enrichment Professional Development Plans and suggestions made for improvement strategies. If the principal has positive feelings about the teacher and his or her value to the school, these feelings should be shared. Often, anxiety about the summative conference can be reduced if the principal works to make it an honest experience. A teacher should be able to say that he or she understands why the principal made a judgment even though the teacher may disagree with it. Effective communication before, during, and after the conference is important.

Feelings of animosity, dislike, and distrust toward particular individuals are part of human nature. The principal must guard against his or her reaction to such feelings by the teacher and not let those feelings bias professional judgments made in the summative phase. Principals must understand that teachers will express negative feelings about the principal as a means of grasping to save their own self-concept. Understanding, sensitivity, and compassion are better administrative behaviors at this time than are the emotional, defensive behaviors of aggressiveness and authoritativeness. Teachers who are struggling professionally usually know they have problems. They usually realize they are unhappy, and if they have serious competence problems, they usually know they are in the wrong profession. Those are difficult problems for some people to admit, especially to their supervisor. But there are ways to talk about performance and skill in the teaching profession without attacking the teacher as an individual. Teaching is not an easy profession to master, and unsuccessful teachers can be very successful in other professions. Honesty tempered with understanding, sensitivity, and compassion are important for the difficult summative conference.

REVIEW AND APPEAL PROCESSES

All evaluation systems should contain some avenue of review and appeal for the teacher who feels wrongly judged. In most districts, the distinction between the terms *review, appeal,* and *grievance* needs clarification.

Principle 29
Review and appeal procedures are
a basic part of the evaluation process.

In PBDE a *review* is defined as the right to request that the judgments made by the principal during the formative process be reviewed by the principal's immediate supervisor.

An *appeal* is defined in PBDE as the right to request that the appropriateness of ratings made on the Summative Evaluation Report be appealed to the principal's immediate supervisor and appropriate personnel. The appeal process is usually more complex procedurally than the review process because the judgments made have a greater impact on the teacher's career.

In Example 2.2 of Chapter 2, a PBDE process was presented. The review and appeal portion of that process is presented in Example 8.2 to demonstrate specific wording for the review and appeal procedures.

EXAMPLE 8.2
Review and Appeal Procedures

A teacher may request a review of, or an appeal of, a professional judgment. This review or appeal is not to be confused with a grievance. Whereas a grievance is related to a perceived violation of the evaluation process, a review is related to a professional judgment made by the supervisor during the formative process, and an appeal is related to a professional judgment made by the supervisor during the summative process.

A teacher has the right to request a *review* of data on a Formative Data Form or a Professional Development Plan by the building principal's immediate supervisor. The request must be made in writing to the principal's supervisor within two working days after receipt of the form or plan. The principal's supervisor will review the request and discuss it with the teacher and principal. The principal's supervisor will append a written statement to the form or plan noting the review and the decision about the review.

A teacher has the right to *appeal* the ratings on the Summative Evaluation Report. The appeal must be in writing to the District Evaluation Review Committee within five working days after receipt of the report. It must identify the reason for the request, including an explanation of the information supporting the appeal. The appeal will be reviewed by the District Evaluation Review Committee. The committee will recommend either that the appeal is justified and the summative report should be changed or that the appeal is not justified and the report should not be changed. The committee will process the appeal within ten working days of receipt and forward all information and their recommendation to the principal's supervisor for a decision about the appeal. The appeal will be processed by the principal's supervisor within ten working days of receipt from the committee. The principal's supervisor will respond in writing and in person to the teacher during that time. The teacher has the right to have a mutually acceptable nonparticipating observer present during this conference.

In all references to review and appeal in this section, if the supervisor was an assistant principal, rather than the principal, the first course of review and appeal must be to the principal. If the issue is not resolved with the principal, the official review and appeal procedures begin.

The District Evaluation Review Committee will include three teachers and three administrators. The teachers will be appointed by the local teacher association and the administrators by the superintendent.

In most school systems and in PBDE, a *grievance* is the right to appeal a procedural infraction during the evaluation process. It is not a review or an appeal of a professional judgment made during the implementation of correct evaluative procedures. Rather, it should be an appeal of due process.

EMPLOYMENT RECOMMENDATIONS

Whether or not the principal should make an employment recommendation on the Summative Evaluation Report is an issue that must be discussed by the District Evaluation Committee developing the evaluation system. Although the board of education is the governing body that makes the employment decision, the summative report should be the basis for that decision. The board's decision should be supported by data from the entire evaluation process.

Including a place to indicate the employment decision on the Summative Evaluation Report (Example 8.1) formalizes the principal's role and eliminates any question in a teacher's mind about the principal's perception of whether or not that teacher should return. In the unusual event that the board of education makes a decision contrary to the principal's recommendation, at least the principal can know with a clear conscience that he or she made the best possible professional recommendation. Also, the teacher knows that it was the board's decision to override the principal's recommendation. Procedurally, it would be very unusual for a board to dismiss a teacher for professional incompetence if the principal deems that the teacher's performance meets expectations and recommends retention. In such cases the board must be certain they have the necessary grounds for dismissal.

```
              Principle  30
A  recommendation  about  employment
    is  made  on  the  summative  report.
```

Operational procedures within the district can be implemented to reduce the likelihood of differing opinions about competence. The identification of teachers receiving Professional Development Plans calling for improvement should be a required practice. Identification by mid-year of any teacher who might possibly be considered as appropriate for nonrenewal or dismissal during that school year should also be required. The dialogue that should accompany this process will prepare the central office, the board, and the principal for differences of opinion. Such differences can usually be resolved before the evaluation recommendation is made on the summative report.

The Summative Evaluation Report in Example 8.1 gives the principal the option of completing the report without making any employment recommendation. This option provides more time for the principal and teacher to work together before the principal must make the recommendation. Use of this option should be an early warning to the teacher that a major concern about the employment recommendation exists. The principal may choose to complete a summative report ahead of schedule to get the teacher's attention and clarify the significance of the concern. The principal would then complete another summative report at a later date and make a recommendation at that time.

INCENTIVE PROGRAMS

Following the National Commission on Excellence in Education's report, *A Nation at Risk* (1983), policymakers and educators developed renewed interest in incentive programs to entice, reward, and retain competent teachers. By 1990, twenty-two states were providing special funding for teacher incentive programs (Southern Regional Educational Board, 1990). The concept of incentive programs is discussed in this chapter because of the frequent linkage between incentive programs and summative evaluation procedures. Too often, educators state that "To have a quality incentive program, one must have an effective evaluation program." Such statements reinforce the belief that a strong relationship must exist between the two if a district is to have an incentive program.

Incentive programs appear to have a much higher rate of failure than success. Merit pay has been up and down the incentive trail time after time. Even the relatively new career ladder incentives have questionable long-term value. Inextricably tying the evaluation process, and more specifically the summative evaluation, to the promise of monetary or other incentive rewards reinforces the mental set that evaluation is a summative rather than a developmental judgment. The focus brought to the summative process is counterproductive to all that has been discussed throughout this book. As stated many times, if evaluation is to be a developmental process in which teachers and principals work in an atmosphere of openness and trust to improve professional performance, the evaluation system must be thought of as a formative process, not a summative process.

Some current incentive programs have been more successful than most. The Missouri Career Ladder program is a good example of efforts to divorce the concept of incentives from the evaluation program. Implemented voluntarily by school districts in a state with an established, effective process for teacher evaluation, the program was tied by statute to performance evaluation. Fortunately, the only linkage was that the criteria in the district's evaluation system must be used to determine if the teacher could apply for admission into the career ladder plan, rather than being a condition for accomplishing the career plan. The Missouri Department of Education encouraged participating school systems not to use their Summative Evaluation Reports as the basis for determining ability to apply. Instead, a voucher approach was developed which listed the performance criteria and required that the teacher making application provide information supporting a self-assessment rating on each criterion. The role of the principal was to review the teacher's voucher and validate the accuracy of the statements. Thus, the voucher system forced teacher self-assessment, forced the teacher to provide support evidence for exemplary performance on the criteria, and eliminated the need for principals to complete a summative report every time a teacher wanted to apply for movement onto or up the ladder. The voucher system moved the emphasis from the judgments made by the principal in the evaluation process to the data on the voucher developed by the teacher.

Any incentive program that brings attention and pressure to the decisions made on the summative report has the potential to detract from the philosophy, and hence the effectiveness, of a developmental evaluation system. If an incentive program is used, and if it must be linked to evaluative judgments, the district leadership should consider developing a separate evaluation process for the incentive program. Incentive programs are usually short-lived because of their dependency on funding. Although a separate evaluation system for the incentive program may seem impractical, it may be a better alternative than permitting the negative impact on a developmental evaluation process that has the potential to improve personnel performance for many years.

> **Principle 31**
> **Developmental evaluation is not used to meet the needs of incentive programs.**

There are no quick fixes in the education business. Although the success of incentive programs is difficult to predict, they appear to have had little impact on improving the image of education as a profession and even less impact on increasing the value society gives to the education of young people. If educators are concerned about attracting outstanding persons to the profession and about maintaining and rewarding outstanding teachers, programs more sophisticated than the typical politically based incentives will need to be developed. Perhaps the starting point can be found in the writings of Goodlad, Sizer, and others trying to understand the overall function and delivery of education. It is doubtful that high-quality reforms will be found in legislated incentive programs.

SUMMARY

If a performance-based developmental evaluation process is properly developed and implemented, adequate and appropriate data are identified to make and defend the difficult decisions for nonrenewal or dismissal of ineffective teachers. The procedures that provide the data for those difficult decisions also provide reassurances to good teachers that their effectiveness has been noted and efforts are ongoing to help them be even more effective.

An effective evaluation process provides confidence that staff will be treated fairly and humanely and that the stated procedures will be followed. The emphasis on personnel improvement so delicately sculpted during months of work in the formative process can be crushed with insensitive comments or circumvention of procedures. Sensitivity to people and attention to process are crucial at that time. Progress made over the year is easily washed out to sea in a tide of unnecessary anxiety. Although the summative process is a necessity, its image must be scaled down and the important links between formative and summative processes must be stressed. Teachers need, and deserve, constant reassurances that the evaluation system was designed and implemented to ensure professional fairness.

REFERENCES

Davis, J. W. (1988). *The relationship between selected performance evaluation procedures and principals' perceptions about performance evaluation.* Doctoral dissertation, University of Missouri–Columbia, 1988. (*Dissertation Abstracts International,* 50/04, 837-A)

National Commission on Excellence in Education. (1983). *A nation at risk: The imperative for educational reform.* Washington, DC: U.S. Government Printing Office.

Popham, W. J. (1988). Judgment-based teacher evaluation. In S. J. Stanley & W. J. Popham (Eds.), *Teacher evaluation: Six prescriptions for success* (pp. 56–77). Alexandria, VA: Association for Supervision and Curriculum Development.

Southern Regional Education Board. (1990). *Career ladder clearinghouse* [newsletter], January. Atlanta, GA: Southern Regional Educational Board.

Valentine, J. W. (1990). *A national survey of state teacher evaluation policies.* Columbia: University of Missouri, Department of Educational Administration. (See Appendix A.)

CHAPTER 9

Evaluating Special Teachers

Personally, I'm always ready to learn, although I do not always like being taught.
—Winston Churchill

THE PROFESSIONAL COMPOSITION of a school faculty changed noticeably from 1960 to 1990. Between 1960 and 1985, the total number of educational staff in the United States doubled, going from about 2 million to a little over 4 million. The number of regular classroom teachers grew from 1.4 million to 2.2 million, but as a proportion of total staff they declined from 65 percent to 53 percent as the hiring of other types of administrative and support staff increased more rapidly (Office of Educational Research and Improvement, 1987). When a principal looked into the faces of teachers in a faculty meeting in the early 1960s, the principal saw regular classroom teachers, with only a few exceptions, perhaps a librarian or a counselor. If that same principal were to view a faculty in 1990, the faces would have represented not only regular classroom teachers but numerous special teachers as well. In addition to noting more librarians and counselors, the principal might have seen several teachers trained to work with students who were mentally handicapped, who had learning disabilities, or who had speech or hearing impairments. The principal might also have noted that the "librarian" had a co-worker called a "media specialist" and, further, that both were often referred to as "instructional materials specialists." The counseling staff might have included both a social worker and a psychologist. Finally, among the faculty seated before the principal might have been several paraprofessionals with teaching degrees who worked as aides or assistants to the classroom teachers.

A principal must be prepared to work with this myriad population of professionals in the same way the principal works with regular classroom teachers. The special teachers deserve the same procedures for developmental evaluation granted to the other staff members. The purpose of this chapter is to provide suggestions for the developmental evaluation of these special teachers. To accomplish this purpose, the chapter is divided into four sections. The first section is devoted to the developmental evaluation of special education teachers, followed by sections for instructional materials specialists, counselors, and paraprofessionals. Each section includes a discussion of evaluative procedures and forms and a suggested list of performance criteria and descriptors.

Throughout this chapter, the term *regular* will be used to describe the typical classroom teacher—for example, the second-grade teacher, the history teacher, the math teacher, the reading teacher. This term *regular* is used to provide the necessary mental contrast between the job responsibilities of the more traditional classroom position and the position of a "special services" teacher.

SPECIAL EDUCATION TEACHERS

Public Law (P.L.) 94-142, the Education for All Handicapped Children Act, was passed by the Ninety-fourth Congress and signed into law by President Gerald Ford on November 29, 1975. The purpose of that landmark legislation was to guarantee special education programs to the handicapped children of our nation. Section 504 of P.L. 93-112, the Vocational Rehabilitation Act Amendments of 1973, preceded P.L. 94-142 and provided that a handicapped individual shall not be discriminated against in any program or activity receiving federal assistance. From the foundation of these two bills sprang a massive effort by the public schools of the United States to meet the needs of handicapped students in a fair and equitable manner. The legal basis for special education was periodically refined and reinforced through later legislation. The more notable of these laws were the Handicapped Act Amendments of 1986 (P.L. 99-457) and the Handicapped Childrens Protection Act of 1986 (P.L. 99-372). The Carl D. Perkins Vocational Act (P.L. 98-524) also included provisions that assured handicapped individuals of access to quality vocational education programs. Undergraduate and graduate programs designed to prepare special education teachers prospered during the 1970s and 1980s as universities attempted to provide enough adequately trained teachers to meet the growing demands for special education teachers. Equipped with special skills and many nontraditional teaching responsibilities, special education teachers provided fresh insights into working with "special" students. And the evaluative strategies and performance criteria that might have been used for regular classroom teachers were questioned by these special education teachers, who saw them as inappropriate to their job demands.

Performance Criteria

The criteria and descriptors selected for this section on special education teachers were developed in 1988 by a committee of special education teachers and administrators in the Special School District of St. Louis County, Missouri. The district employs over 2,000 special educators to meet the needs of handicapped students in twenty-three school districts in St. Louis County. It is one of the largest and most comprehensive special educational systems in the country. The district made a commitment to performance-based evaluation in 1983 and, since that time, has reviewed and refined the evaluative procedures in an effort to implement a PBDE approach for all professional staff.

The criteria and descriptors for the special education teachers of the Special School District of St. Louis County are presented in Example 9.1. The most notable difference between these criteria and those for the regular classroom teacher are found in the performance area entitled "Assessment Process." The criteria for the performance areas of Instructional Process, Interpersonal Relationships, and Professional Responsibilities are similar to those for regular classroom teachers presented in Chapter 3.

EXAMPLE 9.1
Special Education Teachers: Performance Areas, Criteria,
and Descriptors

I. Assessment process (performance area)
   The special education teacher:
   A. Follows screening procedures (criterion).
      —Implements and interprets various screening instruments and procedures (descriptor).
      —Follows the guidelines and procedures established by the district.

(text continues on page 157)

—Utilizes the screening information to determine further specific assessment instruments.

B. Identifies appropriate diagnostic tests/methods for assessment.

—Demonstrates knowledge of the appropriate assessment methods/instruments for use with the different handicapping conditions or functional levels.

—Utilizes existing behavioral and academic data, as well as teacher input, in selecting the appropriate assessment methods/instruments.

—Considers age, functioning level, and other relevant factors when selecting the appropriate assessment methods/instruments.

—Develops an Individual Evaluation Plan by identifying instruments, procedures, and personnel needed for the evaluation process.

C. Demonstrates appropriate administration of assessment methods/instruments.

—Follows administrative procedures and standardization requirements in the test materials.

—Demonstrates knowledge of scoring procedures as outlined in the test manuals.

—Demonstrates effective techniques in the administration of informal assessments (e.g., structured interview techniques, rating scales).

D. Demonstrates interpretation of assessment methods/instruments.

—Evaluates test results in order to identify students' strengths and weaknesses.

—Integrates test results with information from all pertinent sources in order to generate appropriate conclusions and recommendations.

—Demonstrates ability to utilize assessment results in determining programming needs.

—Demonstrates ability to relate assessment results to parents and professionals in a meaningful fashion.

—Writes reports in a manner which substantiates the conclusions reached through the assessments.

E. Initiates/processes evaluations/reevaluations.

—Utilizes available academic and behavioral data in initiat-

(continued)

EXAMPLE 9.1 continued

---

ing referrals (e.g., intake, placement change, prevocational/vocational, and related services).
—Participates as appropriate in the preparation/completion of activities for the evaluation/reevaluation process.
—Participates in conferences/staffings as required.

II. Instructional process
The special education teacher:
A. Demonstrates appropriate preparation for instruction and/or intervention.
—Selects activities which are appropriate to the abilities, needs, and interests of the students.
—Designs lessons in a clear, logical, and sequential format.
—Incorporates content from previous lessons into daily planning to ensure continuity and sequence.
B. Demonstrates a knowledge of instructional needs of handicapping conditions.
—Displays a knowledge of strategies in programming for handicapped students.
—Selects materials appropriate to the educational needs of the student.
—Provides direct and consultative services to students, staff, and parents as needed.
C. Demonstrates a knowledge of subject matter/curriculum.
—Displays a competent knowledge of curriculum and subject matter.
—Selects and presents subject matter which is accurate.
—Selects materials appropriate to the subject matter/curriculum.
D. Selects/implements instructional objectives effectively.
—Communicates learning objectives to students.
—Uses learning activities designed to achieve stated objectives.
—Assigns work to students which requires application of instructional objectives.
—Utilizes current events and unexpected situations for their educational value.
E. Selects/implements a variety of effective educational techniques.

—Provides for instructional set, comprehension checks, and closure during lessons.

—Employs a variety of educational techniques appropriate to the functioning level of students and the instructional objectives (e.g., lecturing, modeling, demonstrating, questioning, experimentation, self-teaching, role-playing, multisensory strategies).

—Relates current lessons to previous learning.

—Modifies lesson/treatment plans, techniques, and educational experiences as the learning situation requires.

—Provides opportunities for students to explore problems and weigh alternatives in decision making.

F. Provides opportunities for individual differences.

—Groups students for each instructional activity in a manner which best assists the learning process.

—Uses a variety of questioning levels effectively.

—Provides support materials that are coordinated with the learning experiences and the developmental level of the child.

—Provides a variety of activities which promote maximum student involvement.

—Provides activities and/or solicits help for remediation and enrichment.

—Reteaches if assessment results indicate it is appropriate.

G. Uses a variety of effective materials/resources.

—Uses materials which enhance multisensory learning (e.g., tactile, visual, and auditory).

—Is resourceful in finding, developing, and using materials to aid instruction.

—Uses available community resources relevant to instruction.

H. Uses instructional/intervention time effectively.

—Begins activities promptly.

—Provides for appropriate learning activities throughout the instructional/intervention time.

—Avoids unnecessary delays during the lesson/activity.

—Avoids inappropriate digressions during the lesson/activity.

—Implements a time schedule individualized for student needs.

(*continued*)

EXAMPLE 9.1 continued

I. Demonstrates ability to motivate students.
—Strives to encourage and involve students who show little or no interest.
—Presents activities which simulate relevant situations outside the school.
—Responds positively to students' requests for help.
—Gives frequent and prompt feedback to students.
—Stimulates and encourages creative and critical thinking.
—Selects and utilizes appropriate reinforcers to promote learning.
—Provides students with the opportunity to meet with success.
—Provides activities which promote student independence.

J. Demonstrates ability to communicate effectively with students.
—Communicates expectations to students.
—Uses correct oral and written communication.
—Uses vocabulary commensurate with the student's language skills.
—Presents ideas logically.
—Gives directions that are clear, concise, and reasonable.
—Uses a variety of verbal and nonverbal techniques (e.g., signing, cues, proximity, physical contact).
—Makes an effort to understand the student's communication system.
—Elicits and responds to student questions.
—Summarizes effectively.

K. Provides students with specific evaluative feedback.
—Makes appropriate use of both formal and informal assessments to provide students with evaluative feedback.
—Provides timely feedback of daily performance.
—Provides students with written and/or verbal comments, in addition to scores, to clarify performance.
—Makes opportunities for one-to-one conferences.
—Assesses students as a group and provides individual feedback.
—Assists students in evaluating their own performance.

L. Designs Individualized Educational Plans.
—Exhibits evidence of preparation for conference.

—Organizes comprehensive Present Level of Performance reflecting relevant assessment data.

—Identifies areas for developing appropriate goals based upon diagnostic and present level information.

—Specifies objectives with required components.

—Specifies appropriate pupil placement and justification for placement.

—Completes all item/components of IEP (e.g., dates, page numbers, adaptations and modifications attachment).

—Submits IEP and attachments per department procedures.

M. Designs/implements Individual Implementor Plans.

—Writes IIPs which contain critical elements necessary to implement corresponding IEP objectives.

—Develops IIP data recording systems that are easily understood and accessible to other professional staff.

—Uses data-recording systems consistently.

—Modifies instructional design based on data derived from recording systems.

III. Management of learning environment

The special education teacher:

A. Organizes environment to promote learning.

—Communicates classroom procedures clearly.

—Maintains the classroom in a functional, attractive, and orderly environment conducive to student learning.

—Assesses the learning environment and knows how and when to change the environment.

—Ensures that materials and information can be read, seen, and/or heard by students.

—Promotes an atmosphere conducive to good health and safety.

—Organizes classroom space to match instructional plans and individual needs.

—Provides adequate management plans for substitute teachers.

B. Manages student behavior in a constructive manner.

—Establishes and clearly communicates behavioral expectations and consequences.

—Manages the behavior of individuals, thus maximizing group learning.

(continued)

EXAMPLE 9.1 continued

—Promotes self-discipline.

—Reinforces appropriate behavior.

—Uses effective techniques (e.g., social approval, contingent activities, keeping students on task) to maintain appropriate behavior.

—Identifies and ignores inconsequential behavior problems.

—Manages disruptive behavior in a constructive, timely manner.

—Endeavors to find and eliminate causes of undesirable behavior.

—Manages discipline problems in accordance with administrative regulations, school board policies, and legal requirements.

IV. Interpersonal relationships
   The special education teacher:
   A. Demonstrates effective interpersonal relationships with students.
      —Demonstrates a respect, understanding, and acceptance of each student as an individual, regardless of sex, race, ethnic origin, cultural or socioeconomic background, religion, or handicapping condition.
      —Recognizes that a student's emotional well-being affects learning potential.
      —Encourages students to develop to their full potential.
      —Communicates with students empathetically.
      —Gives time willingly to provide for a student's academic and personal needs.
      —Displays effective active listening skills.
      —Uses discretion in handling sensitive information confided by a student.
      —Gives constructive feedback which promotes self-esteem.
      —Assists students in dealing with success and failure.
      —Respects the individual's right to hold different views.
      —Recognizes and deals effectively with crisis issues (e.g., substance abuse, child abuse, suicidal behavior, or mood changes).
      —Shows sensitivity to physical development and special health needs of students.

—Creates a classroom climate which encourages mutually respectful relationships.

—Uses and appreciates humor in proper perspective.

B. Demonstrates effective interpersonal relationships with educational staff.

—Demonstrates a respect, understanding, and acceptance of each person as an individual, regardless of sex, race, ethnic origin, cultural or socioeconomic background, religion, or handicapping condition.

—Works cooperatively with colleagues in planning educational activities which reflect the best interest of the students.

—Shares ideas, materials, and methods with other staff.

—Makes appropriate use of support/ancillary staff.

—Works cooperatively with administrators to implement policies, regulations, and procedures.

—Informs administrators and/or appropriate personnel of school-related matters.

—Coordinates responsibilities, implements training, and evaluates teacher assistant/aide.

—Demonstrates ability to promote a positive image of the district.

—Fulfills responsibilities in situations requiring a team approach.

—Demonstrates acceptance of the right of others to hold differing views and values.

—Uses discretion in handling sensitive and/or confidential information.

—Displays effective active listening skills.

C. Demonstrates effective interpersonal relationships with parents/patrons.

—Demonstrates a respect, understanding, and acceptance of each person as an individual, regardless of sex, race, ethnic origin, cultural or socioeconomic background, religion, or handicapping condition.

—Provides a climate which opens up communications between staff and parent.

—Supports and participates in parent–staff activities.

—Promotes patron involvement with building/district.

—Maintains ongoing communication with parents/patrons.

(continued)

EXAMPLE 9.1 continued

—Demonstrates ability to promote a positive image of school district services within the community.

—Uses discretion in handling sensitive and/or confidential information.

—Initiates and utilizes effective oral and written communication with parents/patrons when appropriate.

—Demonstrates acceptance of the right of others to hold differing views and values.

—Interacts with parents/patrons in a friendly, respectful manner.

—Displays effective active listening skills.

—Cooperates with parents in the best interest of the students.

V. Professional responsibilities

The special education teacher:

   A. Participates in professional growth activities.

   —Demonstrates commitment by participation in professional activities (e.g., coursework, workshops, conferences).

   —Takes advantage of opportunities to learn from colleagues, students, parents, and community.

   —Is knowledgeable about current developments and issues in special/vocational education.

   B. Follows the communicated policies and procedures of the school district.

   —Demonstrates awareness of policies, regulations, and procedures applicable to his/her position.

   —Works cooperatively with other educators to implement policies, regulations, and procedures.

   —Selects appropriate channels for resolving concerns/problems when implementing policies, regulations, and procedures.

   C. Assumes responsibilities outside of the classroom in the best interest of the student.

   —Assumes fair share of noninstructional responsibilities.

   —Exercises responsibility for student management throughout the school campus (e.g., hallway, cafeteria, playground).

D. Demonstrates a sense of professional responsibility.
—Meets obligations in a prompt fashion (i.e., punctuality, attendance, etc.).
—Carries out duties in accordance with job description in a professional manner.
—Exhibits personal self-control.
—Utilizes supervisory/evaluative feedback to change behavior.
—Utilizes a problem-solving approach in dealing with areas of concern.
—Demonstrates effective organizational skills as previously defined by supervisor.
—Is knowledgeable about relevant community resources.

E. Processes district/departmental records and data.
—Monitors and forwards various pupil data forms.
—Completes appropriate referrals for ancillary program service.
—Completes forms/records per established time lines (i.e., district forms, referrals, supply/text requisitions, student attendance, etc.).
—Provides accurate data to the school and district as requested for management purposes.

Evaluative criteria and descriptors for special education teachers and paraprofessionals and the procedures for evaluating paraprofessionals are the possession of the Special School District of St. Louis County. They are used by permission of the District. Dennis Buhr, Director of Personnel of the Special School District of St. Louis County, and Arthur Allen, Director for Special Education of the Jefferson City Public Schools, provided special assistance in the preparation of the information for special education teachers.

Evaluative Procedures

An example of a developmental evaluation process for regular classroom teachers is presented in Chapter 2. In PBDE, special education teachers should be evaluated using the same operational procedures. This includes orienting teachers to the process and criteria; defining the evaluation cycle; implementing a formative phase that includes data collection, documentation procedures, conferences, and Professional Development Plans; and concluding with a summative evaluation.

Although the stated evaluative procedures are the same for regular and special education teachers, implementation of these procedures requires commonsense adaptation, especially in the collection and application of data. For example, the special education teacher is often the key person on a staffing team responsible for designing an Individualized Education Program (IEP) for a student. Some observation data for a special education teacher might come from a staffing meeting. Other observation data might be gathered while the teacher is working in a one-to-one setting with a student, or in a small group setting. Nonobserved data might be solicited from the "regular" classroom teacher who works with the special teacher to provide for mainstreaming of a student. Parents will be a common source of unsolicited data about a special education teacher. District-level supervisors frequently work closely with special education teachers and are an excellent source of both planned and unplanned data. The supervisor simply needs to consider the nature of the job—the tasks and responsibilities—and adjust the data collection process accordingly.

As with the regular teacher, the basic requirements of one scheduled and one unscheduled observation during the evaluation cycle are appropriate. However, the Preobservation Worksheet used with regular classroom teachers may need to be modified to meet the needs of special education teachers. Example 9.2, the Preobservation Worksheet for special education teachers, differs slightly from Example 4.1, the Preobservation Worksheet for regular teachers.

The procedures for documenting data (Chapter 5) and conferencing (Chapter 6) that apply to all regular teachers also apply to special education teachers. As with the regular teachers, a Formative Data Form is recommended for documenting information prior to and during the conference. A Formative Data Form for special education teachers is presented in Example 9.3.

The Formative Data Short Form discussed and presented in Chapter 5 is particularly useful for special education teachers. The short form used for special education teachers is the same as used for regular classroom teachers.

Professional Development Plans (PDPs) are recommended for all teachers (Chapter 7). As with regular classroom teachers, the PDP for special education teachers should focus on a performance criterion. Like the Formative Data Short Form, the PDP form is the same as for regular classroom teachers and is not repeated in this chapter.

The summative evaluation procedures discussed in Chapter 8

(text continues on page 165)

EXAMPLE 9.2
Preobservation Worksheet—Special Education Teachers

Teacher	Date	School

Subject Area	Grade/Level	Observation Time

Teacher completes this form and discusses content with principal prior to observation.

1. What are the objectives of the activity?

2. What strategies will be used to accomplish the objectives?

3. How are you going to monitor progress toward, and mastery of, the objectives?

4. Are there any specific behaviors you especially want monitored?

5. Are there any special circumstances of which the supervisor should be aware?

NOTES:

Teacher's Signature/Date	Principal's Signature/Date

(Signatures imply the content of this document has been discussed.)

EXAMPLE 9.3
Formative Data Form—Special Education Teachers

Teacher	Date	School

Content	Grade/Level	Observation Time

Data: ___Scheduled Obs. ___Unscheduled Obs. ___Non-observed ___Artifact

I. **Assessment Process**
   A. **Follows screening procedures.**

   B. **Identifies appropriate diagnostic tests/methods for assessment.**

   C. **Demonstrates appropriate administration of assessment methods/instruments.**

   D. **Demonstrates interpretation of assessment methods/instruments.**

   E. **Initiates/processes evaluations/re-evaluations.**

II. Instructional Process
   A. Demonstrates appropriate preparation for instruction and/or intervention.

   B. Demonstrates a knowledge of instructional needs of handicapping conditions.

   C. Demonstrates a knowledge of subject matter/curriculum.

   D. Selects/implements instructional objectives effectively.

   E. Selects/implements a variety of effective educational techniques.

   F. Provides opportunities for individual differences.

(continued)

EXAMPLE 9.3 continued

G. Uses a variety of effective materials/resources.

H. Uses instructional/intervention time effectively.

I. Demonstrates ability to motivate students.

J. Demonstrates ability to communicate effectively with students.

K. Provides students with specific, evaluative feedback.

L. Designs Individualized Educational Plans.

M. Designs/implements Individual Implementor Plans.

III. Management of Learning Environment
    A. Organizes classroom environment to promote learning.

    B. Manages student behavior in a constructive manner.

IV. Interpersonal Relationships
    A. Demonstrates effective interpersonal relationships with students.

    B. Demonstrates effective interpersonal relationships with educational staff.

    C. Demonstrates effective interpersonal relationships with parents/patrons.

V. Professional Responsibilities
    A. Participates in professional growth activities.

(continued)

EXAMPLE 9.3 continued

B. Follows the communicated policies and procedures of the school district.

C. Assumes responsibilities outside of the classroom in the best interest of the student.

D. Demonstrates a sense of professional responsibility.

E. Processes district/departmental records and data.

Comments:

Teacher's Signature/Date   Supervisor's Signature/Date

(Signatures indicate the data have been read and discussed. Copies to teacher and supervisor.)

apply to special education teachers. The Summative Evaluation Report is different only in that the performance criteria for the special education teachers are unique to their respective job responsibilities. A copy of a Summative Evaluation Report for special education teachers is provided in Example 9.4.

INSTRUCTIONAL MATERIALS SPECIALISTS

The school library of 1990 bore only a slight resemblance to the library of 1960. Still present were the rows of books, but computerized files had displaced card catalogues. Gone were the 35 mm film projectors, displaced by video cassette recorders. Other additions included portable television recording equipment, desktop computers, and electronic checkout and surveillance. The electronic media have made a mark on education, and today's librarian is no longer merely a disseminator of printed matter.

Even with these technological changes, librarians, media specialists, or instructional materials specialists remain key staff members of good schools. They provide essential support services to faculty and students. The physical complexion of the room may have changed, but the crucial importance of the role remains constant.

The evaluative criteria and procedures that follow were developed for application with instructional materials specialists, whether the job title was librarian, media specialist, or instructional materials specialist. As mentioned previously for special education teachers, this section does not stand alone. It should be read and considered only in the context of the discussion of developmental evaluation presented in the previous eight chapters.

Performance Criteria

The criteria and descriptors selected for this section were published in 1985 by the Missouri Department of Elementary and Secondary Education. They were developed by a state study committee of librarians and media specialists representing the Missouri Librarians Association. These criteria and descriptors, presented in Example 9.5, have been used in schools throughout Missouri and other states and have proved to be an excellent set of criteria and descriptors for developmental evaluation.

(text continues on page 171)

EXAMPLE 9.4
Summative Evaluation Form—Special Education Teachers

TEACHER:_____School_____

Performance Area: Assessment Process

A.   Follows screening procedures.

☐ Meets expectations   ☐ Does not meet expectations

B.   Identifies appropriate diagnostic tests/methods for assessment.

☐ Meets expectations   ☐ Does not meet expectations

C.   Demonstrates appropriate administration of assessment
methods/instruments.

☐ Meets expectations   ☐ Does not meet expectations

D.   Demonstrates interpretation of assessment
methods/instruments.

☐ Meets expectations   ☐ Does not meet expectations

E.   Initiates/processes evaluations/re-evaluations.

☐ Meets expectations   ☐ Does not meet expectations

Comments:

II. Instructional Process

   A. Demonstrates appropriate preparation for instruction and/or intervention.

   ☐ Meets expectations   ☐ Does not meet expectations

   B. Demonstrates a knowledge of instructional needs of handicapping conditions.

   ☐ Meets expectations   ☐ Does not meet expectations

   C. Demonstrates a knowledge of subject matter/curriculum.

   ☐ Meets expectations   ☐ Does not meet expectations

   D. Selects/implements instructional objectives effectively.

   ☐ Meets expectations   ☐ Does not meet expectations

   E. Selects/implements a variety of effective educational techniques.

   ☐ Meets expectations   ☐ Does not meet expectations

   F. Provides opportunities for individual differences.

   ☐ Meets expectations   ☐ Does not meet expectations

   G. Uses a variety of effective teaching materials/resources.

   ☐ Meets expectations   ☐ Does not meet expectations

   H. Uses instructional/intervention time effectively.

   ☐ Meets expectations   ☐ Does not meet expectations

   I. Demonstrates ability to motivate students.

   ☐ Meets expectations   ☐ Does not meet expectations

(continued)

EXAMPLE 9.4 continued

J.   Demonstrates ability to communicate effectively with students.

☐ Meets expectations   ☐ Does not meet expectations

K.   Provides students with specific, evaluative feedback.

☐ Meets expectations   ☐ Does not meet expectations

L.   Designs Individualized Educational Plans.

☐ Meets expectations   ☐ Does not meet expectations

M.   Designs/implements Individual Implementor Plans.

☐ Meets expectations   ☐ Does not meet expectations

Comments:

III. Management of Learning Environment

A.   Organizes classroom environment to promote learning.

☐ Meets expectations   ☐ Does not meet expectations

B.   Manages student behavior in a constructive manner.

☐ Meets expectations   ☐ Does not meet expectations

Comments:

IV. Interpersonal Relationships
   A. Demonstrates effective interpersonal relationships with students.

   ▢ Meets expectations   ▢ Does not meet expectations

   B. Demonstrates effective interpersonal relationships with educational staff.

   ▢ Meets expectations   ▢ Does not meet expectations

   C. Demonstrates effective interpersonal relationships with parents/patrons.

   ▢ Meets expectations   ▢ Does not meet expectations

Comments:

V. Professional Responsibilities
   A. Participates in professional growth activities.

   ▢ Meets expectations   ▢ Does not meet expectations

   B. Follows the communicated policies and procedures of the school district.

   ▢ Meets expectations   ▢ Does not meet expectations

   C. Assumes responsibilities outside of the classroom in the best interest of the student.

   ▢ Meets expectations   ▢ Does not meet expectations

   D. Demonstrates a sense of professional responsibility.

   ▢ Meets expectations   ▢ Does not meet expectations

   E. Processes district/departmental records and data.

   ▢ Meets expectations   ▢ Does not meet expectations

Comments:

(continued)

EXAMPLE 9.4 continued

Administrator's Recommendation:

☐ Reemployment recommended.

☐ Reemployment not recommended.

☐ No recommendation made at this time.

Teacher's Comments:

Administrator's Comments:

Teacher's Signature/Date   Administrator's Signature/Date
(Signatures imply the content of this document has been discussed. Explanatory comments required for all ratings not meeting expected performance.)

Evaluative Procedures

Developmental evaluation for instructional materials specialists includes the same basic operational components used for all teachers: orientation to the process and criteria, clarification of the evaluation cycle, and implementation of a formative and summative phase. The

---

EXAMPLE 9.5
Instructional Materials Specialists: Performance Areas,
Criteria, and Descriptors

I. Management and administration of the library/media center
The instructional materials specialist:
  A. Recognizes the critical role of information retrieval in the future of education.
    —Makes long-range plans which guide the development of the library/media center.
    —Encourages the use of new technologies.
  B. Establishes and maintains an environment in which students and staff can work at productive levels.
    —Develops and implements policies and procedures for the operation of the library/media center.
    —Uses initiative to promote the flexible use of the library/media center by individuals, small groups, and large groups for research, browsing, recreational reading, viewing, or listening.
    —Maintains the library/media center in a functional, attractive, and orderly environment conducive to student learning.
    —Arranges and uses space and facilities in the library/media center to support the objectives of the instructional program, providing areas for various types of activities.
    —Communicates health and safety needs of the library/media center to the proper authorities.
    —Assumes responsibility for proper use and care of library/media center facilities, materials, and equipment.
  C. Manages student behavior in a constructive manner.
    —Promotes appropriate learner behavior.
    —Encourages student self-direction and responsibility for

(continued)

EXAMPLE 9.5 continued

---

learning; maintains a productive balance between freedom and control.
—Exercises consistency in discipline policies.
—Corrects disruptive behavior constructively.
D. Demonstrates competency in selection, acquisition, circulation, and maintenance of materials and equipment.
—Uses a district-approved selection policy based on state guidelines.
—Selects materials and equipment which support the curriculum and promote the school's educational philosophy.
—Uses approved business procedures for ordering and receiving materials and equipment.
—Classifies, catalogues, processes, and organizes for circulation the educational media and equipment according to professional standards established by national, state, and local sources.
—Uses clearly stated circulation procedures.
—Informs staff and students of new materials and equipment.
—Establishes and/or follows procedures for maintenance and repair of media equipment.
—Periodically reviews and evaluates the collection to assure a current, attractive, and well-balanced collection.
—Assists in production of materials as feasible.
E. Prepares statistical records and reports needed to administer the library/media center.
—Maintains a current inventory of holdings to assure accurate records.
—Prepares and submits to administrators such reports as are needed to promote short- and long-term goals of the library/media center.
—Prepares and submits reports to other officials as requested.
F. Trains and supervises library/media center personnel to perform duties efficiently.
—Trains and supervises clerks, aides, student assistants, and/or adult volunteers in clerical tasks.
—Trains and supervises library/media center personnel to circulate materials and equipment.
—Trains and supervises library/media center personnel to

assist students and staff in the use of the library/media center.

G. Administers budgets according to needs and objectives of the library/media center within administrative guidelines.
—Submits budget proposals based on needs and objectives of the library/media center.
—Plans expenditures of allocated funds to meet short- and long-term goals.
—Keeps accurate records of all disbursements for the library/media center.

H. Evaluates library/media center programs, services, facilities, and materials to assure optimum use.
—Evaluates programs, services, facilities and materials informally and formally on a continuous basis, identifying strengths and weaknesses.
—Provides periodically for evaluation by faculty and students.
—Develops plans for making changes based on evaluations.

I. Uses time effectively, efficiently, and professionally.
—Prioritizes demands on time to provide maximum support of library/media center programs and services.
—Streamlines or eliminates time-consuming or nonessential routines when possible, without lowering the quality of programs and services.

II. Instructional process

The instructional materials specialist:

A. Exercises leadership and serves as a catalyst in the instructional program.
—Serves as instructional resource consultant and media specialist to teachers and students.
—Uses an appropriate variety of media and teaching techniques in instructional situations.
—Provides leadership in using newer technologies for instruction.
—Provides inservice training and library/media center orientation as needed.
—Plans and/or participates in special projects or proposals.
—Serves on committees involved with designing learning experiences for students, curriculum revision, or textbook adoption.

(continued)

EXAMPLE 9.5 continued

—Administers resource sharing, interlibrary loan, and/or networking activities.

B. Plans and implements the library/media center program of library/media skills.

—Considers long-range objectives when planning instruction appropriate to subject and grade levels.

—Develops sequential, short-range objectives which facilitate progress toward defined long-range objectives.

—Demonstrates knowledge of the general curriculum and observes recommended steps of teaching when in formal instructional situations.

—Plans with teachers to identify and implement the library/media center skills curriculum within the classroom curriculum.

—Continually instructs students and staff, individually or in groups, in the use of the library/media center media and equipment.

—Encourages independent use of the facility, collection, and equipment by students and staff.

—Guides students and staff in selecting appropriate media from a wide range of learning alternatives.

—Guides and supervises students and staff in research activities and in the use of reference materials.

—Communicates effectively with students and staff.

C. Promotes the development of reading skills and reading appreciation.

—Conveys enthusiasm for books and reading.

—Develops activities and/or provides individual guidance to motivate reading.

D. Supports classroom teachers in their instructional units.

—Provides a wide variety of resources and supplementary materials.

—Assists in choosing and collecting appropriate materials.

—Cooperatively plans and teaches content appropriate to library/media center objectives.

—Cooperates with teachers in designing and implementing a functional study skills program.

E. Provides resources for professional growth of faculty and staff.

—Identifies and encourages use of materials from the library/media center and professional library.

—Informs staff of new materials, equipment, and research in which they have special interest.

—Suggests resources outside of the library/media center collections.

III. Interpersonal relationships
The instructional materials specialist:
A. Demonstrates positive interpersonal relations with students.
   —Interacts with individual students in a mutually respectful and friendly manner.
   —Strives to be an available personal resource for all studonto.
   —Protects each user's right to privacy and confidentiality in library/media center use.
   —Demonstrates understanding and acceptance of different views and values.
   —Gives constructive criticism and praise when appropriate.
B. Demonstrates positive interpersonal relations with educational staff.
   —Initiates interaction with colleagues in planning instructional activities for students.
   —Shares ideas and methods with other teachers and staff.
   —Makes appropriate use of support staff services.
   —Works cooperatively with the school's administration to implement policies and regulations for which the school is responsible.
   —Informs administrators and/or appropriate personnel of school-related matters.
C. Demonstrates positive interpersonal relations with parents/patrons.
   —Provides a climate which encourages communication between the library/media center and parents or patrons.
   —Cooperates with parents in the best interests of students.
   —Supports and participates in parent–teacher activities.
   —Promotes patron involvement with the library/media center.
   —Handles complaints and/or challenged materials in a firm but friendly manner.

(*continued*)

EXAMPLE 9.5 continued

—Identifies community resource persons who may serve to bring the community into the educational process.

IV. Professional responsibilities
The instructional materials specialist:
A. Participates in professional growth activities.
   —Keeps abreast of developments in library science and issues related to teaching.
   —Demonstrates commitment by participating in professional activities (e.g., professional organizations, coursework, workshops, conferences).
   —Takes advantage of opportunities to learn from colleagues, students, parents, and the community.
B. Follows the policies and procedures of the school district.
   —Strives to stay informed about policies and regulations applicable to his/her position.
   —Selects appropriate channels for resolving concerns/problems.
C. Demonstrates a sense of professional responsibility.
   —Completes duties promptly, dependably, and accurately in accordance with established job description.
   —Demonstrates a responsible attitude for student management throughout the entire building.

Evaluative criteria and descriptors for counselors and instructional materials specialists are presented by permission of the Missouri Department of Elementary and Secondary Education, Robert Bartman, Commissioner. The criteria and descriptors were developed by members of the Missouri Performance Evaluation Committee, chaired by Turner Tyson, and members of the Missouri Librarians' Association and the Missouri School Counselors' Association.

formative phase includes data collection, documentation, conferences, and Professional Development Plans. The summative phase includes the Summative Evaluation Report and conference.

The application of the formative procedures differs slightly from the approach for regular classroom teachers. Although planned scheduled and unscheduled observations remain important, the setting for these specialists is obviously different than for regular classroom teachers. The principal may observe the instructional materials specialist working with students, assisting teachers with materials, helping teachers in the library or in the classroom, or managing the operation of the media facility. Because of the nature of the job, more unplanned than planned observation data may be used.

The role of the administrator remains the same as when gathering data for the regular classroom teacher: to observe performance, document performance, discuss performance, and develop growth plans. As with the developmental evaluation of special education teachers, a commonsense adaptation of the procedures for the regular classroom teachers is all that is needed to make developmental evaluation work effectively for instructional materials specialists.

The Preobservation Worksheet used with regular classroom teachers needs slight modification to meet the needs of instructional materials specialists. Example 9.6 can be contrasted with the Preobservation Worksheet presented as Example 4.1. The most important differences are found in the first two questions. For the regular teacher, the first two questions are "What are the lesson objectives?" and "What teaching/learning activities will be used?" For the instructional materials specialist, the questions might be "What program objectives do you hope to accomplish during the day of the observation?" and "What activities will be observed that relate to those objectives?" The purpose of the preobservation conference with the instructional materials specialist is to identify the goals the specialist plans to accomplish that day so the same issue can be addressed effectively during the postobservation conference.

The Formative Data Form and the Summative Evaluation Report for the instructional materials specialist are similar in format but different in content from those for regular classroom teachers or other special teachers such as the special education teachers described previously in this chapter. A Formative Data Form for the instructional materials specialist is presented in Example 9.7. A Summative Evaluation Report form is provided in Example 9.8.

SCHOOL COUNSELORS

Educational counselors provide a valuable service to students. When done properly, the job goes well beyond administering standardized tests and keeping track of student academic records. I vividly recall a comment made in 1972 by a veteran high school principal bemoaning the performance of his counselors. He said: "I can hire an hourly clerk to keep track of cumulative records. What I need are counselors who can help kids and teachers survive adolescence!" That principal had no

(text continues on page 188)

EXAMPLE 9.6
Preobservation Worksheet—
Instructional Materials Specialist

Instructional Materials Specialist   Date   School

Content   Grade/Level   Observation Time

Instructional Materials Specialist completes this form and discusses content with principal prior to observation.

1. What program objectives will you be working toward today?

2. What activities will be used to accomplish the objectives?

3. How are you going to monitor progress toward, and completion of, the objectives?

4. Are there any specific behaviors you especially want monitored?

5. Are there any special circumstances of which the supervisor should be aware?

NOTES:

Instructional Materials Specialist's Signature/Date   Principal's Signature/Date
(Signatures imply the content of this document has been discussed.)

EXAMPLE 9.7
Formative Data Form—Instructional Materials Specialist

Teacher	Date	School

Content	Grade/Level	Observation Time

Data: ___Scheduled Obs. ___Unscheduled Obs. ___Non-observed ___Artifact

I. **Management and Administration of the Library/Media Center**
The Instructional Materials Specialist:
A. Recognizes the critical role of information retrieval in the future of education.

B. Establishes and maintains an environment in which students and staff can work at productive levels.

C. Manages student behavior in a constructive manner.

D. Demonstrates competency in selection, acquisition, circulation, and maintenance of materials and equipment.

(continued)

Example 9.7 continued

E. Prepares statistical records and reports needed to administer the library/media center.

F. Trains and supervises library/media center personnel to perform duties efficiently.

G. Administers budgets according to needs and objectives of the library/media center within administrative guidelines.

H. Evaluates library/media center programs, services, facilities, and materials to assure optimum use.

I. Uses time effectively, efficiently and professionally.

II. Instructional Process
   The Instructional Materials Specialist:
   A. Exercises leadership and serves as a catalyst in the instructional program.

   B. Plans and implements the library/media center program of library/media skills.

   C. Promotes the development of reading skills and reading appreciation.

   D. Supports classroom teachers in their instructional units.

   E. Provides resources for professional growth of faculty and staff.

(*continued*)

EXAMPLE 9.7 continued

III. Interpersonal Relationships
   The Instructional Materials Specialist:
   A. Demonstrates positive interpersonal relations with
       students.

   B. Demonstrates positive interpersonal relations with
       educational staff.

   C. Demonstrates positive interpersonal relations with
       parents/patrons.

IV. Professional Responsibilities
   The Instructional Materials Specialist:
   A. Participates in professional growth activities.

B. Follows the policies and procedures of the school district.

C. Demonstrates a sense of professional responsibility.

Comments:

_____   _____
Teacher's Signature/Date   Supervisor's Signature/Date
(Signatures indicate the data have been read and discussed. Copies to teacher and supervisor.)

EXAMPLE 9.8
Summative Evaluation Form—
Instructional Materials Specialist

School:_____ Teacher:_____

I. Management and Administration of the Library/Media Center

> The Instructional Materials Specialist:
> A. Recognizes the critical role of information retrieval in the future of education.

☐ Meets expectations. ☐ Does not meet expectations.

> B. Establishes and maintains an environment in which students and staff can work at productive levels.

☐ Meets expectations ☐ Does not meet expectations

> C. Manages student behavior in a constructive manner.

☐ Meets expectations. ☐ Does not meet expectations.

> D. Demonstrates competency in selection, acquisition, circulation, and maintenance of materials and equipment.

☐ Meets expectations. ☐ Does not meet expectations.

> E. Prepares statistical records and reports needed to administer the library/media center.

☐ Meets expectations. ☐ Does not meet expectations.

> F. Trains and supervises library/media center personnel to perform duties efficiently.

☐ Meets expectations. ☐ Does not meet expectations.

G. Administers budgets according to needs and objectives of the library/media center within administrative guidelines.

☐ Meets expectations.   ☐ Does not meet expectations.

H. Evaluates library/media center programs, services, facilities, and materials to assure optimum use.

☐ Meets expectations.   ☐ Does not meet expectations.

I. Uses time effectively, efficiently and professionally.

☐ Meets expectations.   ☐ Does not meet expectations.

Comments:

II. Instructional Process
The Instructional Materials Specialist:

A. Exercises leadership and serves as a catalyst in the instructional program.

☐ Meets expectations.   ☐ Does not meet expectations.

B. Plans and implements the library/media center program of library/media skills.

☐ Meets expectations.   ☐ Does not meet expectations.

C. Promotes the development of reading skills and reading appreciation.

☐ Meets expectations.   ☐ Does not meet expectations.

D. Supports classroom teachers in their instructional units.

☐ Meets expectations.   ☐ Does not meet expectations.

E. Provides resources for professional growth of faculty and staff.

☐ Meets expectations.   ☐ Does not meet expectations.

Comments:

(continued)

EXAMPLE 9.8 continued

III. **Interpersonal Relationships**
The Instructional Materials Specialist:

A. Demonstrates positive interpersonal relations with students.

☐ Meets expectations.   ☐ Does not meet expectations.

B. Demonstrates positive interpersonal relations with educational staff.

☐ Meets expectations.   ☐ Does not meet expectations.

C. Demonstrates positive interpersonal relations with parents/patrons.

☐ Meets expectations.   ☐ Does not meet expectations.
Comments:

IV. **Professional Responsibilities**
The Instructional Materials Specialist:

A. Participates in professional growth activities.

☐ Meets expectations.   ☐ Does not meet expectations.

B. Follows the policies and procedures of the school district.

☐ Meets expectations.   ☐ Does not meet expectations.

C. Demonstrates a sense of professional responsibility.

☐ Meets expectations.   ☐ Does not meet expectations.
Comments:

Administrator's Recommendation:

☐ Reemployment recommended.

☐ Reemployment not recommended.

☐ No recommendation made at this time.

Instructional Materials Specialist's Comments:

Administrator's Comments:

Specialist's Signature/Date	Administrator's Signature/Date

(Signatures imply the content of this document has been discussed. Explanatory comments required for all ratings not meeting expected performance.)

intention of allowing his counselors to use their days managing paperwork behind closed doors. He wanted them among the students, developing relationships and building bridges that could be used someday to help the students cross turbulent water. Like any job, counseling has its share of routine paperwork as well as its opportunities for leadership and impact. The principal or supervisor must work with the counselor to assess performance of the mundane as well as the challenging aspects of the job. PBDE procedures for counselors, like those for regular classroom teachers, special education teachers, and instructional materials specialists, should include an orientation to the process and criteria, clarification of the evaluation cycle, and implementation of formative and summative phases. The formative phase should include data collection, documentation, conferences, and Professional Development Plans. The summative phase should include a Summative Evaluation Report and conference. As with all the special teachers discussed in this chapter, the procedures and forms for evaluating counselors should not be implemented without careful analysis of the information presented in previous chapters.

Performance Criteria

The criteria and descriptors selected for this section and presented in Example 9.9 were published in 1985 by the Missouri Department of Elementary and Secondary Education. They were developed by a special study committee representing the Missouri Counselors' Association. These counseling criteria and descriptors have been used in hundreds of schools and represent typical statements of responsibility and performance for school counselors.

EXAMPLE 9.9
School Counselors: Performance Areas, Criteria,
and Descriptors

I. The guidance and counseling process
The counselor:
A. Creates a climate conducive to counseling.
—Displays a nonjudgmental and accepting attitude.
—Shows respect for others through active listening.
—Maintains the confidentiality of student interviews.

(text continues on page 192)

—Provides opportunities for students to explore problems and weigh alternatives in decision making.

—Encourages students to set goals and assume responsibility for meeting them.

B. Employs a variety of effective guidance and counseling procedures.

—Counsels with students individually.

—Counsels with students in small groups.

—Conducts class/large-group sessions on appropriate topics.

—Consults with parents and staff.

—Provides inservice workshops for interested staff and parents.

C. Provides for individual differences effectively.

—Responds positively to students' requests for help.

—Provides developmental activities emphasizing positive mental health.

—Communicates with students in a manner appropriate to age and level of understanding.

—Uses and interprets cumulative data to assist students.

—Assists in appropriate educational planning and placement with individual students.

—Systematically contacts students who need assistance.

D. Displays competent knowledge of guidance and counseling.

—Demonstrates knowledge of child/adolescent growth and development.

—Selects and administers appropriate test instruments and uses results appropriately.

—Displays knowledge of environmental factors and situations which affect students' behavior and development.

—Selects and uses guidance materials appropriate for the abilities and interests of students.

—Communicates knowledge of methods and techniques used to change student behavior.

E. Uses guidance and counseling time effectively.

—Allots a realistic amount of time for specified guidance activities.

—Is available to students at appointed times.

—Begins activities on time.

—Uses time effectively for each designated activity.

F. Implements guidance programs effectively.

(continued)

EXAMPLE 9.9 continued

—Implements activities related to career exploration and planning.
—Provides activities to assist with educational planning.
—Provides opportunities to enhance knowledge of self and others.
—Implements additional activities which meet the program objectives.
—Provides and implements testing program when appropriate.
G. Demonstrates the ability to communicate effectively with students.
  —Uses correct oral and written communication.
  —Uses appropriate vocabulary.
  —Presents ideas logically.
  —Gives directions that are clear, concise, and reasonable.
  —Uses a variety of verbal and nonverbal techniques.
  —Elicits and responds to questions.
  —Summarizes effectively.

II. Guidance program management
The counselor:
  A. Organizes a systematic, developmental guidance program.
    —Uses formal and informal methods to assess student needs.
    —Sets priorities for the guidance and counseling program based on student needs.
    —Develops goals and objectives for a comprehensive guidance program.
    —Determines desired student outcomes based on program goals and objectives.
    —Develops a sequence of guidance program activities to meet stated goals and objectives.
    —Communicates information concerning the objectives of the guidance program to students, staff, and others.
    —Designs and implements a system for the evaluation of the guidance program.
  B. Develops a structure for implementing the guidance program.
    —Maintains an annual schedule of guidance events as well as a daily activity schedule.
    —Establishes a referral process for counseling services and disseminates the procedure to staff and students.

—Coordinates and maintains a file of pupil guidance information, including cumulative data, referrals, plans, and goals.

—Provides resources and guidance materials to meet program goals.

—Keeps an up-to-date listing of referral sources available outside of the school system.

—Maintains an attractive and accessible office environment.

—Provides informative materials or activities designed to enhance the image of the guidance program.

III. Interpersonal relationships
The counselor:
A. Demonstrates positive interpersonal relations with students.
   —Promotes positive self image in students.
   —Promotes students' self-control.
   —Makes an effort to know each student as an individual.
   —Interacts with students in a mutually respectful and friendly manner.
   —Gives constructive criticism and praise when appropriate.
   —Is reasonably available to all students.
   —Acknowledges the rights of others to hold differing views or values.
   —Demonstrates understanding and acceptance of different racial, ethnic, cultural, and religious groups.
   —Uses discretion in handling confidential information and difficult situations.
B. Demonstrates positive interpersonal relations with educational staff.
   —Works cooperatively with colleagues in planning counseling activities.
   —Shares ideas, materials, and methods with other staff members.
   —Makes appropriate use of support staff.
   —Works cooperatively with the school's administration to implement policies and regulations for which the school is responsible.
   —Informs administrators and/or appropriate personnel of school-related matters.
C. Demonstrates positive interpersonal relations with parents/patrons.
   —Cooperates with parents in the best interest of the students.

(continued)

EXAMPLE 9.9 continued

—Provides a climate which opens up communication be-
tween counselor and parent.
—Supports and participates in parent–teacher activities.
—Promotes patron involvement with school.
—Initiates communication with parents when appropriate.

IV. Professional responsibilities
   The counselor:
   A. Participates in professional growth activities.
      —Demonstrates commitment by a participation in profes-
      sional activities (e.g., professional organizations, course-
      work, workshops, conferences).
      —Takes advantage of opportunities to learn from col-
      leagues, students, parents, and community.
      —Keeps abreast of developments in the counseling profes-
      sion.
   B. Follows the policies and procedures of the school district.
      —Strives to stay informed about policies and regulations ap-
      plicable to his/her position.
      —Selects appropriate channels for resolving concerns/prob-
      lems.
   C. Assumes responsibilities outside the counseling center as
      they relate to the school.
      —Assumes necessary noncounseling responsibilities.
      —Exercises responsibility for student management through-
      out the entire building.
   D. Demonstrates a sense of professional responsibility.
      —Completes duties promptly and accurately.
      —Is punctual.
      —Provides accurate data to the school and district as re-
      quested for management purposes.
      —Carries out duties in accordance with established job de-
      scription.

Evaluative criteria and descriptors for counselors and instructional materials specialists are presented by permission of the Missouri Department of Elementary and Secondary Education, Robert Bartman, Commissioner. The criteria and descriptors were
developed by members of the Missouri Performance Evaluation Committee, chaired
by Turner Tyson, and members of the Missouri Librarians' Association and the Missouri School Counselors' Association.

Evaluative Procedures

A suggested copy of a Preobservation Worksheet for counselors is presented in Example 9.10. In application and format, it is similar to the form used for regular classroom teachers. In content it is more similar to the form for the instructional materials specialist than to that for the classroom teacher.

Examples 9.11 and 9.12 are the Formative Data Form and the Summative Evaluation Report for counselors. Except for the content of the criteria, the forms are similar to those presented in previous chapters for regular classroom teachers and in this chapter for the other special teachers.

PARAPROFESSIONALS

To better meet the needs of students, many schools employ teacher aides. These paraprofessionals often have teaching certificates. They seek the role of teacher aide or assistant to "get their foot in the door" for a future job as a teacher, or because the position provides a stimulating professional challenge within the field of education while permitting them to meet personal needs such as working part-time or spending more time with family or on other interests than they could spend if they were teachers. The services provided by these teaching assistants are invaluable to the teachers they support. Their assistance reduces the pupil–teacher ratio in the classroom and facilitates the use of specific teaching strategies such as personalized progress and mastery learning. Because these teachers have direct contact with the students and thus a direct effect on students' academic success, developmental evaluation can serve as a formal evaluative process while improving their performance.

Performance Criteria

Criteria, descriptors, and performance areas for paraprofessionals are presented in Example 9.13. Because special education programs often use many more paraprofessionals than regular classroom programs, many of the criteria listed in Example 9.13 were first developed for special education programs. Of the criteria listed, most were from the paraprofessional evaluation system of the Special School District of St.

EXAMPLE 9.10
Preobservation Worksheet—Counselor

Counselor	Date	School

Content	Grade/Level	Observation Time

Counselor completes this form and discusses content with principal prior to observation.

1. What program objectives will you be working toward today?

2. What activities will be used to accomplish the objectives?

3. How are you going to monitor progress toward, and completion of, the objectives?

4. Are there any specific behaviors you especially want monitored?

5. Are there any special circumstances of which the supervisor should be aware?

NOTES:

Counselor's Signature/Date   Principal's Signature/Date
(Signatures imply the content of this document has been discussed.)

Louis County, a system that employs and evaluates more than 400 paraprofessionals. As with other listings of criteria in this chapter, the reader should be familiar with information in previous chapters before beginning to implement an evaulation process in a school system.

(text continues on page 207)

EXAMPLE 9.11
Formative Data Form—Counselors

Counselor	Date	School

Activity	Observation Time

Data: ___Scheduled Obs. ___Unscheduled Obs. ___Non-observed ___Artifact

I. **The Guidance and Counseling Process**
The Counselor:
A. Creates a climate conducive to counseling.

B. Employs a variety of effective guidance and counseling procedures.

C. Provides for individual differences effectively.

D. Displays competent knowledge of guidance and counseling.

E. Uses guidance and counseling time effectively.

F. Implements guidance programs effectively.

G. Demonstrates the ability to communicate effectively with students.

(continued)

EXAMPLE 9.11 continued

II. Guidance Program Management
   The Counselor:
   A. Organizes a systematic, developmental guidance program.

   B. Develops a structure for implementing the guidance program.

III. Interpersonal Relationships
   The Counselor:
   A. Demonstrates positive interpersonal relations with students.

   B. Demonstrates positive interpersonal relations with educational staff.

   C. Demonstrates positive interpersonal relations with parents/patrons.

IV. Professional Responsibilities
The Counselor:
A. Participates in professional growth activities.

B. Follows the policies and procedures of the school district.

C. Assumes responsibilities outside the counseling center as they relate to the school.

D. Demonstrates a sense of professional responsibility.

Comments:

Counselor's Signature/Date   Supervisor's Signature/Date

(Signatures indicate the data have been read and discussed. Copies to counselor and supervisor.)

EXAMPLE 9.12
Summative Evaluation Form—Counselor

School:_____   Counselor:_____

I.   The Guidance and Counseling Process
     The Counselor:
     A. Creates a climate conducive to counseling.

     ☐ Meets expectations   ☐ Does not meet expectations

     B. Employs a variety of effective guidance and counseling procedures.

     ☐ Meets expectations   ☐ Does not meet expectations

     C. Provides for individual differences effectively.

     ☐ Meets expectations   ☐ Does not meet expectations

     D. Displays competent knowledge of guidance and counseling.

     ☐ Meets expectations   ☐ Does not meet expectations

     E. Uses guidance and counseling time effectively.

     ☐ Meets expectations   ☐ Does not meet expectations

     F. Implements guidance programs effectively.

     ☐ Meets expectations   ☐ Does not meet expectations

     G. Demonstrates the ability to communicate effectively with
        students.

     ☐ Meets expectations   ☐ Does not meet expectations

Comments:

II. Guidance Program Management
The Counselor:
A. Organizes a systematic, developmental guidance program.

☐ Meets expectations   ☐ Does not meet expectations

B. Develops a structure for implementing the guidance program.

☐ Meets expectations   ☐ Does not meet expectations

Comments:

III. Interpersonal Relationships
The Counselor:
A. Demonstrates positive interpersonal relations with students.

☐ Meets expectations   ☐ Does not meet expectations

B. Demonstrates positive interpersonal relations with educational staff.

☐ Meets expectations   ☐ Does not meet expectations

C. Demonstrates positive interpersonal relations with parents/patrons.

☐ Meets expectations   ☐ Does not meet expectations

Comments:

(*continued*)

EXAMPLE 9.12 continued

IV. Professional Responsibilities
The Counselor:
A. Participates in professional growth activities.

☐ Meets expectations   ☐ Does not meet expectations

B. Follows the policies and procedures of the school district.

☐ Meets expectations   ☐ Does not meet expectations

C. Assumes responsibilities outside the counseling center as they relate to the school.

☐ Meets expectations   ☐ Does not meet expectations

D. Demonstrates a sense of professional responsibility.

☐ Meets expectations   ☐ Does not meet expectations

Comments:

Administrator's Recommendation:

☐ Reemployment recommended.

☐ Reemployment not recommended.

☐ No recommendation made at this time.

Counselor's Comments:

Administrator's Comments:

_____   _____
Counselor's Signature/Date   Administrator's Signature/Date
(Signatures imply the content of this document has been discussed.
Explanatory comments required for all ratings not meeting expected
performance.)

EXAMPLE 9.13
Paraprofessionals: Performance Areas, Criteria,
and Descriptors

I. Instructional process (performance area)
The paraprofessional:
  A. Assists with preparation for instruction (criterion).
   —Provides input in selecting activities appropriate to the abilities, needs, and interests of the students (descriptor).
   —Assists in the preparation of appropriate teaching materials.
   —Organizes materials for instruction.
  B. Demonstrates a knowledge of subject matter/curriculum.
   —Displays a competent knowledge of curriculum and subject matter.
   —Presents subject matter which is accurate.
  C. Implements effective teaching techniques to accomplish instructional objectives.
   —Employs a variety of teaching techniques appropriate to the functioning level of students and the instructional objectives as demonstrated by the teacher (e.g., lecturing, modeling, demonstrating, questioning, experimentation, self-teaching, role-playing, multisensory strategies).
   —Implements modifications of lessons plans, teaching techniques, and educational experiences as the learning situations require.
   —Provides opportunities for students to experience success in instructional activities.
   —Demonstrates an ability to allow for individual student differences.
   —Uses support materials that are coordinated with the learning experiences and developmental level of the child.
   —Promotes maximum student involvement in instructional activities.
   —Follows instructional prescriptions for remediation and/or enrichment.
  D. Uses instructional time effectively.
   —Begins activities promptly.
   —Implements appropriate learning activities throughout the instructional time.
   —Avoids unnecessary delays during the lesson.
   —Avoids inappropriate digressions during the lesson.

—Implements a time schedule individualized for student needs.

E. Demonstrates ability to motivate students.
   —Strives to encourage and involve students who show little or no interest.
   —Responds positively to students' requests for help.
   —Gives frequent and prompt feedback to students.
   —Stimulates and encourages creative and critical thinking.
   —Utilizes appropriate reinforcers to promote learning.
   —Provides students with the opportunity to meet with success.
   —Utilizes activities which promote student independence.

F. Demonstrates ability to communicate effectively with students.
   —Communicates expectations to students.
   —Uses correct oral and written communication.
   —Uses vocabulary commensurate with the student's language skills.
   —Presents ideas logically.
   —Gives directions that are clear, concise, and reasonable.
   —Uses a variety of verbal and nonverbal techniques (e.g., signing, cues, proximity, physical contact).
   —Makes an effort to understand the student's communication system.
   —Elicits and responds to student questions.
   —Summarizes effectively.

G. Assists teacher in providing students with specific evaluative feedback.
   —Provides timely feedback of daily performance.
   —Provides students with written and/or verbal comments, in addition to scores, to clarify performance.
   —Provides teacher with information on student performance.
   —Assists students in evaluating their own performances.
   —Completes required data charts, graphs, grades, etc., as required by the teacher.
   —Assists the teacher in maintaining student progress reports.

H. Assists the teacher in maintaining classroom equipment and physical arrangement.
   —Maintains physical organization of classroom.

(*continued*)

EXAMPLE 9.13 continued

—Secures, operates, and returns audiovisual and computer equipment.

II. Classroom management
The paraprofessional:
   A. Assists in organizing classroom environment to promote learning.
      —Follows and reinforces classroom procedures established by the teacher.
      —Assists in maintaining the classroom in a functional, attractive, and orderly environment conducive to student learning.
      —Cooperates with the teacher to assess the learning environment and makes suggestions for how and when to change the environment.
      —Ensures that materials and information can be read, seen, and/or heard by students.
      —Works with the teacher to organize classroom space to match instructional plans and individual needs.
   B. Manages student behavior in a constructive manner.
      —Implements the behavior system as directed by the classroom teacher.
      —Manages the behavior of individuals, thus maximizing group learning.
      —Promotes self-discipline.
      —Reinforces appropriate behavior.
      —Uses effective techniques to maintain appropriate behavior.
      —Identifies and ignores inconsequential behavior problems.
      —Manages disruptive behavior in a constructive, timely manner.
      —Communicates to the teacher information regarding student behavior.
      —Manages discipline problems in accordance with administrative regulations, school board policies, and legal requirements.

III. Interpersonal relationships
The paraprofessional:
   A. Demonstrates effective interpersonal relationships with students.

—Demonstrates a respect, understanding, and acceptance of each student as an individual, regardless of sex, race, ethnic origin, cultural or socioeconomic background, religion, or handicapping condition.

—Recognizes that a student's emotional well-being affects learning potential.

—Encourages students to develop to their full potential.

—Communicates with students with empathy.

—Gives time willingly to provide for students' academic and personal needs.

—Displays effective active listening skills.

—Uses discretion in handling sensitive information confided by a student.

—Gives constructive feedback which promotes self-esteem.

—Assists students in dealing with success and failure.

—Respects the individual's right to hold different views.

—Recognizes and follows procedures for handling crisis issues (e.g., substance abuse, child abuse, suicidal behavior, or mood changes).

—Shows sensitivity to physical development and special health needs of students.

—Works with the teachers to create a classroom climate which encourages mutually respectful relationships.

B. Demonstrates effective interpersonal relationships with educational staff.

—Demonstrates a respect, understanding, and acceptance of each person as an individual, regardless of sex, race, ethnic origin, cultural or socioeconomic background, religion, or handicapping condition.

—Works cooperatively with staff in planning activities which reflect the best interest of the students.

—Shares ideas, materials, and methods with other staff.

—Works cooperatively with administrators to implement policies, regulations, and procedures.

—Informs appropriate personnel of school-related matters.

—Fulfills responsibilities in situations requiring a team approach.

—Demonstrates acceptance of the right of others to differing views and values.

(continued)

EXAMPLE 9.13 continued

—Uses discretion in handling sensitive and/or confidential information.
—Displays effective active listening skills.
C. Demonstrates effective interpersonal relationships with parents/patrons.
    —Demonstrates a respect, understanding, and acceptance of each person as an individual, regardless of sex, race, ethnic origin, cultural or socioeconomic background, religion, or handicapping condition.
    —Demonstrates ability to promote a positive image of district services within the community.
    —Uses discretion in handling sensitive and/or confidential information.
    —Demonstrates acceptance of the right of others to hold differing views and values.
    —Interacts with parents/patrons in a friendly, respectful manner.
    —Displays effective active listening skills.

IV. Professional responsibilities
    The paraprofessional:
    A. Participates in professional growth activities.
        —Participates in available educational activities that may enhance professional competence.
        —Takes advantage of opportunities to learn from colleagues, students, parents, and community.
        —Is knowledgeable about current developments and issues in education.
    B. Follows the communicated policies and procedures of the school district.
        —Demonstrates awareness of policies, regulations, and procedures applicable to his or her position.
        —Works cooperatively with other educators to implement policies, regulations, and procedures.
        —Utilizes appropriate channels for resolving concerns/problems.
    C. Assumes responsibilities outside the classroom.
        —Assumes noninstructional responsibilities (e.g., committees, public relations, special programs) as appropriate.
        —Exercises responsibility for student management through-

out the school campus (e.g., hallway, cafeteria, playground).

D. Demonstrates a sense of professional responsibility.
—Meets obligations in a prompt fashion (i.e., punctuality, attendance, etc.).
—Carries out duties in accordance with job description in a professional manner.
—Takes initiative in completing expected responsibilities.
—Completes duties in an accurate and timely manner.
—Manages time effectively.
—Exhibits personal self-control.
—Utilizes supervisory evaluative feedback to change behavior.
—Utilizes a problem-solving approach in dealing with areas of concern.
—Demonstrates effective organizational skills.
—Knows emergency procedures.

E. Performs clerical responsibilities as assigned by the teacher.
—Maintains accurate records such as attendance, lunch counts, grades, etc.
—Reproduces materials for learning activities such as copies, worksheets, etc.
—Assists in the preparation/dissemination of correspondence.

Evaluative criteria and descriptors for special education teachers and paraprofessionals and the procedures for evaluating paraprofessionals are the possession of the Special School District of St. Louis County. They are used by permission of the District. Dennis Buhr, Director of Personnel of the Special School District of St. Louis County, and Arthur Allen, Director for Special Education of the Jefferson City Public Schools, provided special assistance in the preparation of the information for special education teachers.

Evaluative Procedures

The role and responsibility of the paraprofessional is sufficiently different from the regular classroom teacher that specific evaluative procedures should be developed for that position. The procedures should clarify (1) who will be responsible for implementing the evaluation process, (2) the evaluation cycle, (3) the formative steps, (4) the summative steps, and (5) the appeal process. Recommended procedures for the evaluation of paraprofessionals are presented in Example 9.14.

(text continues on page 214)

EXAMPLE 9.14
Evaluative Process for Paraprofessionals

The following is an explanation of the procedures for performance-based evaluation of paraprofessionals. The process begins with orientation for the paraprofessionals and continues through the implementation of the formative and summative phases.

I. ORIENTATION

A. Supervisors

Prior to initiating the evaluation process, each teacher and administrator who supervises a paraprofessional will receive appropriate inservice training in the evaluation process. Annual inservice sessions will be conducted by the district to improve the consistency and quality of the supervisors' skills.

B. Paraprofessionals

New paraprofessionals shall receive orientation about performance-based paraprofessional evaluation at the beginning of their employment as paraprofessionals. All paraprofessionals shall receive additional inservice conducted by the district every two years. These sessions will be conducted to review roles and responsibilities of the paraprofessionals and the teachers with whom they work.

II. EVALUATION CYCLE

A. Regular Status

A Summative Evaluation Report will be completed at least once every three years for regular-status paraprofessionals. The Summative Evaluation Report will be completed prior to May 1 of the final year of the three-year cycle. Additional Summative Evaluation Reports may occur as deemed necessary by the supervisor or as requested by the paraprofessional. If a Summative Evaluation Report of a regular-status paraprofessional is going to occur more frequently than once every three years, the paraprofessional will be notified by the supervisor as soon as practical. Typical examples of reasons for more frequent Summative Evaluation Reports are transfer requests, reassignments, administrative concerns, and paraprofessionals' requests.

B. Probationary Status

A Summative Evaluation Report will be completed after each year for paraprofessionals in their first three years of an assignment. The report will be completed prior to May 1 for each probationary paraprofessional. A paraprofessional achieves regular status for the purposes of the evaluation cycle after three years of continuous employment in the same position.

III. FORMATIVE PHASE

The formative phase is the ongoing process for professional improvement. This phase is crucial to the success of performance evaluation and the development of paraprofessionals. The formative phase begins after a Summative Evaluation Report is written and concludes with the writing of the next Summative Evaluation Report. Following are the essential components of the formative phase.

A. Data Collection

Effective supervision includes the collection and sharing of information about a paraprofessional's performance. The data may be planned or unplanned. Each type may include observed data, non-observed data, and artifact data. The most typical planned observations are scheduled and unscheduled observations of performance. Following is an explanation of each.

1. Scheduled Observation Data

Scheduled observations provide focused and comprehensive information. A minimum of one scheduled observation will occur during each formative phase.

Prior to a scheduled observation, the paraprofessional and the supervisor (teacher or administrator) will establish the time and date of the observation. The paraprofessional and supervisor will discuss the activity to be observed.

Unexpected events may necessitate a change in the scheduled observation time. If so, the paraprofessional and supervisor will work together to identify an appropriate time for another observation and the need for another preobservation discussion.

The supervisor will make notes during the observation and transfer them to a Formative Data Form. The length of the scheduled ob-

(continued)

EXAMPLE 9.14 continued

---

servation shall be determined during the preobservation discussion. A postobservation conference will follow a scheduled observation.

2. Unscheduled Observation Data

Unscheduled observations may be planned or unplanned. They provide focused and comprehensive information about performance. A minimum of one planned unscheduled observation will occur during each school year.

During planned observations the supervisor will make notes and then transfer those notes to a Formative Data Form.

Unplanned observations of performance that the supervisor chooses to document must be recorded on the Formative Data Form. An observation is not valid for evaluative purposes unless the information is recorded on the Formative Data Form and discussed in a postobservation conference.

3. Nonobserved Data

Planned nonobserved data comprise information the supervisor seeks from others who are familiar with the paraprofessional's performance. Examples include evaluations by other supervising teachers or administrators, and discussions with other paraprofessionals, staff, students, or parents. Planned nonobserved data are seldom used without the endorsement of the paraprofessional being evaluated. The data are documented on the Formative Data Form and discussed with the paraprofessional.

Unplanned nonobserved data are those types of information that come to the attention of the supervisor indirectly. These are data that are not observed by the supervisor; examples include telephone calls and personal conversations. The supervisor should make appropriate notations regarding such information, seek to validate the information, and determine if it is significant. If it is determined to be significant, the supervisor will document the information on the Formative Data Form and discuss the issue with the paraprofessional within a realistic time frame, usually a few working days.

4. Artifact Data

Planned artifact data consist of information that should enhance the supervisor's understanding of the skill of the paraprofessional as related to specific criteria. Planned artifact data are typically identified at the beginning of the formative phase and are collected during the formative phase. Examples include clerical work, displays, records, and prepared materials. Performance relative to planned artifact data are documented on the Formative Data Form.

Unplanned artifact data include information that comes to the attention of the supervisor indirectly. These are data that the supervisor did not solicit; examples include letters, memos, and notes about the paraprofessional's performance. The responsibility of the supervisor is to determine if the information is significant. If it is determined to be significant, the supervisor will document the information on the Formative Data Form and discuss the issue with the paraprofessional within a realistic time frame, usually a few working days.

B. Formative Data Form

The Formative Data Form provides the format for documenting all data collected in the formative process. The role of the supervisor is to record pertinent data on the form. The data on the form become the basis for discussion between the paraprofessional and supervisor about job performance. The paraprofessional and supervisor will retain a copy of the form.

C. Conferencing

After recording pertinent data on the Formative Data Form, the paraprofessional and supervisor will discuss the data as they relate to the criteria. This conference should occur, when practical, within two working days after any planned scheduled or unscheduled observation.

If more than five attendance days (days when supervisor and paraprofessional are at school) transpire between a planned scheduled or unscheduled observation and conferencing, either party has the option to reject the observation and request another.

For planned nonobserved data and for all unplanned data, the conference should occur when the data have been determined to be significant.

At the conclusion of the conference, the paraprofessional and supervisor both sign the Formative Data Form, indicating the criteria have been discussed. Both parties will have the opportunity to make written comments on the Formative Data Form at that time. Additional written comments by either party must be shared within five working days, appended to the Formative Data Form, and discussed as soon as practical.

(continued)

EXAMPLE 9.14 continued

D. Professional Development Plans

Professional Development Plans are used to improve professional skill as defined by the criteria. The Professional Development Plan includes identifiable, precise objective(s) and appropriate means for achieving the objective(s).

A Professional Development Plan will be developed with each paraprofessional at some time during the formative phase. The plan may make a transition through more than one evaluation cycle, especially for probationary-status paraprofessionals. The plan will represent an effort to enhance skill on a criterion on which current performance is considered effective (enrichment plan) or on one on which performance is not considered effective (improvement plan).

If a supervisor recognizes a need for improvement on a criterion, the supervisor will identify the criterion and work with the paraprofessional to develop and implement a plan. Supervisors are responsible for coordinating all Professional Development Plans and may seek assistance from other personnel, if appropriate. A paraprofessional will not be rated "does not meet expectations" unless a Professional Development Plan for improvement noting a deficiency for that criterion preceded the Summative Evaluation Report.

Paraprofessionals not identified as needing a Professional Development Plan to improve a deficiency will meet with the supervisor sometime during the formative phase to develop an enrichment plan. The paraprofessional and supervisor will discuss the criterion on which the paraprofessional will focus. The supervisor and the paraprofessional will develop the plan, with the paraprofessional implementing the plan and sharing the progress/results of the plan with the supervisor prior to the end of the evaluation cycle.

The supervisor serves as a resource person to assist the paraprofessional with the plan, including efforts to facilitate participation in activities that may occur outside of, and/or during, the school day.

IV. SUMMATIVE PHASE

The summative phase constitutes the review and synthesis of formative data pertaining to the performance of the paraprofessional.

A. Summative Evaluation Report

The Summative Evaluation Report is the document used to summarize the evaluator's rating of performance for each criterion.

B. Summative Conference

After the evaluator has completed the Summative Evaluation Report, a conference between the paraprofessional and the evaluator will be conducted to review the information on the report. The Summative Evaluation Report and the conference will be completed by May 1 of the appropriate school year.

The conference will be conducted by the supervisor. If input was provided by other supervisors, such input shall be clarified on the report.

The paraprofessional and supervisor will both sign the Summative Evaluation Report, indicating the document has been read and discussed. Both parties will have the opportunity to make written comments on the report at that time. Additional written comments by either party must be shared within five working days and appended to the original copy of the Summative Evaluation Report. Copies of the Summative Evaluation Report will be retained by the paraprofessional, the supervisor, the principal (if the principal was not the supervisor), and the personnel director.

V. REVIEW/APPEAL

A paraprofessional may request a review of, or an appeal of, a professional judgment. This review or appeal is not to be confused with a grievance. A grievance is related to a violation of evaluation process; review or appeal is related to professional judgment.

A paraprofessional has the right to request a review of data on a Formative Data Form or a Professional Development Plan by the supervisor's immediate supervisor. The immediate supervisor will review the information and discuss it with the paraprofessional and the supervisor.

A paraprofessional has a right to appeal the ratings on the summative report. The appeal must be presented in writing within five working days after receipt of the Summative Evaluation Report and must identify the reason for the request, including an explanation of the information supporting the appeal. The appeal will be re-

(continued)

EXAMPLE 9.14 continued
---

viewed by the supervisor's immediate supervisor. That supervisor will process the appeal within ten working days of receipt and will respond both in writing and in person to the paraprofessional during that time. The paraprofessional has the right to have a mutually acceptable, nonparticipating observer present during this conference.

VI. SYSTEM REVIEW

The school district administration will review the paraprofessional evaluation system every five years to promote the maintenance of an effective, fair, and efficient system that is comprehensive and performance-based. This review will be made by a committee composed of a majority of paraprofessionals, with supervising teachers and administrators completing the committee membership.

The forms necessary to implement paraprofessional evaluation are similar to those for the other teaching positions presented throughout this book. The Preobservation Worksheet, the Formative Data Forms, the Professional Development Plan, and the Summative Evaluation Report would be prepared using the paraprofessional criteria arranged in the same format as on the evaluative forms for the other types of teaching positions.

SUMMARY

The special teachers discussed in this chapter provide essential services to the students of a school system. Over the past fifty years, new types of special teachers have emerged and become accepted as commonplace in the school setting. As new positions emerge in the future— and they surely will—the developmental evaluative procedures presented in this chapter can be adapted easily to the specific responsibilities of the positions.

REFERENCE

Office of Educational Research and Improvement. (1987). *The condition of education: A statistical report.* Washington, DC: U.S. Government Printing Office.

CHAPTER 10

Evaluating Coaches

*The mediocre teacher tells. The good teacher explains. The superior
teacher demonstrates. The great teacher inspires.*
—William Arthur Wood

SCHOOLING IS MORE than the acquisition of knowledge in science,
history, and other "courses." A high-quality educational program provides for the development of interests and abilities beyond the regular
classroom. Although the cost of athletic programs, at the expense of
classroom programs, might be arguable in periods of austerity, the
value to students of co-curricular activities is consistently demonstrated in schools throughout the year.

Finding good coaches is obviously an important first step in the
development of a high-quality athletic program. But once the athletic
programs are staffed, a supervisor such as an athletic director, principal, or assistant principal must evaluate each coach's ability to accomplish the goals of the particular sports program. As discussed in previous chapters, the beginning tasks in the development of a good
evaluation system include defining a philosophy of evaluation, determining the job-related expectations (criteria) for coaches, and identifying the procedures appropriate for assessing those expectations. Evaluative forms must then be developed to implement the procedures.
While this chapter provides specific information for each of those
tasks, it should be read in context with the other chapters in this book.
The principles and related discussions presented in chapters 1 through

The author appreciates the help of the many principals he visited with across the
country who shared their thoughts, procedures, and forms for evaluating coaches. Of particular value was the information shared by two principals, Thomas Herrick of William
Chrisman High School in Independence, Missouri, and Albert Burr of Clayton High
School in Clayton, Missouri.

8 are essential to an effective understanding of the issues discussed in this chapter. Simply stated, if you haven't attempted to read the first eight chapters, you should not yet be reading this chapter.

A COACHING PHILOSOPHY

The basic function of a coach is to educate the athlete effectively, just as the function of the classroom teacher is to educate the student. The National Interscholastic Athletic Administrators Association makes available to its members an *Athletic Administrators' Reference Manual* (1989). Included in this manual is a Code of Ethics from the National Federation of Interscholastic Coaches Association (NFICA). This code, presented in Example 10.1, provides statements on which to build a philosophy for coaching and for evaluating coaches. The basic tenets on which an evaluation system is based should be stated clearly before the system is developed. Chapter 2 provides details about the writing of a philosophy statement.

EXAMPLE 10.1
NFICA Coaches' Code of Ethics

The function of a coach is to properly educate students through participation in interscholastic competition. The interscholastic program is designed to enhance academic achievement and should never interfere with opportunities for academic success. Each child should be treated as though they were the coaches' own and their welfare shall be uppermost at all times. In recognition of this, the following guidelines for coaches have been adopted by the NFICA Board of Directors.

The coach must be aware that he or she has a tremendous influence, either good or bad, in the education of the student athlete and, thus, shall never place the value of winning above the value of instilling the highest desirable ideals of character.

The coach must constantly uphold the honor and dignity of the profession. In all personal contact with the student athlete, officials, athletic directors, school administrators, the state high school athletic association, the media and the public, the coach shall strive to set an example of the highest ethical and moral conduct.

The coach shall take an active role in the prevention of drug, alcohol and tobacco abuse and under no circumstances should authorize their use.

The coach shall promote the entire interscholastic program of the school and direct his or her program in harmony with the total school program.

The coach shall be thoroughly acquainted with the contest rules and is responsible for their interpretation to team members. The spirit and letter of rules should be regarded as mutual agreements. The coach shall not try to seek an advantage by circumvention of the spirit or letter of the rules.

Coaches shall actively use their influence to enhance sportsmanship by their spectators, working closely with cheerleaders, pep club sponsors, booster clubs, and administrators.

Contest officials shall have the respect and support of the coach. The coach shall not indulge in conduct which will incite players or spectators against the officials. Public criticism of officials or players is unethical.

Before and after contests, rival coaches should meet and exchange friendly greetings to set the correct tone for the event.

A coach shall not exert pressure on faculty members to give student athletes special consideration.

It is unethical for coaches to scout opponents by any means other than those adopted by the league and/or state high school athletic association.

Reprinted by permission of the National Interscholastic Athletic Administrators' Association.

PROCEDURES FOR EVALUATING COACHES

As with the evaluation of teachers, a distinct set of procedures should be developed for evaluating coaches. The procedures should explain (1) who will be responsible for implementing the evaluation process, (2) the evaluation cycle, (3) the formative steps, (4) the summative steps, and (5) the appeal process. Since each of these concepts was discussed in previous chapters, a detailed explanation is not necessary. However, a suggested process for performance-based developmental evaluation of coaches is presented in Example 10.2 to clarify those procedures unique to coaching.

(text continues on page 224)

EXAMPLE 10.2
Evaluative Process for Coaches

The following is an explanation of the procedures for performance-based developmental evaluation of coaches. The process begins with orientation for the coaches, continues with the formative phase, and culminates in the summative evaluation. This evaluation process is intended to be continuous, constructive, and cooperative.

I. ORIENTATION

A. Supervisors

Prior to initiating the evaluation process, each supervisor will receive appropriate inservice training in the evaluation process. Supervisors include all personnel responsible for supervising/evaluating coaches, including principals, assistant principals, and athletic directors.

B. Coaches

New coaches shall receive orientation about the evaluation process at the beginning of their employment as coaches. All coaches shall receive additional inservice conducted by the district athletic director every two years. These sessions will be conducted to review coaching guidelines, performance expectations and information about the evaluation process.

II. EVALUATION CYCLE

A. Schedule for Experienced Coaches

A Summative Evaluation Report will be completed at least once every three years for experienced coaches (coaches with more than three years' experience in the current coaching assignment). The Summative Evaluation Report will be completed during the final year of the three-year cycle. Additional Summative Evaluation Reports may occur as deemed necessary by the supervisor or as requested by the coach. If a Summative Evaluation Report of an experienced coach is going to occur more frequently than once every three years, the coach will be notified by the supervisor as soon as practical. Typical examples of reasons for more frequent Summative Evaluation Reports are transfer requests, reassignments, administrative concerns, and coaches' requests.

Summative reports will be completed within one month after the end of the sport season. Coaches of more than one sport will be evaluated separately for each sport they coach.

B. Schedule for Coaches New to Assignments

A Summative Evaluation Report will be completed after each appropriate sport season for coaches in their first three years of a coaching assignment. The report will be completed within one month after the end of the appropriate sport season.

III. FORMATIVE PHASE

The formative phase is the ongoing process for professional improvement. This phase is critical to the success of performance evaluation and the development of students and the sports program. The formative phase begins after a Summative Evaluation Report for the appropriate sport is written and concludes with the writing of the next Summative Evaluation Report for that sport. Following are the essential components of the formative phase.

A. Data Collection

Effective supervision includes collecting and sharing information about coaching performance. The data may be planned or unplanned. Each type may include observed data, nonobserved data, and artifact data. The most typical planned observations are scheduled and unscheduled observations of coaching performance. Following is an explanation of each.

1. Scheduled Observation Data

Scheduled observations provide focused and comprehensive information. A minimum of one scheduled observation will occur during each formative phase.

(continued)

EXAMPLE 10.2 continued

Prior to a scheduled observation, the coach and supervisor will establish the time and date of the observation. The coach and supervisor will discuss the activity to be observed. The approximate length of the observation will be determined during the discussion.

Unexpected events may necessitate a change in the scheduled observation time. If so, the coach and supervisor will work together to identify an appropriate time for another observation and the need for another preobservation discussion.

The supervisor will make notes during the observation and transfer them to a Formative Data Form. A postobservation conference will follow a scheduled observation.

2. Unscheduled Observation Data

Unscheduled observations may be either planned or unplanned. They provide focused and comprehensive information about performance. A minimum of one planned unscheduled observation will occur during each sports season. During planned observations, the supervisor will make notes and transfer those notes to a Formative Data Form.

Unplanned observations which the supervisor wishes to document must be recorded on the Formative Data Form. An observation is not valid for evaluative purposes unless the information is recorded on the Formative Data Form and discussed in a postobservation conference.

3. Nonobserved Data

Planned nonobserved data consist of information the supervisor seeks from others who are familiar with the coach's performance. Examples include evaluations by assistant coaches and athletes, and discussions with other coaches, teachers, athletes, and parents. Planned nonobserved data are seldom used without the endorsement of the coach being evaluated. The data are documented on the Formative Data Form and discussed with the coach.

Unplanned nonobserved data include those types of information that come to the attention of the supervisor indirectly. These are data that are not observed by the supervisor; examples include telephone calls and personal conversations. The supervisor should make appropriate notations regarding the information, seek to validate the information, and determine if it is significant. If it is determined to be significant, the supervisor will document the information on the Formative Data Form and discuss the issue with the coach within a realistic time frame, usually a few working days.

4. Artifact Data

Planned artifact data include information that should enhance the supervisor's understanding of the skill of the coach with respect to specific criteria. Planned artifact data are typically identified at the beginning of the formative phase and collected during the formative phase. Examples might include budgets, worksheets, inventories, game plans, playbooks, discipline referrals, and workshop handouts. Performance relative to artifact data is documented on the Formative Data Form.

Unplanned artifact data include information that comes to the attention of the supervisor indirectly. These are data that the supervisor did not solicit; examples include letters, memos, and notes about the coach's performance. The responsibility of the supervisor is to determine if the information is significant. If it is determined to be significant, the supervisor will document the information on the Formative Data Form and discuss the issue with the coach within a realistic time frame, usually a few working days.

B. Formative Data Form

The Formative Data Form provides the format for documenting all data collected in the formative process. The role of the supervisor is to record pertinent data on the form. The data on the form become the basis for discussion between the coach and supervisor about job performance. The coach and the supervisor will each retain a copy of the form.

C. Conferencing

After recording pertinent data on the Formative Data Form, the coach and supervisor will discuss the data as they relate to the criteria. This conference should occur, when practical, within two working days after any planned scheduled or unscheduled observation.

If more than five attendance days (days when the supervisor and the coach are at school) transpire between a planned scheduled or unscheduled observation and conferencing, either party has the option to reject the observation and request another.

(continued)

EXAMPLE 10.2 continued

For planned nonobserved and artifact data and for all unplanned data, the conference should occur when the supervisor determines that the data are significant.

At the conclusion of the conference, the coach and supervisor sign the Formative Data Form, indicating the criteria have been discussed. Either party will have the opportunity to make written comments on the Formative Data Form at that time. Additional written comments by either party must be shared within five working days, appended to the Formative Data Form, and discussed as soon as practical.

D. Professional Development Plans

Professional Development Plans are used to improve professional skill as defined by the criteria. The Professional Development Plan includes identifiable, precise objective(s) and appropriate means for achieving the objective(s).

A Professional Development Plan will be developed with each coach at some time during the formative phase. The plan may make a transition through more than one evaluation cycle, especially for coaches new to the assignment, who are receiving a Summative Evaluation Report for three seasons in succession. The plan will represent an effort to enhance skill on a criterion on which the coach is considered effective (enrichment plan) or on a criterion on which the coach is considered deficient (improvement plan).

If a supervisor recognizes a need for improvement on a criterion, the supervisor will identify the criterion and work with the coach to develop and implement a plan. Supervisors are responsible for coordinating all Professional Development Plans and may seek assistance from other appropriate personnel. A coach will not be rated "does not meet expectations" unless an improvement plan noting the deficiency on that criterion preceded the Summative Evaluation Report.

Coaches not identified as needing a Professional Development Plan to improve a deficiency will meet with the supervisor sometime during the formative phase to develop an enrichment plan. The coach and supervisor will discuss the criterion on which the coach will focus. The supervisor and the coach will develop the plan, with the coach implementing the plan and keeping the supervisor apprised of progress.

The supervisor serves as a resource person to assist the coach with the plan, including efforts to facilitate participation in activities that may occur either outside of or during the school day.

IV. SUMMATIVE PHASE

The summative phase is the review and synthesis of formative data pertaining to the performance of the coach.

A. Summative Evaluation Report

The Summative Evaluation Report is the document used to summarize the evaluator's rating of performance for each criterion.

B. Summative Conference

After the evaluator has completed the Summative Evaluation Report, a conference between the coach and supervisor will be conducted to review the information in the report. The Summative Evaluation Report and the conference will be completed within one month after the end of the respective sports season.

The conference will be conducted by the supervisor. If input was provided by other supervisors, such input shall be clarified on the report.

The coach and supervisor will sign the Summative Evaluation Report, indicating that the document has been read and discussed. Either party will have the opportunity to make written comments on the report at that time. Additional written comments by either party must be shared within five working days and appended to the original copy of the Summative Evaluation Report. Copies of the Summative Evaluation Report will be retained by the coach, the supervisor, the principal (if the principal was not the supervisor), and the personnel director.

V. REVIEW/APPEAL

A coach may request a review of, or an appeal of, a professional judgment. This review or appeal is not to be confused with a grievance. A grievance is related to a violation of evaluation process. Both a review and an appeal are related to professional judgment.

(*continued*)

EXAMPLE 10.2 continued

A coach has the right to request a review of information on a Formative Data Form or a Professional Development Plan by the supervisor's immediate supervisor. The immediate supervisor will review the information and discuss it with the coach and the supervisor.

A coach has a right to appeal the ratings on a Summative Evaluation Report. The appeal must be made in writing within five working days after receipt of the Summative Evaluation Report and must identify the reason for the request, including an explanation of the information supporting the appeal. The appeal will be reviewed by the supervisor's immediate supervisor. The immediate supervisor will process the appeal within ten working days of receipt and will respond both in writing and in person to the coach during that time. The coach has the right to have a mutually acceptable, nonparticipating observer present during this conference.

VI. SYSTEM REVIEW

The administration of the school district shall provide for a review of the evaluation system every five years to promote the maintenance of an effective, fair, and efficient system that is comprehensive and performance-based. This review will be made by a committee composed of an equal number of coaches and administrators.

CRITERIA AND DESCRIPTORS

Criteria represent the performance expectations for coaches with similar responsibilities. Because coaching responsibilities are common across all sports, a basic list of criteria can be used to evaluate all head coaches. The same list can also be used to evaluate all assistant coaches by instructing the supervisor to mark "not applicable" for those criteria that might not apply to an assistant coach's responsibilities.

If separate criteria and descriptors for assistant coaches are desired, two approaches appear most feasible. One is to develop a separate list of criteria and descriptors for assistant coaches. The shortcoming of this is that different assistant coaches usually have different responsibilities. It would be time-consuming to develop distinct lists, and a supervisor would still have to use "not applicable" for some criteria. The second approach is to use the same criteria for all coaches and develop separate descriptors for the assistant coaches. This, too, would be time-consuming.

A review of the criteria and descriptors listed in Example 10.3 demonstrates how the criteria can be written so head coaches and assistant coaches for all sports can be evaluated using the same criteria. This is the most efficient process to develop and implement. It minimizes the number of different forms that must be used and the number of criteria and descriptors that must be understood and interpreted by the supervisors. Also, notice the consistency between the coaching criteria and the teaching criteria presented in previous chapters. This consistency reduces confusion about the meaning of the factors used to evaluate personnel.

(text continues on page 232)

EXAMPLE 10.3
Coaches: Performance Areas, Criteria, and Descriptors

I. Leadership
The coach:
A. Provides positive direction for the program.*
—Develops short- and long-range goals for the program.
—Involves program staff, administrators, and support groups in the development of program goals.
—Uses needs assessment data for goal development.
B. Develops and maintains student participation in the program.
—Demonstrates the ability to promote and maintain a quality program.
—Encourages students to participate in the program.
—Gives all students who meet program requirements equal opportunity to be selected for the program.
—Conducts the program in the best interest of the students.
C. Develops and maintains a good public relations program for the sport.

(continued)

EXAMPLE 10.3 continued

—Makes information available to students, parents, and community members.

—Represents the sports program to community organizations when asked.

—Keeps students, parents, and community members informed of program activities, schedules, etc.

—Works effectively with the media.

D. Demonstrates effective problem-solving and decision-making skills.

—Identifies and analyzes pertinent elements in a problem situation.

—Establishes priorities and seeks relevant data.

—Considers alternative solutions before making decisions.

—Makes logical decisions based on available data.

—Knows when to make a decision and when to gather more data or be patient.

E. Demonstrates effective organizational skills.

—Manages time efficiently and effectively.

—Prioritizes tasks and functions accordingly.

—Utilizes resources in an optimal manner.

—Delegates responsibility and authority when appropriate.

—Completes duties accurately and in a timely manner.

—Begins activities promptly.

—Maintains effective time on task during activities.

F. Provides leadership for the other staff members in the program.*

—Establishes roles and responsibilities for staff.

—Supervises staff effectively.

—Provides assistance and development for all staff.

—Promotes the establishment of high standards of performance for staff.

—Promotes staff awareness of new developments and ideas in the sport.

—Demonstrates skill in the recruitment, selection, and assignment of program staff.

G. Follows the policies, regulations, and procedures of the school and district.

—Demonstrates awareness of policies, regulations, and procedures of the school and district.

—Works cooperatively with other educators to implement

school and district policies, regulations, procedures, and goals.

—Selects appropriate channels and procedures for resolving concerns and problems.

—Complies with school policy on attendance and punctuality.

—Completes duties promptly and accurately.

—Maintains and provides accurate records/data.

—Provides plans and materials for substitutes in case of absence.

—Demonstrates effective organizational skills in managing professional responsibilities.

—Handles confidential information ethically and with discretion,

—Keeps personal interests/problems separate from professional responsibilities and duties.

—Recognizes and deals effectively with crisis issues (e.g., substance abuse, child abuse, suicidal behavior, mood changes).

H. Ensures effective management of the fiscal resources of the program.

—Follows building and district guidelines for fiscal management.

—Meets time lines for development and implementation of fiscal issues.

—Selects appropriate channels for resolving fiscal problems.

—Plans for long-range fiscal needs.

—Supervises fund-raising activities according to program, building, and district guidelines.

—Maintains appropriate inventories of program supplies and equipment.

I. Establishes and maintains a positive and safe environment for the program.

—Establishes efficient practice and game routines.

—Establishes and communicates expectations and parameters for student conduct.

—Establishes a program climate of mutual trust, respect, and purpose.

—Provides a physical environment conducive to good health and safety.

(*continued*)

EXAMPLE 10.3 continued

    —Monitors, reports, endeavors to correct, and follows up on unsafe conditions.

    —Organizes facilities to match instructional activities and program needs.

    —Maintains facilities in good, safe working condition.

J. Manages student behavior in a constructive manner.

    —Manages discipline problems in accordance with program, building, and district guidelines.

    —Is courteous and sensitive but firm and professional when dealing with student behavior problems.

    —Anticipates and corrects disruptive behavior in a constructive and timely manner.

    —Recognizes inconsequential behavior and responds accordingly.

    —Endeavors to identify and resolve causes of undesirable behavior.

    —Manages the behavior of individuals, thus maximizing the learning for the group.

    —Promotes positive self-image for students while managing their behavior.

    —Maintains a positive attitude toward student management.

    —Uses effective techniques to promote self-discipline and maintain appropriate behavior.

K. Demonstrates a commitment to professional growth.**

    —Participates actively in the supervisory process for ongoing professional growth.

    —Maintains current knowledge in coaching and teaching/learning theory and practice.

    —Participates in professional organizations and activities as available.

    —Participates in school and district inservice activities as appropriate.

    —Exhibits personal self-control.

    —Gives serious consideration and appropriate action to parental comments and criticism.

II. Program instruction

The coach:

A. Demonstrates evidence of effective planning and preparation for instruction of students.

—Prepares practices and game plans based on program philosophy and goals.

—Prepares activities designed to effectively teach and challenge participants.

—Designs activities that build on present skills and progress toward higher skills.

—Has needed equipment and materials readily available.

B. Uses effective teaching techniques and strategies.

—Develops a mental and physical readiness for learning the knowledge, skills, and attitudes of the sport.

—Explains the objectives of the learning activities and skills to the athletes.

—Uses a variety of techniques to teach the knowledge, skills, and attitudes of the sport.

—Gives clear, concise, reasonable directions.

—Monitors student progress during the learning process.

—Provides effective opportunities for practicing the appropriate skills.

C. Demonstrates an understanding of the sport, including the knowledge, skills, strategies, and attitudes associated with the particular sport.

—Teaches in accordance with the philosophy of the program.

—Displays competent knowledge of the rules and regulations of the sport.

—Displays competent knowledge of the athletic skills needed for the sport.

—Understands and implements appropriate coaching strategies during practice and contests.

—Promotes among participants a proper attitude for enjoyment of the sport.

—Selects content and skills appropriate to the level of performance of the athletes.

D. Evaluates student progress effectively.

—Uses evaluation strategies consistent with program philosophy and goals.

—Uses both mental and physical assessment strategies to determine student progress.

—Provides evaluative feedback in a sensitive and timely manner.

(*continued*)

EXAMPLE 10.3 continued

—Uses a variety of techniques for communicating progress (e.g., film, written and verbal information, individual and group discussion).
E. Provides for individual differences while promoting team development.
—Groups students for each activity in a manner that best facilitates learning.
—Uses knowledge of various learning styles of students.
—Determines and applies remediation and enrichment activities based on individual needs.
—Understands and applies child development principles in the conditioning and teaching process.
—Provides activities and materials coordinated with the developmental level of each athlete.
F. Demonstrates ability to motivate students.
—Communicates challenging expectations.
—Provides all athletes with opportunities to succeed.
—Stimulates and encourages creative, critical thinking, and problem-solving skills.
—Gives constructive feedback frequently and promptly.
—Involves all athletes in appropriate activities.
—Responds positively to athletes' requests for assistance.
—Helps athletes develop positive self-concepts.
—Demonstrates enthusiasm.

III. Interpersonal relationships
The coach:
A. Demonstrates positive interpersonal relationships with students.
—Demonstrates respect, understanding, and acceptance of each student as an individual, regardless of sex, race, ethnic origin, cultural or socioeconomic background, religion, or handicapping condition.
—Interacts with students in a mutually respectful, empathetic, just manner.
—Respects the individual's right to hold differing views.
—Communicates effectively in oral and written form (e.g., grammar, syntax, vocabulary, spelling).
—Uses effective active listening skills.

—Encourages students to develop to their full potential.

—Recognizes that student's emotional well-being affects learning potential.

—Gives time willingly to provide for a student's academic, athletic, and personal needs.

—Assists students in dealing with success and failure.

—Gives praise and constructive criticism.

—Makes an effort to know each student as an individual.

—Shows sensitivity to physical development and special health needs of students.

B. Demonstrates positive interpersonal relationships with educational staff.

—Demonstrates respect, understanding, and acceptance of each staff member as an individual, regardless of sex, race, ethnic origin, cultural or socioeconomic background, religion, or handicapping condition.

—Interacts with other staff in a mutually respectful, empathetic, just manner.

—Respects the individual's right to hold differing views.

—Communicates effectively in oral and written form (e.g., grammar, syntax, vocabulary, spelling).

—Uses effective active listening skills.

—Provides positive encouragement to other staff.

—Works cooperatively with colleagues in planning and implementing educational activities that reflect the best interests of the student.

—Shares ideas, materials, and methods with other staff.

—Works effectively with support/ancillary staff.

C. Demonstrates positive interpersonal relationships with parents and other members of the school community.

—Demonstrates respect, understanding, and acceptance of each parent/patron as an individual, regardless of sex, race, ethnic origin, cultural or socioeconomic background, religion, or handicapping condition.

—Interacts with parents/patrons in a mutually respectful, empathetic, just manner.

—Respects the individual's right to hold differing views.

—Communicates effectively in oral and written form (e.g., grammar, syntax, vocabulary, spelling).

—Uses effective active listening skills.

(*continued*)

EXAMPLE 10.3 continued

—Provides positive encouragement to parents working to resolve student problems.

—Works cooperatively with parents in planning and implementing activities that reflect the best interests of the student.

—Supports and participates in parent–staff activities.

—Initiates and maintains communication with parents.

—Promotes a positive image of the school within the community.

Note: Descriptors provide examples of specific behaviors and skills often associated with the criterion. Descriptors are presented to help communicate the meaning of the criterion. They are not an inclusive listing of the behaviors or skills that might relate to the criterion.

*These criteria may not be appropriate for assistant coaches.

**The coach is responsible for providing the supervisor with a listing of pertinent information for the current evaluation cycle.

EVALUATION FORMS

After the procedures for evaluating coaches and the criteria on which they will be evaluated are determined, the forms necessary to implement the process must be developed. These include a Formative Data Form for recording information during the formative process, a Professional Development Plan form for identifying strategies for growth, and a Summative Evaluation Report form for summarizing the data and making recommendations about continued involvement in the program. As with all the sections of this chapter on coaching evaluation, the information presented about forms must be placed in perspective through the detail presented in chapters 1 through 8. Use of the forms without an understanding of their basic philosophy, purpose, and appropriate application will lead to misuse. Each form serves a specific purpose in the overall game plan to promote a positive, developmental approach to the evaluation of coaching personnel.

Forms for the evaluation of coaches are presented in Examples 10.4, 10.5, 10.6, and 10.7. The forms match the criteria and procedures presented in previous sections of this chapter. The forms are also con-

(text continues on page 243)

EXAMPLE 10.4
Formative Data Form—Coaches

| Coach | Date | School |

| Sport/Activity | Observation Time |

Data: ___Scheduled Obs. ___Unscheduled Obs. ___Non-observed ___Artifact

I. **Program Leadership**
A. **Provides positive direction for the program.***

B. **Develops and maintains student participation in the program.**

C. **Develops and maintains a good public relations program for the sport.**

D. **Demonstrates effective problem-solving and decision-making skills.**

(continued)

EXAMPLE 10.4 continued

E. Demonstrates effective organizational skills.

F. Provides leadership for the other staff members in the program.*

G. Follows the policies, regulations, and procedures of the school and district.

H. Ensures effective management of the fiscal resources of the program.

I. Establishes and maintains a positive and safe environment for the program.

J. Manages student behavior in a constructive manner.

K. Demonstrates a commitment to professional growth.**

II. Program Instruction

A. Demonstrates evidence of effective planning and preparation for instruction of students.

B. Uses effective teaching techniques and strategies.

C. Demonstrates and understanding of the sport, including the knowledge, skills, strategies, and attitudes associated with the sport.

D. Evaluates student progress effectively.

E. Provides for individual differences while promoting team development.

(continued)

EXAMPLE 10.4 continued

F. Demonstrates ability to motivate students.

III. Interpersonal Relationships
A. Demonstrates positive interpersonal relationships with students.

B. Demonstrates positive interpersonal relationships with educational staff.

C. Demonstrates positive interpersonal relationships with parents and other members of the school community.

Comments:

Coach's Signature/Date   Supervisor's Signature/Date
(Signatures indicate the data have been read and discussed. Copies to coach and supervisor.)
*These criteria may not be appropriate for assistant coaches.
**The coach is responsible for providing the supervisor with a listing of pertinent information for the current evaluation cycle.

EXAMPLE 10.5
Formative Data Short Form—Coaches

Coach	Date	School

Sport/Activity

Data: ___Scheduled Obs. ___Unscheduled Obs. ___Non-observed ___Artifact
This form is used in lieu of the longer form when only one or two criteria are being documented.

Criterion:

Data:

Criterion:

Data:

Coach's Signature/Date	Supervisor's Signature/Date

(Signatures indicate the data have been read and discussed. Copies to coach and supervisor.)

EXAMPLE 10.6
Professional Development Plan—Coaches

Coach:_____   Sport:_____

School: _____ _____   Date:_____

CRITERION:

OBJECTIVE(S):

PROCEDURES FOR ACHIEVING OBJECTIVE(S):

ASSESSMENT METHOD AND DATES:

COMMENTS:

This Professional Development Plan is developed to: (check one)
_____Enrich Effective Performance   _____Improve Below Expected Performance
Plan Developed:_____   _____
                Coach's Signature/Date   Supervisor's Signature/Date
If Plan Revised (Date/Initials):_____
If Alternate Plan Developed (Date/Initials): _____
Plan Achieved:_____   _____
                Coach's Signature/Date   Supervisor's Signature/Date
One PDP is used for one criterion. Form is completed by the supervisor during discussion with the coach. Additional comments will be permanently appended to this form and initialed by coach and supervisor. Signatures/initials imply this Plan has been discussed.

EXAMPLE 10.7
Summative Evaluation Form—Coaches

COACH:_____SCHOOL_____SPORT_____YEAR___

PERFORMANCE AREA: Program Leadership

A. Provides positive direction for the program.*

☐ Meets expectations   ☐ Does not meet expectations

B. Develops and maintains student participation in the program.

☐ Meets expectations   ☐ Does not meet expectations

C. Develops and maintains a good public relations program for the sport.

☐ Meets expectations   ☐ Does not meet expectations

D. Demonstrates effective problem-solving and decision-making skills.

☐ Meets expectations   ☐ Does not meet expectations

E. Demonstrates effective organizational skills.

☐ Meets expectations   ☐ Does not meet expectations

F. Provides leadership for the other staff members in the program.*

☐ Meets expectations   ☐ Does not meet expectations

G. Follows the policies, regulations, and procedures of the school and district.

☐ Meets expectations   ☐ Does not meet expectations

H. Ensures effective management of the fiscal resources of the program.

☐ Meets expectations   ☐ Does not meet expectations

(continued)

EXAMPLE 10.7 continued

I. Establishes and maintains a positive and safe environment for the program.

☐ Meets expectations ☐ Does not meet expectations

J. Manages student behavior in a constructive manner.

☐ Meets expectations ☐ Does not meet expectations

K. Demonstrates a commitment to professional growth.**

☐ Meets expectations ☐ Does not meet expectations

Comments:

PERFORMANCE AREA: PROGRAM INSTRUCTION

A. Demonstrates evidence of effective planning and preparation for instruction of students.

☐ Meets expectations ☐ Does not meet expectations

B. Uses effective teaching techniques and strategies.

☐ Meets expectations ☐ Does not meet expectations

C. Demonstrates and understanding of the sport, including the knowledge, skills, strategies, and attitudes associated with the sport.

☐ Meets expectations ☐ Does not meet expectations

D. Evaluates student progress effectively.

☐ Meets expectations ☐ Does not meet expectations

E. Provides for individual differences while promoting team development.

☐ Meets expectations   ☐ Does not meet expectations

F. Demonstrates ability to motivate students.

☐ Meets expectations   ☐ Does not meet expectations

Comments:

PERFORMANCE AREA: Interpersonal Relationships

A. Demonstrates positive interpersonal relationships with students.

☐ Meets expectations   ☐ Does not meet expectations

B. Demonstrates positive interpersonal relationships with educational staff.

☐ Meets expectations   ☐ Does not meet expectations

C. Demonstrates positive interpersonal relationships with parents and other members of the school community.

☐ Meets expectations   ☐ Does not meet expectations

Comments:

(continued)

EXAMPLE 10.7 continued

II. Supervisor's Recommendation:

☐ Reemployment for same assignment recommended.

☐ Reemployment for different assignment recommended.

☐ Reemployment as a coach not recommended.

☐ No recommendation made at this time.

III. Coach's Comments:

IV. Supervisor's Comments:

Coach's Signature/Date   Supervisor's Signature/Date
(Signatures imply the content of this document has been discussed.)
*These criteria may not be appropriate for assistant coaches.
**The coach is responsible for providing the supervisor with a listing of pertinent information for the current evaluation cycle.

sistent with the developmental strategies and forms presented throughout this book.

SUMMARY

Coaches make significant contributions to the development of students each year. Many student-athletes would be less successful in school were it not for the nurturance and guidance of coaches and/or the desire of the students to participate in specific sports. Coaches have an obligation to promote the overall development of the student-athlete, not just the development of athletic prowess. Students who participate in sports should be students in the classroom first and athletes second. Yet, a good athletic program, staffed by competent coaches, can develop the body, improve the mind, and shape attitudes that will also remain with the student for life. Such a program is an important supplement to high-quality classroom experiences.

The evaluation process described in this chapter is based on the belief that coaches must strive to fulfill the goal of "development of the total student-athlete"—that is, developing both the mind and the body. The evaluator of coaches, like the evaluator of the classroom teacher, must be willing to invest the time and energy necessary to observe and understand the skills of the coach and then help coaches to refine those skills so they can best meet the needs of student-athletes. The principles of evaluation described throughout this book apply to the evaluation of coaches just as they do to the evaluation of classroom teachers. A developmental evaluation process based on those principles can make a difference in the quality of the coaching students receive. Development of the total student-athlete is an important and realistic goal of an athletic program.

REFERENCE

Athletic Administrator's Reference Manual. (1989). Kansas City, MO: National Interscholastic Athletic Administrator's Association.

CHAPTER 11

Evaluating Sponsors

*In teaching it is the method and not the content that is the message
... the drawing out not the pumping in.*
—Ashley Montagu

CO-CURRICULAR ACTIVITIES are a fixture in today's educational system. They include the many school-sponsored teams, clubs, and other organizations that are not a part of the regular classroom curriculum. As a result, principals are constantly faced with the challenge of staffing the co-curricular programs. Seldom does a principal, particularly a secondary principal, have the luxury of hiring an English teacher who will only teach English. Given the number of activities in a typical high school, the English teacher may need to coach girls' basketball, direct the debating team, sponsor the literary magazine, or supervise the literature club. In many high schools, over half of the teachers have extra-duty responsibilities. In a middle school, extra-duty assignments are almost as common, although the emphasis should be more on clubs, organizations, and intramural sports than on interscholastic sports. At the elementary level, the need for sponsors appears to be on the increase as more elementary schools provide before- and after-school club programs on topics such as drama, science, aerospace, computers, and wellness. Today's teacher is seldom just a high school math teacher or an elementary school fifth-grade teacher.

In addition to assigning the staff for the co-curricular programs, the principal must evaluate the teachers' effectiveness in supervising the programs. Principals seldom formally evaluate teachers' performance as sponsors of co-curricular programs. Unless complaints or concerns are raised by those served, principals often assume the sponsor is meeting the students' needs. In most cases, the principal is pleased and relieved to find a person willing to sponsor the organization, and spends relatively little time evaluating the sponsor or the program.

244

The assignment and assessment of sponsors changed noticeably during the 1970s and 1980s because of an understanding of the importance of these programs and particularly because of the difficulty of securing sponsors for the numerous organizations. Some school systems began issuing teachers' contracts contingent on sponsorship of a club or activity. If the teacher desired to withdraw as the sponsor of the organization stipulated in the contract, the district could choose to dismiss the teacher in order to secure another person to sponsor the activity.

Whether or not a teacher's contract is linked with the sponsorship of an organization, the principal has the responsibility to ensure that a quality co-curricular program is being implemented. To do so, the principal must determine the effectiveness of the teacher as sponsor of the program and work with the teacher to meet a level of expected performance that will assure a high-quality program for the students. Performance-based developmental evaluation of co-curricular sponsors is as vital to a school's overall educational mission as the evaluation of the teacher in the regular curricular program.

Although the evaluation of noncoaching co-curricular sponsors described in this chapter is similar to the evaluation of coaches described in the previous chapter, enough differences exist to warrant separate chapters for the two roles. Presenting the procedures and forms separately should serve as a practical convenience for school systems interested in implementing or refining evaluation systems for coaches, for sponsors, or for both.

THE THIRD CURRICULUM

In the Foreword to *The Third Curriculum: Student Activities,* Dale Hawley, Director of Student Activities for the National Association of Secondary School Principals, credits Robert Frederick with the origination of the term *third curriculum* to describe the co-curricular programs offered in today's schools (Biernat & Klesse, 1989). Hawley explains that the first curriculum is the coursework required to earn a high school diploma, the second curriculum is the elective or exploratory program that permits students to choose areas of specialization, and the third curriculum is the student activities program. The activities program includes the athletic teams described in the previous chapter and the clubs and other school organizations about which this chapter was written.

The value of this third curriculum is without question. Through co-curricular programs, students learn many of the carryover skills for adult life. They develop abilities in leadership, followership, character, communications, teamwork, decision making, self-worth, and individual potential (Biernat & Klesse, 1989).

Students who participate in co-curricular activities generally do better academically and have better attendance records than do non-participators (Minnesota State High School League, 1984; Slotz, 1984; Biernat & Klesse, 1989). Co-curricular programs are an ideal training ground for development of the social skills associated with good citizenship (Erbeck, 1961). College admissions officers realize the importance of recruiting students who have co-curricular activities listed on their applications (Biernat & Klesse, 1989). Co-curricular programs provide vital opportunities for student development not possible through the regular classroom curriculum.

EVALUATION PROCEDURES

The procedures for evaluating sponsors described in this chapter are consistent with the developmental philosophy of evaluation presented throughout this book. Although they are similar to the procedures discussed in previous chapters for the evaluation of classroom teachers, and particularly to those for coaches, enough differences exist to warrant the detailed description provided in Example 11.1. These procedures include the identification of persons responsible for implementing the evaluation process, and descriptions of the evaluation cycle, the formative process, the summative process, and the appeal process. These procedures are based on detailed explanations presented in chapters 1 through 8 and should be implemented only after reviewing those chapters.

EXAMPLE 11.1
Evaluative Process for Sponsors

The following is an explanation of the procedures for performance-based evaluation of noncoaching co-curricular sponsors. The process begins with orientation for the sponsors, continues with the for-

(text continues on page 253)

mative phase, and culminates in the summative evaluation. This evaluation process is intended to be continuous, constructive, and cooperative.

I. ORIENTATION

A. Supervisors

Prior to initiating the evaluation process, each supervisor will receive appropriate inservice training in the PBDE. Supervisors include all personnel responsible for supervising/evaluating sponsors, including principals, assistant principals, and activities directors.

B. Sponsors

New sponsors shall receive orientation about the evaluation process at the beginning of their employment as sponsors. All sponsors shall receive additional inservice conducted by the district activities director every two years. These sessions will be conducted to review responsibilities, performance expectations, and the evaluation process.

II. EVALUATION CYCLE

A. Schedule for Experienced Sponsors

A Summative Evaluation Report will be completed at least once every three years for experienced sponsors (sponsors with more than three years experience in the current co-curricular assignment). The Summative Evaluation Report will be completed during the final year of the three-year cycle. Additional Summative Evaluation Reports may occur as deemed necessary by the supervisor or as requested by the sponsor. If a Summative Evaluation Report of an experienced sponsor is going to occur more frequently than once every three years, the sponsor will be notified by the supervisor as soon as practical. Typical examples of reasons for more frequent Summative Evaluation Reports are transfer requests, reassignments, administrative concerns, and sponsors' requests.

(*continued*)

EXAMPLE 11.1 continued

Summative reports will be completed within one month after the end of the co-curricular activity for which the sponsor was responsible. Sponsors of more than one co-curricular activity will be evaluated separately for each activity they sponsor.

B. Schedule for Sponsors New to Assignments

A Summative Evaluation Report will be completed after each appropriate activity for sponsors in their first three years of the co-curricular assignment. The report will be completed within one month after the end of the appropriate activity.

III.   FORMATIVE PHASE

The formative phase is the ongoing process for professional improvement. This phase is crucial to the success of performance evaluation and the development of staff who work with co-curricular programs. The formative phase begins after a Summative Evaluation Report for the appropriate activity is written and concludes with the writing of the next Summative Evaluation Report. Following are the essential components of the formative phase.

A. Data Collection

Effective supervision includes the collection and sharing of information about the sponsor's performance. The data may be planned or unplanned. Each type may include observed data, nonobserved data, and artifact data. The most typical planned observations are scheduled and unscheduled observations of the sponsor's performance. Following is an explanation of each.

1. Scheduled Observation Data
Scheduled observations provide focused and comprehensive information. A minimum of one scheduled observation will occur during each formative phase.

Prior to a scheduled observation, the sponsor and supervisor will establish the time and date of the observation. The sponsor and supervisor will discuss the activity to be observed. The length of the scheduled observation will be determined during the preobservation discussion.

Unexpected events may necessitate a change in the scheduled observation time. If so, the sponsor and supervisor will work together to identify an appropriate time for another observation and the need for another preobservation discussion.

The supervisor will make notes during the observation and transfer them to a Formative Data Form. A postobservation conference will follow a scheduled observation.

B. Unscheduled Observation Data

Unscheduled observations may be either planned or unplanned. They provide focused and comprehensive information about performance. A minimum of one planned unscheduled observation will be made by the supervisor each school year for each co-curricular program. During planned observations, the supervisor will make notes and transfer those notes to a Formative Data Form.

Unplanned observations which the supervisor chooses to document must be recorded on the Formative Data Form. An observation is not valid for evaluative purposes unless the information is recorded on a Formative Data Form and discussed in a postobservation conference.

2. Nonobserved Data

Planned nonobserved data include information the supervisor seeks from others who are familiar with the sponsor's performance. Examples include discussions with other sponsors, teachers, students, or parents. Planned nonobserved data are seldom used without the endorsement of the sponsor being evaluated. The data are documented on the Formative Data Form and discussed with the sponsor.

Unplanned nonobserved data are those types of information that come to the attention of the supervisor indirectly. They are data that are not observed by the supervisor; examples include telephone calls and personal conversations. The supervisor should make appropriate notations regarding such information, seek to validate the information, and determine if it is significant. If it is determined to be significant, the supervisor will document the information on a For-

(continued)

EXAMPLE 11.1 continued

---

mative Data Form and discuss the issue with the sponsor within a realistic time frame, usually a few working days.

3. Artifact Data

Planned artifact data consist of information that should improve the supervisor's understanding of the sponsor's skill in terms of specific criteria. Planned artifact data are typically identified at the beginning of the formative phase and are collected during the formative phase. Examples include budgets, worksheets, inventories, curricular plans, activities lists, discipline referrals, and workshop handouts. Performance data from artifacts are documented on the Formative Data Form.

Unplanned artifact data include information that comes to the attention of the supervisor indirectly. These are data that the supervisor did not solicit; examples include letters, memos, and notes about the sponsor's performance. The responsibility of the supervisor is to determine if the information is significant. If it is determined to be significant, the supervisor will document the information on the Formative Data Form and discuss the issue with the sponsor within a realistic time frame, usually a few working days.

C. Formative Data Form

The Formative Data Form provides the format for documenting all data collected in the formative process. The role of the supervisor is to record pertinent data on the form. The data on the form become the basis for discussion between the sponsor and the supervisor about job performance. Both the sponsor and the supervisor will retain a copy of the form.

D. Conferencing

After recording pertinent data on the Formative Data Form, the sponsor and supervisor will discuss the data as they relate to the criteria. This conference should occur, when practical, within two working days after any planned scheduled or unscheduled observation.

If more than five attendance days (days when supervisor and sponsor are at school) transpire between a planned scheduled or unscheduled observation and conferencing, either party has the option to reject the observation and request another.

For planned nonobserved and artifact data and all unplanned data, the conference will occur when the supervisor determines the data are significant.

At the conclusion of the conference, the sponsor and supervisor sign the Formative Data Form, indicating that the criteria have been discussed. Either party will have the opportunity to make written comments on the Formative Data Form at that time. Additional written comments by either party should be shared within five working days, appended to the Formative Data Form, and discussed as soon as practical.

E. Professional Development Plans

Professional Development Plans are used to improve professional skill as defined by the criteria. The Professional Development Plan includes identifiable, precise objective(s) and appropriate means for achieving the objective(s).

A Professional Development Plan will be developed with each sponsor at some time during the formative phase. The plan may make a transition through more than one evaluation cycle, especially for sponsors new to the assignment, who are receiving a Summative Evaluation Report for three years in succession. The plan will represent an effort to enhance skill on a criterion on which the sponsor is considered effective (enrichment plan) or to improve skill on a criterion on which the sponsor is considered deficient (improvement plan).

If a supervisor indicates a need for an improvement plan, the supervisor will identify the criterion and work with the sponsor to develop and implement a plan. Supervisors are responsible for coordinating all Professional Development Plans and may seek assistance from other personnel, if appropriate. A sponsor will not be rated "does not meet expectations" unless an improvement plan noting a deficiency on that criterion preceded the Summative Evaluation Report.

Sponsors not identified as needing a Professional Development Plan to improve a deficiency will meet with the supervisor sometime during the formative phase to develop an enrichment plan. The sponsor and supervisor will discuss the criterion on which the sponsor will focus. The supervisor and the sponsor will develop the plan, with the sponsor implementing the plan and keeping the supervisor apprised of progress.

(*continued*)

EXAMPLE 11.1 continued

The supervisor serves as a resource person to assist the sponsor with the plan, including efforts to facilitate participation in activities that may occur both outside of and during the school day.

IV. SUMMATIVE PHASE

The summative phase is the review and synthesis of formative data pertaining to the performance of the sponsor.

A. Summative Evaluation Report

The Summative Evaluation Report is the document used to summarize the evaluator's rating of performance for each criterion.

B. Summative Conference

After the supervisor has completed the Summative Evaluation Report, a conference between the sponsor and the supervisor will be conducted to review the information on the report. The summative report and the conference will be completed within one month after the end of the respective co-curricular program.

The conference will be conducted by the supervisor. If input was provided by other supervisors, such input shall be clarified on the report.

The sponsor and supervisor will sign the Summative Evaluation Report, indicating that the document has been read and discussed. Both parties will have the opportunity to make written comments on the report at that time. Additional written comments by either party must be shared within five working days and appended to the original copy of the Summative Evaluation Report. Copies of the Summative Evaluation Report will be retained by the sponsor, the supervisor, the principal (if the principal was not the supervisor), and the personnel director.

V. REVIEW AND APPEAL

A sponsor may request a review, or an appeal, of a professional judgment. This review or appeal is not to be confused with a grievance. A grievance is related to a violation of evaluation process. A review or appeal is related to professional judgment.

A sponsor has the right to request a review of information of a Formative Data Form or a Professional Development Plan by the supervisor's immediate supervisor. The immediate supervisor will review the information and discuss it with the sponsor and supervisor.

A sponsor has a right to appeal the ratings on a Summative Evaluation Report. The appeal must be made in writing within five working days after receipt of the summative report and must identify the reason for the request, including an explanation of the information supporting the appeal. The appeal will be reviewed by the supervisor's immediate supervisor. The immediate supervisor will process the appeal within ten working days of receipt and will respond both in writing and in person to the sponsor during that time. The sponsor has the right to have a mutually acceptable, nonparticipating observer present during this conference.

VI.   SYSTEM REVIEW

The school district administration shall provide for a review of the evaluation system every five years to promote the maintenance of an effective, fair, and efficient system that is comprehensive and performance-based. This review will be made by a committee composed of an equal number of sponsors and administrators.

CRITERIA AND DESCRIPTORS

Criteria are the performance expectations for all co-curricular sponsors with similar responsibilities. Because co-curricular responsibilities are so common across the various programs, a basic list of criteria can be used to evaluate all sponsors. If a particular criterion does not apply to the role of a sponsor, the supervisor can simply mark "not applicable." A list of criteria and descriptors are provided in Example 11.2. The criteria parallel, insofar as feasible, those for other job responsibilities presented in previous chapters. This consistency reduces confusion about the meaning of the issues on the basis of which personnel are evaluated.

(text continues on page 260)

EXAMPLE 11.2
Co-curricular Sponsors: Performance Areas, Criteria,
and Descriptors

I. Leadership
The sponsor:
A. Provides positive direction for the program.*
—Develops short- and long-range goals for the program.
—Involves program staff, administrators, and support groups in the development of program goals.
—Uses needs assessment data for goal development.
B. Develops and maintains student participation in the program.
—Demonstrates the ability to promote and maintain a quality program.
—Encourages students to participate in the program.
—Gives all students who meet program requirements equal opportunity to be selected for the program.
—Conducts the program in the best interest of the students.
C. Develops and maintains a good public relations program for the co-curricular program.
—Makes information available to students, parents, and community members.
—Represents the program to community organizations when asked.
—Keeps students, parents, and community members informed of program activities, schedules, etc.
—Works effectively with the media.
D. Demonstrates effective problem-solving and decision-making skills.
—Identifies and analyzes pertinent elements in a problem situation.
—Establishes priorities and seeks relevant data.
—Considers alternative solutions before making decisions.
—Makes logical decisions based on available data.
—Knows when to make a decision and when to gather more data or be patient.
E. Demonstrates effective organizational skills.
—Manages time efficiently and effectively.
—Prioritizes tasks and functions accordingly.
—Utilizes resources in an optimal manner.

—Delegates responsibility and authority when appropriate.

—Completes duties accurately and in a timely manner.

—Begins activities promptly.

—Maintains effective time on task during activities.

F. Provides leadership for the other staff members in the program.*

—Establishes roles and responsibilities for staff.

—Supervises staff effectively.

—Provides assistance and development for all staff.

—Promotes the establishment of high standards of performance for staff.

—Promotes staff awareness of new developments and ideas in the program.

—Demonstrates skill in the recruitment, selection, and assignment of program staff.

G. Follows the policies, regulations, and procedures of the school and district.

—Demonstrates awareness of policies, regulations, and procedures of the school and district.

—Works cooperatively with other educators to implement school and district policies, regulations, procedures, and goals.

—Selects appropriate channels and procedures for resolving concerns and problems.

—Complies with school policy on attendance and punctuality.

—Completes duties promptly and accurately.

—Maintains and provides accurate records/data.

—Provides plans and materials for substitutes in case of absence.

—Demonstrates effective organizational skills in managing professional responsibilities.

—Handles confidential information ethically and with discretion.

—Keeps personal interests/problems separate from professional responsibilities and duties.

—Recognizes and deals effectively with crisis issues (e.g., substance abuse, child abuse, suicidal behavior, mood changes).

H. Ensures effective management of the fiscal resources of the program.

(continued)

EXAMPLE 11.2 continued

  —Follows building and district guidelines for fiscal management.
  —Meets time lines for development and implementation of fiscal issues.
  —Selects appropriate channels for resolving fiscal problems.
  —Plans for long-range fiscal needs.
  —Supervises fund-raising activities according to program, building, and district guidelines.
  —Maintains appropriate inventories of program supplies and equipment.

I. Establishes and maintains a positive and safe environment for the program.
  —Establishes and communicates expectations and parameters for student conduct.
  —Establishes a program climate of mutual trust, respect, and purpose.
  —Provides a physical environment conducive to good health and safety.
  —Monitors, reports, endeavors to correct, and follows up on unsafe conditions.
  —Organizes facilities to match instructional activities and program needs.
  —Maintains facilities in good, safe working condition.

J. Manages student behavior in a constructive manner.
  —Manages discipline problems in accordance with program, building, and district guidelines.
  —Is courteous and sensitive but firm and professional when dealing with student behavior problems.
  —Anticipates and corrects disruptive behavior in a constructive and timely manner.
  —Recognizes inconsequential behavior and responds accordingly.
  —Endeavors to identify and resolve causes of undesirable behavior.
  —Manages the behavior of individuals, thereby maximizing the learning for the group.
  —Promotes positive self-image for students while managing their behavior.

—Maintains a positive attitude toward student management.
—Uses effective techniques to promote self-discipline and maintain appropriate behavior.
K. Demonstrates a commitment to professional growth.**
—Participates actively in the supervisory process for ongoing professional growth.
—Maintains current knowledge in the program area and in teaching/learning theory and practice.
—Participates in professional organizations and activities as available.
—Participates in school and district inservice activities as appropriate.
—Exhibits personal self-control.
—Gives serious consideration and appropriate action to parental comments and criticism.

II. Program instruction
The sponsor:
A. Demonstrates evidence of effective planning and preparation for instruction of students.
—Prepares activities based on program philosophy and goals.
—Prepares activities designed to teach and challenge participants effectively.
—Designs activities that build upon present skills and progress toward higher skills.
—Has needed equipment and materials readily available.
B. Uses effective teaching techniques and strategies.
—Develops a mental and physical readiness for learning the knowledge, skills, and attitudes appropriate to the program.
—Explains the objectives of the learning activities and skills to the participants.
—Uses a variety of techniques to teach the knowledge, skills, and attitudes appropriate to the program.
—Gives clear, concise, reasonable directions.
—Monitors student progress during the learning process.
—Provides effective opportunities for practicing the appropriate skills.
C. Demonstrates an understanding of the program, including the knowledge, skills, strategies, and attitudes associated with the particular program.

(*continued*)

EXAMPLE 11.2 continued

—Teaches in accordance with the philosophy of the program.
—Displays competent knowledge of any rules and regulations associated with the program.
—Displays competent knowledge of the skills associated with the program.
—Understands and implements appropriate strategies during practice and contests.
—Promotes among participants a proper attitude for enjoyment of the program.
—Selects content and skills appropriate to the level of performance of the participants.

D. Evaluates student progress effectively.
—Uses evaluation strategies consistent with program philosophy and goals.
—Uses both mental and physical assessment strategies to determine student progress.
—Provides evaluative feedback in a sensitive and timely manner.
—Uses a variety of techniques for communicating progress (e.g., film, written and verbal information, individual and group discussion).

E. Provides for individual differences.
—Groups students for each activity in a manner that best facilitates learning.
—Uses knowledge of various learning styles of students.
—Determines and applies remediation and enrichment activities based on individual needs.
—Understands and applies child development principles in the activities used in the program.
—Provides activities and materials coordinated with the developmental level of each participant.

F. Demonstrates ability to motivate students.
—Communicates challenging expectations.
—Provides all participants with opportunities to succeed.
—Stimulates and encourages creative, critical thinking, and problem-solving skills.
—Gives constructive feedback frequently and promptly.
—Involves all participants in appropriate activities.
—Responds positively to participants' requests for assistance.

—Helps participants develop positive self-concepts.
—Demonstrates enthusiasm.

III. Interpersonal relationships
The sponsor:
A. Demonstrates positive interpersonal relationships with students.
 —Demonstrates respect, understanding, and acceptance of each student as an individual, regardless of sex, race, ethnic origin, cultural or socioeconomic background, religion, or handicapping condition.
 —Interacts with students in a mutually respectful, empathetic, just manner.
 —Respects the individual's right to hold differing views.
 —Communicates effectively in oral and written form (e.g., grammar, syntax, vocabulary, spelling).
 —Uses effective active listening skills.
 —Encourages students to develop to their full potential.
 —Recognizes that students' emotional well-being affects their learning potential.
 —Gives time willingly to provide for a student's academic and personal needs.
 —Assists students in dealing with success and failure.
 —Gives praise and constructive criticism.
 —Makes an effort to know each student as an individual.
 —Shows sensitivity to physical and mental development and special health needs of students.
B. Demonstrates positive interpersonal relationships with educational staff.
 —Demonstrates respect, understanding, and acceptance of each staff member as an individual, regardless of sex, race, ethnic origin, cultural or socioeconomic background, religion, or handicapping condition.
 —Interacts with other staff in a mutually respectful, empathetic, just manner.
 —Respects the individual's right to hold differing views.
 —Communicates effectively in oral and written form (e.g., grammar, syntax, vocabulary, spelling).
 —Uses effective active listening skills.
 —Provides positive encouragement to other staff.

(continued)

EXAMPLE 11.2 continued

—Works cooperatively with colleagues in planning and implementing educational activities that reflect the best interests of the student.

—Shares ideas, materials, and methods with other staff.

—Works effectively with support/ancillary staff.

C. Demonstrates positive interpersonal relationships with parents and other members of the school community.

—Demonstrates respect, understanding, and acceptance of each parent/patron as an individual, regardless of sex, race, ethnic origin, cultural or socioeconomic background, religion, or handicapping condition.

—Interacts with parents/patrons in a mutually respectful, empathetic, just manner.

—Respects the individual's right to hold differing views.

—Communicates effectively in oral and written form (e.g., grammar, syntax, vocabulary, spelling).

—Uses effective active listening skills.

—Provides positive encouragement to parents working to resolve student problems.

—Works cooperatively with parents in planning and implementing activities that reflect the best interests of the student.

—Supports and participates in parent–staff activities.

—Initiates and maintains communication with parents.

—Promotes a positive image of the school within the community.

Note: Descriptors provide examples of specific behaviors and skills often associated with the criterion. Descriptors are presented to help communicate the meaning of the criterion. They are not an inclusive listing of the behaviors or skills that might relate to the criterion.

*These criteria may not be appropriate for sponsors who assist another sponsor in a co-curricular program–for example, a freshman debate coach who assists a varsity debate coach.

**The sponsor is responsible for providing the supervisor with a listing of pertinent information for the current evaluation cycle.

EVALUATION FORMS

Following the development of the procedures for evaluating co-curricular sponsors and the criteria on which they will be evaluated, the forms necessary to implement the process must be developed. The forms include a Formative Data Form for recording information during the formative process, a Professional Development Plan form for identifying strategies for growth, and a Summative Evaluation Report form for summarizing the data and making recommendations about continued involvement in the program. As stated in the chapter on coaching evaluation, the forms presented in this chapter must be understood in the context of information presented in previous chapters. Each form serves a specific purpose in the developmental approach to the evaluation of sponsors.

Forms for the evaluation of sponsors are presented in Examples 11.3, 11.4, 11.5, and 11.6. These forms match the criteria and procedures presented previously in this chapter. As with any evaluation process, the criteria become the important content on which the forms are based. As with all the forms in this book, the similarity between the forms for the classroom teachers and those for the co-curricular sponsors provide additional consistency among all evaluative processes and facilitate ease of understanding and use.

SUMMARY

Co-curricular activities promote the development of students in ways not available in the regular classroom. This "third curriculum" is a vital part of the total educational program. Opportunities to organize and plan, to assume leadership roles, to gain recognition and identity, to experience self-governance, and to mature socially come, to a significant degree, through student activities programs. Participation develops talent, maturity, and responsibility (Biernat & Klesse, 1989). The accomplishments of adults are often linked with the nonacademic accomplishments of youth. Student activities are of extraordinary importance to the development of adult leaders.

Principals have an obligation to provide high-quality programs and to assure the community that the teachers who sponsor co-curricular programs meet standards of performance as defined by the criteria for co-curricular sponsors in the school district. Too often co-curricular programs receive little attention relative to the potential impact they can have on developing students into complete citizens. The middle-level schools that operate their co-curricular programs during the school day in order to involve all students in a program may have the right idea. All students can benefit from the development of socialization skills, leadership, and self-confidence that can be provided through a good co-curricular program.

EXAMPLE 11.3
Formative Data Form—Sponsors

Sponsor   Date   School

Program/Activity   Observation Time

Data: ___Scheduled Obs. ___Unscheduled Obs. ___Non-observed ___Artifact

I.   **Program Leadership**
     A. Provides positive direction for the program.*

     B. Develops and maintains student participation in the program.

     C. Develops and maintains a good public relations program for the cocurricular program.

     D. Demonstrates effective problem-solving and decision-making skills.

Formative Data Form-Sponsors, Page 2

E. Demonstrates effective organizational skills.

F. Provides leadership for the other staff members in the program.*

G. Follows the policies, regulations, and procedures of the school and district.

H. Ensures effective management of the fiscal resources of the program.

I. Establishes and maintains a positive and safe environment for the program.

J. Manages student behavior in a constructive manner.

(continued)

EXAMPLE 11.3 continued

Formative Data Form-Sponsors, Page 3

    K. Demonstrates a commitment to professional growth.**

II. Program Instruction

    A. Demonstrates evidence of effective planning and preparation for instruction of students.

    B. Uses effective teaching techniques and strategies.

    C. Demonstrates an understanding of the program, including the knowledge, skills, strategies, and attitudes associated with the particular program.

    D. Evaluates student progress effectively.

    E. Provides for individual differences.

Formative Data Form-Sponsors, Page 4

F. Demonstrates ability to motivate students.

III. Interpersonal Relationships
A. Demonstrates positive interpersonal relationships with students.

B. Demonstrates positive interpersonal relationships with educational staff.

C. Demonstrates positive interpersonal relationships with parents and other members of the school community.

Comments:

_____   _____
Sponsor's Signature/Date   Supervisor's Signature/Date
(Signatures indicate the data have been read and discussed. Copies to sponsor and supervisor.)
*These criteria may not be appropriate for sponsors who assist another sponsor in a cocurricular program, e.g. a freshman debate coach who assists a varsity debate coach.
**The sponsor is responsible for providing the supervisor with a listing of pertinent information for the current evaluation cycle.

EXAMPLE 11.4
Formative Data Short Form—Sponsors

| Sponsor | Date | School |

Program/Activity

Data: ___Scheduled Obs. ___Unscheduled Obs. ___Non-observed ___Artifact
This form is used in lieu of the longer form when only one or two criteria are being documented.

Criterion:

Data:

Criterion:

Data:

Sponsor's Signature/Date   Supervisor's Signature/Date
(Signatures indicate the data have been read and discussed. Copies to sponsor and supervisor.)

EXAMPLE 11.5
Professional Development Plan—Sponsors

Sponsor:_____   Activity:_____

School: _____   Date:_____

CRITERION:

OBJECTIVE(S):

PROCEDURES FOR ACHIEVING OBJECTIVE(S):

ASSESSMENT METHOD AND DATES:

COMMENTS:

This Professional Development Plan is developed to: (check one)

_____Enrich Effective Performance   _____Improve Below Expected Performance

Plan Developed:_____   _____

           Sponsor's Signature/Date   Supervisor's Signature/Date

If Plan Revised (Date/Initials):_____

If Alternate Plan Developed (Date/Initials): _____

Plan Achieved:_____   _____

           Sponsor's Signature/Date   Supervisor's Signature/Date

One PDP is used for one criterion. Form is completed by the supervisor during discussion with the sponsor. Additional comments will be permanently appended to this form and initialed by sponsor and supervisor. Signatures/initials imply this Plan has been discussed.

EXAMPLE 11.6
Summative Evaluation Form—Sponsors

SPONSOR:＿＿＿＿＿＿＿   SCHOOL＿＿＿＿＿＿＿＿＿＿

PROGRAM＿＿＿＿＿＿＿＿＿＿＿＿＿＿＿＿   Year＿＿＿＿＿

PERFORMANCE AREA: Program Leadership

A. Provides positive direction for the program.*

☐ Meets expectations   ☐ Does not meet expectations

B. Develops and maintains student participation in the program.

☐ Meets expectations   ☐ Does not meet expectations

C. Develops and maintains a good public relations program for the cocurricular program.

☐ Meets expectations   ☐ Does not meet expectations

D. Demonstrates effective problem-solving and decision-making skills.

☐ Meets expectations   ☐ Does not meet expectations

E. Demonstrates effective organizational skills.

☐ Meets expectations   ☐ Does not meet expectations

F. Provides leadership for the other staff members in the program.*

☐ Meets expectations   ☐ Does not meet expectations

G. Follows the policies, regulations, and procedures of the school and district.

☐ Meets expectations   ☐ Does not meet expectations

H. Ensures effective management of the fiscal resources of the program.

☐ Meets expectations   ☐ Does not meet expectations

Summative Evaluation Report--Sponsors, Page 2

I. Establishes and maintains a positive and safe environment for the program.

☐ Meets expectations ☐ Does not meet expectations

J. Manages student behavior in a constructive manner.

☐ Meets expectations ☐ Does not meet expectations

K. Demonstrates a commitment to professional growth.**

☐ Meets expectations ☐ Does not meet expectations

Comments:

PERFORMANCE AREA: PROGRAM INSTRUCTION

A. Demonstrates evidence of effective planning and preparation for instruction of students.

☐ Meets expectations ☐ Does not meet expectations

B. Uses effective teaching techniques and strategies.

☐ Meets expectations ☐ Does not meet expectations

C. Demonstrates and understanding of the program, including the knowledge, skills, strategies, and attitudes associated with the program.

☐ Meets expectations ☐ Does not meet expectations

D. Evaluates student progress effectively.

☐ Meets expectations ☐ Does not meet expectations

(*continued*)

EXAMPLE 11.6 continued

Summative Evaluation Report--Sponsors, Page 3

 E. Provides for individual differences.

☐ Meets expectations ☐ Does not meet expectations

 F. Demonstrates ability to motivate students.

☐ Meets expectations ☐ Does not meet expectations

Comments:

PERFORMANCE AREA: Interpersonal Relationships

 A. Demonstrates positive interpersonal relationships with students.

☐ Meets expectations ☐ Does not meet expectations

 B. Demonstrates positive interpersonal relationships with educational staff.

☐ Meets expectations ☐ Does not meet expectations

 C. Demonstrates positive interpersonal relationships with parents and other members of the school community.

☐ Meets expectations ☐ Does not meet expectations

Comments:

Summative Evaluation Report--Sponsors, Page 4

II.   Supervisor's Recommendation:

☐ Reemployment for same assignment recommended.

☐ Reemployment for different assignment recommended.

☐ Reemployment as a sponsor not recommended.

☐ No recommendation made at this time.

III.   Sponsor's Comments:

IV.   Supervisor's Comments:

_____   _____
   Sponsor's Signature/Date   Supervisor's Signature/Date
(Signatures imply the content of this document has been discussed.)
*These criteria may not be appropriate for sponsors who assist another sponsor in a cocurricular program, e.g. a freshman debate coach who assists a varsity debate coach.
**The sponsor is responsible for providing the supervisor with a listing of pertinent information for the current evaluation cycle.

REFERENCES

Biernat, N. A., & Klesse, E. J. (1989). *The Third Curriculum: Student Activities.* Reston, VA: National Association of Secondary School Principals.

Erbeck, R. (1961). Justifying the extracurricular program. *School Activities,* February, pp. 178–179.

Minnesota State High School League. (1984). Reported in: Minnesota finds student athletes get better grades, *Education Week,* May 2.

Slotz, D. F. (1984). Athletes and achievement—making the grade. *Interscholastic Athletic Administration,* Winter, pp. 4–7.

CHAPTER 12

Outcome-Based Goals

Judge a tree from its fruit, not its leaves.
—Euripides

FOR ELEVEN CHAPTERS, components of evaluation systems that have been tried, tested, and described as effective in schools across the United States have been presented and discussed. The outcome-based component discussed in this chapter has not been as extensively implemented and researched. It is more theoretical than proved. However, it represents a process that all school systems should discuss and consider when developing or refining a teacher evaluation system.

Outcome-based evaluation, as presented in this chapter, is not to be confused with evaluation approaches that are designed to hold teachers accountable for improving student gains on nationally normed standardized tests. Rather, it is a process of working with teachers to identify meaningful educational outcomes for students that have resulted because of the teachers' performance. Each teacher is responsible for establishing the desired outcomes, which should reflect the unique needs of the students in the teacher's care. This process both supplements and complements the performance-based developmental evaluation approach discussed in previous chapters.

A RATIONALE

In Chapter 7 strategies for writing and implementing Professional Development Plans were described. The intent of the Professional Development Plan is to work with the teacher to create a focus of improvement. Literally, this means an effort to improve *personal* skill on a specific performance criterion.

In contrast, outcome-based goals are the desired outcomes the teacher has for the students. The intent of the outcome-based goal process is to create a focus on improvement for the students. In the classroom, this means goals designed to have an impact on the students of the class. Outside the traditional classroom, such as on the athletic field or in the French Club, it means goals designed to have an impact on the students with whom the teacher is working. An outcome-based goal describes the impact the teacher will have on the student, perhaps in cognitive development, skill development, socialization, or in other ways only the creative genius of the teacher can describe.

When good teachers begin a lesson, they know what outcomes they want their students to attain as a result of the lesson. When good teachers begin a school year, they soon have some understanding of the outcomes they want for their students as a result of that year's experiences. When good sponsors hold the first meeting of the Drama Club in September, they know what they want the students to accomplish by June. Outcome-based goals are those desired student accomplishments.

In developing and writing outcome-based goals, it is easy to drift from the language of student outcomes to the teacher's own personal goals. The following, for example, are *not* outcome-based goals: "Complete a graduate degree." "Develop skill in higher order questioning." "Develop a curriculum guide for the seventh-grade math program." These may be tasks worthy of effort, but they are not statements that address the ultimate responsibility of all teachers—having an impact on students. Each of a teacher's outcome-based goals should be described in terms of the impact on the student. If it cannot be described in terms of the student, it is not appropriate as an outcome-based goal.

Why the emphasis on outcome-based goals? Why not just ask teachers to identify two or three professional goals they would like to accomplish during the year? Why do the goals have to be stated in student terms? The answers to these questions were formulated from the experience of observing teachers write goal statements. Teachers who are asked to write down their goals will generally, and with the best of intentions, write down personal goals that seldom make a difference for students. Or their goals may describe tasks the teacher was planning to do anyway—or has already completed. Astute teachers will write goals they know they will accomplish, for no one wants to describe a goal he or she is not sure of achieving. Such goals often make little difference for students because they lack relevance, sophistication, and proper intent. Goals like these are written in an effort to meet the need to write goals, not to meet the needs of students.

How are outcome-based goals different? What guarantee is there that the goals will be written in such a manner as to make a difference for students? There is no guarantee, but at least there is a better chance that teachers' goals will have an impact on students if they must be written in terms of desired student outcomes. There is a better chance of having an impact on students if the teachers and administrators continue to ask the question, "How does this goal affect students?" And there is a better chance that the goals will have an impact on students if the principal and the teacher both understand that the place to address a personal goal is through a Professional Development Plan for the appropriate performance criterion, and the place to address a desired student outcome is through the outcome-based goal.

WRITING THE GOALS

Four issues should be considered when writing an outcome-based goal: (1) phrasing the goal statement, (2) developing strategies for achieving the goal, (3) identifying support services necessary to accomplish the goal, and (4) describing the methods for assessing the accomplishment of the goal. The Goal Statement Form in Example 12.1 includes these four issues, as well as a place to set a date for a formative progress conference and an approximate date on which the supervisor will assess the accomplishment of the goal. These issues are discussed in the following sections.

The Goal Statement

The goal statement should represent a desired student outcome on which the teacher can have some impact. Teachers will initially have difficulty thinking of desirable goals and stating those goals as desired student outcomes. For that reason, numerous goal statements are listed in Example 12.2. Following each example is the teacher's grade level and/or subject area.

Each of the goal statements in Example 12.2 describes a desired student outcome and a time frame within which that outcome will occur. Some are very specific, such as "Ninety percent . . . will have demonstrated mastery of . . . objectives," and "all students will have

(text continues on page 278)

EXAMPLE 12.1
Goal Statement Form

Teacher	**Current Date**

School	**School Year**

(Use one Goal Statement Form for each goal.)

Goal Statement: (State as desired student outcomes the goal to be accomplished during the school year.)

Achievement Strategies: (List specific activities or tasks to be completed to accomplish the goal.)

Support Services: (Identify physical, fiscal, and personnel resources needed to accomplish the goal.)

Approaisal Method: (Identify the methods to be used to assess accomplishment of the goal.)

Progress Conference Date(s): (Identify the approximate date(s) when the supervisor and teacher will disucss progress toward accomplishment of the goal.)

Summative Conference Date: (Identify the approximate date when the supervisor and teacher will discuss accomplishment of the goal.)

Teacher's Signature/Date	Supervisor's Signature/Date

(Signatures indicate this goal has been discussed.)

EXAMPLE 12.2
Goal Statements

- By the end of the school year, 90 percent of the students in my three Algebra I classes will have demonstrated mastery of the Algebra I curricular objectives using the district criterion-referenced exams. (high school math)
- By the first of March, Larry L, Marty J, and Roger B will have developed enough self-control to remain seated and attentive consistently during class lessons. (sixth-grade language arts)
- By the end of the school year, all students in the debate club will have participated in three formal debates and had the opportunity to serve as judges at the junior high debate festival. (high school debate club sponsor)
- Throughout the school year, Tommy W will continue to improve his pattern of positive social interaction with the other students in the class. (second grade)
- During the basketball season, each member of the team will complete homework assignments, devote specifically determined amounts of time each day to study, and maintain a C or higher level of performance in each academic class. (basketball coach)
- By the end of the school year, all students in my honors physics class will have mastered all objectives and achieved a grade of B or higher. (high school physics)
- By the end of the school year, I will have identified four at-risk students in my classes and made a personal effort to know and work with them in order to maintain their interest in school and in learning. (junior high industrial arts)
- By the end of the year, each child in my class will be receiving regular assistance at home from one of his or her parents because the parent participated in my parents-as-teachers program. (third grade)
- All students in my class will have developed common courtesy behaviors such as "please" and "thank you" and attentive listening by Christmas and will continue to demonstrate those courtesy behaviors for the remainder of the school year. (fourth grade)
- By the end of the first semester, each student in the wellness club will have developed an appreciation for his or her own wellness by describing a change made and maintained in his or her life-style to achieve better wellness. (middle school wellness club sponsor)

participated in three debates." Others may be more general, such as "identified four 'at-risk' students and made a personal effort to . . . " and " . . . will have developed common courtesy behaviors such as . . . " But for each goal, what the teacher wishes to accomplish for the students is clear. And the teacher's intent goes beyond what the curriculum guide might list as desired objectives. The goal represents something meaningful the teacher personally wishes to accomplish with the students.

Goal statements are commonly written in the spring for the upcoming year, or early in the fall, as soon as the teacher becomes familiar with the students in the program. Two or three goals are generally adequate. It is better to have just a couple of special, meaningful goals and do them well than to have several and do them poorly or feel so pressed to accomplish them that their presence is counterproductive.

Unlike Professional Development Plans for enrichment, outcome-based goals should be developed on an annual basis. Therefore, if tenured teachers are evaluated every three years, and outcome-based goals are a part of that summative evaluation, the principal may have as few as three or four or as many as five or six goals to review during the final summative conference at the end of the three-year cycle.

Some outcome-based goals may require more than a year to accomplish. Although this is not common, it may be appropriate when teachers know they will be working with the same student or students for more than a year. For example, a coach or sponsor may develop a two-year goal in an attempt to meet the needs of a particular student or students.

Achievement Strategies

How will the goal be accomplished? What tasks must the teacher complete to reach the goal? What activities must be organized and implemented? What sequential steps must be followed? These are the types of questions that provide guidance for writing achievement strategies. For example, what tasks must be completed to achieve the goal of "90% of the students in my three Algebra I classes will have demonstrated mastery of the Algebra I curricular objectives"? An initial reaction is that if the teacher simply does a good job, the goal should be reached. Yet, identification of specific strategies greatly increases the likelihood the goal will be accomplished. Following are some strategies that might be used with this goal statement about mastery in algebra.

1. Identify the lowest quartile of students on the basis of first-quarter grades. Provide after-school tutoring sessions for these students.

2. Determine which curricular concepts have not been mastered by each student at the end of each quarter. Develop appropriate strategies for reteaching these concepts during regular class hours.

3. Make an initial contact and continue making contacts with parents of students who are not mastering concepts. Provide parents with specific objectives and a schedule indicating approximately when those objectives will be taught. Provide parents with a list of suggestions for monitoring their students' homework.

4. Develop a plan for using the departmental instructional aide to provide additional testing of the students to determine understanding of the concepts.

5. Use additional workbooks and other resource materials to help the students who are having difficulty mastering the concepts.

The strategies listed were developed by the teacher and principal at the beginning of the school year. They are a good starting point. As the year progresses, the teacher and principal may identify additional strategies and add them to the list. Finding the right activities to accomplish the goals and the flexibility to change those activities as necessary are important. The crucial issue is goal accomplishment, not sticking to the strategies at all costs just because that is what you thought would work back in September.

Support Services

Specific physical, fiscal, and personnel resources are often necessary to accomplish a goal. The principal should make an effort to provide these types of resources for teachers. For example, in the goal described in the previous section, the algebra teacher may need assistance from the principal to obtain clerical help to send communiques about student performance and homework assistance home to parents. The teacher may need help from the principal or department chair to secure the additional time of the instructional aide to help test student mastery. The teacher may need money to obtain the supplemental teaching materials.

Appraisal Method

What process will be used to determine if the goal has been accomplished? The answer is often found in the goal statement itself. In the example we have been following, the answer is obvious: "Ninety percent of the students in my three Algebra I classes will have demonstrated mastery of the Algebra I curricular objectives using the district criterion-referenced exams." When will this be determined? What is the time frame for making the assessment? In a well-written goal, the answer is again obvious—in the example, "by the end of the school year."

FORMATIVE GOALS CONFERENCE

The principal and the teacher should make an effort to communicate in person during the school year about progress toward accomplishment of the teacher's goals. For the talented teacher, this formative conference can be conveniently conducted when the principal and teacher are visiting about other instructional issues, such as during a postobservation conference. For the teacher whose performance is marginal or deficient, a separate conference at least once a semester provides the opportunity for more detailed discussion of the teacher's progress toward the goals.

Just before or during the formative goal conference, a brief assessment of progress should be recorded on the Goal Statement Formative Form (Example 12.3) by the teacher. The teacher should make the initial assessment because the teacher knows better than anyone else the degree to which the goal is being accomplished. The principal can simply respond to that assessment statement if a response seems appropriate.

During the formative conference, the principal should review the goal statement, the strategies, and the support services. All concerns should be discussed candidly, with notes made by the principal on the Goal Statement Formative Form during the conference. Any changes in the goal, strategies, support services, or assessment method should also be noted on the form.

EXAMPLE 12.3
Goal Statement Formative Form

_____   _____
            Teacher   **Current Date**

_____   _____
            School   **School Year**

(Because the teacher is the person who usually has the best insight about goal accomplishment, typically the teacher completes this form before the conference and the principal responds during the conference.)

Teacher's assessment of progress toward accomplishment of goal:

Principal's assessment of progress toward accomplishment of goal:

_____   _____
Teacher's Signature/Date   Supervisor's Signature/Date
(Signatures indicate the information on this page has been discussed.)

GOAL STATEMENT SUMMATIVE EVALUATION

At the end of the school year, the principal and teacher should complete a Goal Statement Annual Summative Form (Example 12.4), which indicates the degree to which the goal was accomplished. Like the Goal Statement Formative Form, the Goal Statement Annual Summative Form should first be completed by the teacher. The principal can then visit with the teacher in a summative conference and complete the supervisor's portion of the form during the conference. Having the teacher's written assessment and the opportunity to discuss the accomplishment of the goal with the teacher prior to completing the form provides the principal with the best possible insight into the degree to which the goal was accomplished.

If a school district uses a final Summative Evaluation Report and wishes to include in the report the outcome-based goal process described in this chapter, a page of the report should summarize the goals and indicate whether or not they were accomplished (Example 12.5). The report depicts at a glance whether the "goal was accomplished," whether the "goal was not accomplished but progress was appropriate," or whether "goal progress was not appropriate." Such a summary report is particularly useful if the district's teacher evaluation cycle is longer than one year.

SUMMARY

In concluding this discussion of outcome-based goals, a logical question must be addressed: "Why incorporate both Professional Development Plans (personal performance goals), *and* outcome-based goals (student impact goals) in the same evaluation process?"

Professional Development Plans represent a desire to improve the teacher's performance on a criterion. Outcome-based goals consider performance only as a means to achieve the desired student outcomes. In essence, performance appraisal stops short of the real issue—impact on students. The addition of a good outcome-based component elevates a good performance-based developmental evaluation process to a performance/outcome-based developmental evaluation process.

Several arguments can be made against including outcome-based goals as a part of the evaluation process. One is the amount of time that must be invested to make the process work effectively. For teachers and principals to take the time to plan an outcome-based goal *and* a

(text continues on page 285)

EXAMPLE 12.4
Goal Statement Annual Summative Form

_____   _____
Teacher   **Current Date**

_____   _____
School   **School Year**

(Because the teacher is the person who usually has the best insight about goal accomplishment, typically the teacher completes this form before the conference and the principal responds during the conference.)

Teacher's assessment of the degree to which the goal was accomplished and information to support that assessment:

Principal's assessment of the degree to which the goal was accomplished and information to support that assessment:

_____   _____
Teacher's Signature/Date   Supervisor's Signature/Date

(Signatures indicate the information on this page has been discussed.)

EXAMPLE 12.5
Goal Statement Summative Evaluation Report

| Teacher | Current Date |

| School | School Year |

GOAL STATEMENT:

☐ Goal Accomplished
☐ Progress toward goal was appropriate, but goal was not accomplished.
☐ Progress toward goal was not appropriate and goal was not accomplished.
COMMENTS:

GOAL STATEMENT:

☐ Goal Accomplished
☐ Progress toward goal was appropriate, but goal was not accomplished.
☐ Progress toward goal was not appropriate and goal was not accomplished.
COMMENTS:

GOAL STATEMENT:

☐ Goal Accomplished
☐ Progress toward goal was appropriate, but goal was not accomplished.
☐ Progress toward goal was not appropriate and goal was not accomplished.
COMMENTS:

(An explanation must be written for all goals not accomplished.)

professional development plan is asking too much in school systems where principal and teacher workloads and attitudes are already stretched to the limit.

A second argument is that an adequate research base does not exist that supports the value of outcome-based student goals as a part of the evaluation process. Although the performance/outcome-based approach has been implemented and assessed in principal evaluation (Valentine, 1987; Drummond, 1988; Valentine & Harting, 1988), it is relatively untested in teacher evaluation. It is still a theory, but a theory very long on common sense.

The lack of accuracy of measurement instruments is another shortcoming of an outcome-based student goals strategy. The best goals would be those that describe specific development based on a reliable measurement instrument. Even standardized tests fall short as fair and equitable means for evaluating teacher performance. Too many variables intervene that affect students' ability—and thus their scores—to hold teachers accountable for a measurable degree of growth on a specific standardized test.

But perhaps the most valid argument for using outcome-based student goals is simply altruistic. Using the process makes a statement about the importance of the student and the realization that everything that is done in education should be, ultimately, for the student's benefit.

REFERENCES

Drummond, G. L. (1988). *Perceptions of Missouri secondary school principals about performance-based principal evaluation.* Doctoral dissertation, University of Missouri–Columbia, 1988. (*Dissertation Abstracts International,* 50/04, 838-A)

Valentine, J. W. (1987). *Performance/outcome-based principal evaluation.* Paper presented at the annual meeting of the American Association of School Administrators, New Orleans, February. (ERIC Document Reproduction Service No. ED 281 317)

Valentine, J. W., & Harting, R. D. (1988). *Performance-based principal evaluation in Missouri: A three-year report.* Study prepared for the Missouri Department of Elementary and Secondary Education, Jefferson City, Missouri. (ERIC Document Reproduction Service No. ED 311 589)

CHAPTER 13

Making the Difference

*The deepest personal defeat suffered by human beings is constituted
by the difference between what one was capable of becoming and
what one has in fact become.*
—Ashley Montagu

METAPHORICALLY, AN EFFECTIVE performance-based developmental evaluation system can be compared to a large mosaic. From the
thousands of individual tiles necessary to depict the various scenes
showing the formative and summative processes, a complete mosaic
comes into focus. The quality of the larger scene is dependent on the
quality of each tile and each smaller image. The scene is not complete
unless all the tiles and images are interwoven effectively by the artist.
No singular tile or image or group of images provides the same pictorial
impact as the unification of all the pieces into a work of art.

Evaluation that will make a significant difference in the educational program in a school system and in an individual school is like the
mosaic. Each piece of the process, each individual principle and
practice, must be considered and woven into the system. Using one or
two principles here and a few there is not adequate. The strength of the
process comes from the blending of all aspects, from the initial commitment to personnel improvement, through the development of the system, to the implementation of the formative and summative phases.
The purpose of this final chapter is to reiterate the principles and
practices that enable an evaluation system to come into focus as a total
scene—to make a difference in the educational program.

EVALUATIVE PRINCIPLES

A *principle* is defined as a basic, fundamental law or doctrine. The principles emphasized throughout this book and listed next represent this

definition. Some are so basic to evaluation they have become accepted as fundamental laws of evaluation. Other principles are so essential to the effectiveness of personnel development that they have become basic doctrines or beliefs shared by most who study evaluation. Some principles represent concepts not yet fully proved as laws or completely accepted as doctrines, but assumed to be significant as more and more data about evaluation practices are analyzed. The principles presented throughout this book are restated in the following list as recommendations to consider when developing and implementing an evaluation system.

1. Climate, culture, and the evaluation system should be interdependent, collectively reinforcing a philosophy of developmental evaluation.

2. District leadership should be committed to the concept of developmental evaluation.

3. Teachers and administrators should demonstrate a readiness for change to a more effective evaluative approach.

4. Those affected by the evaluation process should be involved in developing, implementing, evaluating, and refining the system.

5. System developers should study effective teaching, schooling, and evaluation before developing the evaluation system.

6. Criteria that define expected performance of teachers in the school district should be developed.

7. Descriptors that provide examples of teacher behavior that effectively communicate the meaning of each criterion should be developed.

8. Staff should be inserviced about evaluation processes and expectations before implementing the system.

9. Ongoing inservice should be provided to improve knowledge and skill on the criteria.

10. Planned and unplanned data should be an integral part of the evaluation process.

11. Classroom observation data should be emphasized in a developmental evaluation system.

12. Observed, nonobserved, and artifact data should be collected during the evaluation process.

13. Comprehensive and focused data collection strategies should be used.

14. Data should be documented on a Formative Data Form under the appropriate criteria.

15. Specific behaviors, not value judgments about the behaviors, should be documented.

16. Conferences should be held as soon as possible after data are collected.

17. Nonclassroom data and artifact data conferences should be held at least once each evaluation cycle.

18. Effective preparation by the supervisor should precede each conference.

19. Conferencing should be the effective teaching of self-assessment to promote self-directed learning.

20. The criteria on the Formative Data Form should be the content basis for the conference.

21. All significant issues should be clarified during formative conferences.

22. Professional Development Plans should be developed collaboratively.

23. Professional Development Plans should be developed for all staff at some time during the formative phase.

24. Professional Development Plans should be for enrichment and improvement of performance.

25. Effective links between the formative and summative phases are essential to developmental evaluation.

26. Expected, not comparative, performance should be rated on the Summative Evaluation Report.

27. A Professional Development Plan should be in place before giving a "does not meet expectations" rating on the summative report.

28. Summative reports should be used as infrequently as possible.

29. Review and appeal procedures should be a basic part of the evaluation process.

30. A recommendation about employment should be made on the summative report.

31. Developmental evaluation should not be used to meet the needs of incentive programs.

Although there are many subtleties associated with each recommendation, this basic listing is a starting point for reviewing an existing evaluation system or developing a new system.

PBDE IN PERSPECTIVE

An evaluation system should be designed to accomplish specific purposes. The primary purpose for the performance-based developmental evaluation approach discussed throughout this book is improved teacher performance, particularly that performance which most directly affects students. The secondary purpose, and a spin-off from the primary purpose, is employment decision making. In the development and implementation of the system, these purposes must be understood by all personnel and policymakers in the school system. The schema presented in Figure 13.1 depicts the major phases and the specific procedural components of performance-based developmental evaluation.

The developmental phase is the creation of the evaluation system. It is contingent on the purposes of the evaluation system, a commitment from the leadership of the district, and a feeling of need among employees for a change in the evaluation process. The committee responsible for developing the system should be knowledgeable about effective teaching, schooling, and evaluation. After developing a proposed system, they should systematically explain their proposed system to all staff and seek their input. Following input, a proposed system should be recommended to the board of education for approval. The committee members should also plan, and play a major role in presenting, inservice to all staff for the new evaluation system.

The preparatory phase is designed to develop knowledge and skill among all staff in the evaluation system. During the inservice, the teachers and principals should develop a clearer understanding of the evaluative procedures and the skills associated with the criteria. The principals must also develop the skills to implement the formative and summative phases effectively.

The formative phase includes the collection and documentation of

FIGURE 13.1 Performance-based developmental evaluation phases.

DEVELOPMENTAL PHASE		PREPARATORY PHASE	
Commitment by school district leadership to developmental evaluation.	Committee reviews models and literature; develops and recommends system to board. Plans inservice.	Inservice principals in content and process.	Inservice teachers in content and process.

FORMATIVE PHASE

Data Collection of Planned and Unplanned Data. --Observed --Non-observed --Artifacts	Document data using Formative Data Form.	Conference from specific data on Formative Data Form.	Professional Development Plan collaboratively developed with all teachers during cycle.

SUMMATIVE PHASE

Analysis of Planned and Unplanned Data. Review of PDP's developed.	Summative Report prepared from data analysis. Criteria rated. Employment decision made.	Summative Conference conducted from Report.

planned and unplanned data and the conferencing about the data. Professional Development Plans are written for all staff at some time during the formative phase, with clear delineation of whether the plan is for enrichment or improvement.

The summative phase is a synthesis of all data about the teacher's performance so a judgment can be made about performance for each criterion. Any criterion on which a teacher receives a rating of "does not meet expectations" must be preceded by a Professional Development Plan to improve the deficiency. A recommendation about employment is also provided by the principal.

AN EVOLVING REALITY

Imagine a school district in which the teacher evaluation system has a direct impact on instructional improvement, and thus on the quality of schooling each student receives. Imagine a school district in which the teacher association supports the evaluation system because it represents a fair and professional approach to personnel improvement. Imagine a school in which the teachers and principal interact frequently, and without anxiety, about teaching and learning. Imagine a school in which most teachers believe that the principal can help them become what they are capable of becoming as professionals.

The principles and practices discussed and recommended throughout this book are not a panacea for transforming a typical school or school district into the ultimate educational organization. However, they can promote accomplishment of the types of outcomes described in the previous paragraph. For years, school districts have implemented, to some degree, each of the principles and practices described in this book. But seldom was the process woven together in an effective manner. Too many pieces of the mosaic were omitted. Too little thought was given to the interrelatedness of procedures, administrative skills, and organizational culture and climate. Too frequently an evaluation system was implemented by edict, without involvement of the appropriate persons in the development and nurturance of the system. Too often teachers and administrators lacked sufficient knowledge, understanding, and skill to implement the system effectively. Too many times evaluation systems sacrificed the goal of personnel development for the goal of personnel decision making. Too many times evaluation systems promoted feelings of mistrust. The response to these evaluative maladies has too often been to ignore the problems and "plow right on" or to back off and simply go through the motions. Either response falls short of having a positive impact on the educational program in the school district.

In *Walden,* Thoreau wrote, "I have learned this at least by experiment: that if one advances confidently in the direction of his dreams, and endeavors to live the life which he has imagined, he will meet with a success unexpected in common hours." Good administrators dream of implementing an evaluation system that is meaningful to teacher and administrator alike—one that really does make a difference in the educational program of the school and the district. The art and science of evaluation have advanced sufficiently to enable these dreams to become a reality. Performance-based developmental teacher evaluation is a starting point. It is not the definitive answer, but an evolving response based on experiences and data from schools and school districts where administrators and teachers believe performance-based developmental evaluation principles and practices are making a difference.

A National Survey of State Teacher Evaluation Policies

SURVEY DESIGN AND EXPLANATORY NOTES

A SURVEY OF teacher evaluation policies and practices was mailed on November 27, 1989, to the chief state school officer of the department of education in each of the fifty states. The results of this survey appear in tabular form on pages 294–297.

Survey Design

The chief state school officer was asked to delegate the responsibility of responding to the survey to the person on the state department of education staff who was most knowledgeable about the state's teacher evaluation policies and practices. The initial letter generated responses from approximately 60 percent of the states. A follow-up letter and survey were mailed to the nonrespondents in early January 1990. By early February, all but three states had responded. The state department of education in each of the three nonresponding states was telephoned in early February. The study was explained, and an appropriate member of the state department staff was asked to respond to the survey questions. The responses from the fifty states were then compiled as a table, and a copy of the table was mailed to each respondent in early March 1990. The respondents were asked to review the items for their state and notify the researcher immediately if there was an error. The responses were thus validated as accurate by personnel from each state department of education as of mid-April 1990.

National Survey of State Teacher Evaluation Policies

	AL	AK	AZ	AR	CA	CO	CT	DE	FL	GA	HI	ID	IL
1. Does the state have:													
(a) legislation requiring evaluation?			X	X	X	X	X		X	X	X		X
(b) state department of education policy requiring evaluation?	X	X		X			X	X	X	X	X	·	X
(c) litigation which has mandated evaluation?											X		
2. If evaluation is required, are specific evaluative procedures or forms (R)equired or (S)uggested?	R		S	R		R	R	R	R	R	R		R
Which of the following are descriptive of the state's required or suggested evaluation process?													
3. Criteria which define effective teaching are included in the process.	X		X	X	X	X	X	X	X	X			X
4. Descriptors which help define the criteria are included in the process.	X			X		X	X	X	X	X			X
5. Scheduled classroom observations must be made by the supervisor. (#/yr for P/T)*	X		2/1 1/1	2/1 1/1	X	X	3/1 1/3				X		1/2
6. Unscheduled classroom observations must be made by the supervisor. (#/yr for P/T)*	X			1/1 1/1	X		3/1		3/1	X			
7. Supervisors take notes during classroom observations.	X		X	X		X	X	X		X			
8. Supervisors transfer classroom observation notes to a formative form.	X		X	X		X	X		X	X			X
9. Conferences between the teacher and supervisor must follow each observation.	X		X	X	X		X	X		X			
10. Copies of notes/forms must be given to the teacher after each conference.	X		X	X			X	X	X	X			X
11. Non-observed data (information shared with supervisor by others) may be used.	X			X	X			X	X	X			
12. Artifact data such as lesson plans and correspondence are (R)equired or (M)ay be used.	M		M	M	M		M	M		M			M
13. Professional development plans are required of (A)ll teachers or only those with (D)eficiencies.	A		D	A	D	A	D	D	D	A			D
14. Observation data for non-classroom duties are (R)equired or (M)ay be used.	M		M	R	M	M	R	M	R	M			
15. Professional development plans must be written before "below expectation" rating on summative.	X		X	X			X			X			
16. Summative evaluation reports are required in the evaluation process. (#/yr for P/T)*			2/1 1/1	1/1 1/1	1/1	1/1 1/3	1/1	1/1 1/2	1/1	1/1		1/2	1/2

*When provided, information distinguishes between (P)robationary/nontenure and (T)enure/career status, with P listed above T, e.g., 3/1 over 1/1 for Item 5 means three scheduled observations per year for a Probationary teacher and one scheduled observation per year for a Tenured teacher.

Teacher Evaluation Survey, Page 2

	IN	IA	KS	KY	LA	ME	MD	MA	MI	MN	MS	MO	MT
1. Does the state have:													
(a) legislation requiring evaluation?	X	X	X	X	X			X			X	X	
(b) state department of education policy requiring evaluation?	X		X	X				X			X	X	
(c) litigation which has mandated evaluation?											X		
2. If evaluation is required, are specific evaluative procedures or forms (R)equired or (S)uggested?			S	R	R						R	S	
Which of the following are descriptive of the state's required or suggested evaluation process?													
3. Criteria which define effective teaching are included in the process.				X	X						X	X	
4. Descriptors which help define the criteria are included in the process.			X	X	X						X	X	
5. Scheduled classroom observations must be made by the supervisor. (#/yr for P/T)*			2/1 2/1	X	X						2/1	X	
6. Unscheduled classroom observations must be made by the supervisor. (#/yr for P/T)*				X								X	
7. Supervisor takes notes during classroom observations.				X	X						X	X	
8. Supervisors transfer classroom observation notes to a formative form.				X	X						X	X	
9. Conferences between the teacher and supervisor must follow each observation.			X	X	X						X	X	
10. Copies of notes/forms must be given to the teacher after each conference.			X	X	X						X	X	
11. Non-observed data (information shared with supervisor by others) may be used.				X							X	X	
12. Artifact data such as lesson plans and correspondence are (R)equired or (M)ay be used.			M	M	R						R	M	
13. Professional development plans are required of (A)ll teachers or only those with (D)eficiencies.				A	D							D	
14. Observation data for non-classroom duties are (R)equired or (M)ay be used.				M							M	M	
15. Professional development plans must be written before "below expectation" rating on summative.				X	X							X	
16. Summative evaluation reports are required in the evaluation process. (#/yr for P/T)*				1/1 1/3	1/1						1/1	1/1 1/3	

*When provided, information distinguishes between (P)robationary/nontenure and (T)enure/career status, with P listed above T, e.g., 3/1 over 1/1 for Item 5 means three scheduled observations per year for a Probationary teacher and one scheduled observation per year for a Tenured teacher.

Teacher Evaluation Survey, Page 3

	NB	NV	NH	NJ	NM	NY	NC	ND	OH	OK	OR	PA	RI
1. Does the state have:													
(a) legislation requiring evaluation?	X	X		X			X	X		X	X	X	
(b) state department of education policy requiring evaluation?	X			X	X			X		X	X	X	
(c) litigation which has mandated evaluation?				X								X	
2. If evaluation is required, are specific evaluative procedures or forms (R)equired or (S)uggested?	R	S		R	R		R			S	R	R	
Which of the following are descriptive of the state's required or suggested evaluation process?													
3. Criteria which define effective teaching are included in the process.	X			X	X		X			X	X	X	
4. Descriptors which help define the criteria are included in the process.				X			X			X		X	
5. Scheduled classroom observations must be made by the supervisor. (#/yr for P/T)*				3/1 1/1	X		3/1			2/1 1/1	2/1 1/2	2/1 1/1	
6. Unscheduled classroom observations must be made by the supervisor. (#/yr for P/T)*					X							X	
7. Supervisor takes notes during classroom observations.				X			X			X		X	
8. Supervisors transfer classroom observation notes to a formative form.	X			X			X			X		X	
9. Conferences between the teacher and supervisor must follow each observation.	X			X	X		X			X	X		
10. Copies of notes/forms must be given to the teacher after each conference.	X			X			X				X	X	
11. Non-observed data (information shared with supervisor by others) may be used.				X			X						
12. Artifact data such as lesson plans and correspondence are (R)equired or (M)ay be used.	M			M			M			M	M	M	
13. Professional development plans are required of (A)ll teachers or only those with (D)eficiencies.	D				A	A	A			D	D	A	
14. Observation data for non-classroom duties are (R)equired or (M)ay be used.					M		M			M	M	M	
15. Professional development plans must be written before "below expectation" rating on summative.				X						X			
16. Summative evaluation reports are required in the evaluation process. (#/yr for P/T)*	X	4/1 1/1		1/1 1/1	1/1		1/1 1/2			2/1 1/1	1/1 1/2	2/1 1/1	

*When provided, information distinguishes between (P)robationary/nontenure and (T)enure/career status, with P listed above T, e.g., 3/1 over 1/1 for Item 5 means three scheduled observations per year for a Probationary teacher and one scheduled observation per year for a Tenured teacher.

Teacher Evaluation Survey, Page 4	NC	ND	TN	TX	UT	VT	VA	WA	WV	WI	WY	%	%
1. Does the state have:													
(a) legislation requiring evaluation?	X	X	X	X	X		X	X		X	X		68
(b) state department of education policy requiring evaluation?	X	X	X	X			X	X	X	X			60
(c) litigation which has mandated evaluation?			X										10
2. If evaluation is required, are specific evaluative procedures or forms (R)equired or (S)uggested?	R	R	R	R	S		S	R	R			R48 S10	5R 810
Which of the following are descriptive of the state's required or suggested evaluation process?													
3. Criteria which define effective teaching are included in the process.	X	X	X	X	X		X	X	X				58
4. Descriptors which help define the criteria are included in the process.	X		X	X	X		X	X	X				48
5. Scheduled classroom observations must be made by the supervisor. (#/yr for P/T)*	3/1 2/3a	2/1 1/1	X	X	6/1 2/1		X	2/1	X				54
6. Unscheduled classroom observations must be made by the supervisor. (#/yr for P/T)*	2/3a		X										24
7. Supervisors take notes during classroom observations.	X		X	X			X						38
8. Supervisors transfer classroom observation notes to a formative form.			X	X			X						40
9. Conferences between the teacher and supervisor must follow each observation.	X		X	X				X					44
10. Copies of notes/forms must be given to the teacher after each conference.		X	X	X	X			X					46
11. Non-observed data (information shared with supervisor by others) may be used.			X	X					X				28
12. Artifact data such as lesson plans and correspondence are (R)equired or (M)ay be used.	R	M	M	R	R							R10 M38	48
13. Professional development plans are required of (A)ll teachers or only those with (D)eficiencies.		D	A	D			A		D			A22 D28	50
14. Observation data for non-classroom duties are (R)equired or (M)ay be used.	M	M		R					M			R08 M34	42
15. Professional development plans must be written before "below expectation" rating on summative.									X				22
16. Summative evaluation reports are required in the evaluation process. (#/yr for P/T)*	1/1 1/3		1/1 2/5	X	X		1/2	1/1	1/1				58

Information provided by state department of education personnel, 1990. *When provided, information distinguishes between (P)robationary/nontenure and (T)enure/career status, with P listed above T, e.g., 3/1 over 1/1 for Item 5 means three scheduled observations per year for a Probationary teacher and one scheduled observation per year for a Tenured teacher. Jerry W. Valentine, 218 Hill Hall, University of Missouri-Columbia. a: May be scheduled or unscheduled in South Carolina.

Explanatory Notes

1. When provided, information distinguished between policies and practices for probationary/nontenured teachers and tenured/career status teachers. Policies for probationary teachers were listed above those for tenured teachers when the information differed. For example, the response for Arkansas to item 5, scheduled classroom observations, distinguished the difference between observations for probationary teachers (twice a year) and for tenured teachers (once a year).

2. When provided, information clarified the number and frequency of observations or evaluations required or suggested. For example, the response for Delaware to item 5, scheduled classroom observations, indicated that three scheduled observations were made each year for probationary teachers and one scheduled observation was completed every three years for tenured teachers.

3. Information was marked only if it applied. Thus, no marking in a state's column means that the state did not report legislation, state department policy, or litigation requiring teacher evaluation. If a state required that teacher evaluation be conducted, the state was asked (item 2) to indicate whether a specific process or specific forms were "required" or "suggested." Some states (e.g., Alabama) required evaluation and also required specific practices; some (e.g., Arizona) required evaluation but only suggested specific practices; and some states (e.g., Alaska) required evaluation but neither required nor suggested specific evaluative practices.

4. The percentages of responses for each item were listed in the last two columns. The last column reported total percentages for all states for the general question asked. The second-to-last column divided that percentage for questions 2, 12, 13, and 14. For example, the data for item 13 indicated that 50 percent of the states require professional development plans. Of the 50 percent, 22 percent require them for all teachers and 28 percent require them only for teachers with performance deficiencies.

5. Historically, information shared by others has not been a requirement of evaluation procedures. Therefore, item 11 was worded to determine only if nonobserved, secondhand data "may" be used.

6. Because artifact data (item 12) and nonclassroom data (item 14) have become more common components of evaluation systems in recent years, respondents were asked to clarify whether artifact data and

nonclassroom data were "required" or "may be used if not required." For example, in Arizona both types of data were permitted if desired, but in Arkansas artifact data *may* be used and nonclassroom data *must* be used.

These data are based on responses from state department of education personnel assigned the responsibility of responding to the data collection survey. They are accurate only to the degree to which the respondent's answers were correctly reflective of the policies for each state.

APPENDIX B

Postobservation Conferencing Skills

THE FOLLOWING ITEMS are descriptive of behaviors associated with effective postobservation conferencing. They are grouped as seven distinct skill areas. The items were identified by Deborah Pulliam and Jerry Valentine in 1988 from a review of the literature and research of conferencing behavior. For a review of the literature and for instrumentation that can be used to assess postobservation skill, see Deborah Pulliam, "Assessment of Principal Conference Skills," doctoral dissertation, University of Missouri, copyright © 1988. The Pulliam instrument is entitled *Assessment of Postobservation Conferencing Skills* and was developed from research using the conferencing skills listed below.

AREA I: PREPARATION

Before the conference begins, the principal:

1. Collects accurate, thorough, and objective observational data during the classroom observation.

2. Schedules the conference within 48 hours after the observation.

3. Develops a plan of action that includes a mental organization of the events of the conference.

300

4. Labels or categorizes varied teaching behaviors on the observational notes.

5. Transfers examples of specific teaching behaviors from the classroom observation notes to a Formative Data Form.

6. Develops a plan of action that includes identifying from the classroom observation notes specific areas of focus (including areas of strength and/or areas for improvement).

7. Schedules ample time for the conference.

8. Ensures a private setting for the conference.

9. Does not permit routine matters to interrupt the conference.

10. Arranges the seating so the teacher and principal are seated at the corner of a table or desk with the observation notes between them.

11. Encourages the teacher to bring to the conference his or her own assessment of strengths and areas for growth.

12. Assesses the teacher's receptivity (attitude and mental readiness) to improvement.

AREA II: ESTABLISHING SET

At the beginning of the conference, the principal:

13. Clarifies the purpose of the conference.

14. Reviews the procedures to be followed during the conference.

15. Reviews the responsibilities of both participants.

16. Places the conference in perspective with previous instructional improvement activities.

17. Places the conference in perspective with future instructional improvement activities.

18. States the objectives of the conference.

19. Encourages the teacher to take an active role in the conference.

AREA III: DIAGNOSIS

During the conference, the principal

20. Works collegially with the teacher to solve instructional problems.

21. Encourages the teacher to diagnose his or her teaching skill.

22. Assists the teacher in identifying successful strategies from the lesson.

23. Assists the teacher in the identification of less effective teaching behaviors.

24. Maintains focus on specific observation data.

25. Discusses each of the expectations (criteria) of teacher skill, as typically listed on a Formative Data Form.

26. Encourages the teacher to analyze the effectiveness of the lesson.

27. Promotes self-assessment by engaging the teacher in a dialogue about the effectiveness of the lesson.

28. References previous discussions or observations when appropriate to the current conference.

29. Encourages the teacher to analyze the interactions and behaviors from the classroom data.

30. Promotes teacher self-assessment of the lesson.

31. Focuses conference feedback on actual teacher performance as represented by items on the Formative Data Form.

32. Analyzes the lesson and gives specific feedback to the teacher when appropriate.

33. Promotes self-analysis through various questioning strategies.

34. Asks questions that cause the teacher to utilize higher-order thinking skills such as evaluation and synthesis to formulate answers (i.e., questions by the principal are not primarily on the knowledge or recall level).

35. Asks affective questions so the teacher can describe how he or she feels about the lesson and the conference.

36. Asks questions that move the teacher from assessing the over-all effectiveness of the lesson to assessing specific behaviors used during the lesson.

37. Asks questions that provide direction for the conference and future classroom observations.

AREA IV: FOCUS FOR GROWTH

During the conference, the principal:

38. Focuses discussion on the patterns of behavior exhibited during the lesson.

39. Focuses discussion on the strengths in the teacher's performance.

40. Focuses discussion on areas for improvement in the teacher's performance.

41. Works with the teacher in identifying alternative behaviors for improving teaching performance.

42. Offers suggestions for improving less effective teaching behaviors.

43. Provides resources to support desired teaching behavior.

44. Assists the teacher in setting realistic goals for improvement in teaching performance.

45. Considers the teacher's needs in developing a strategy for improvement.

46. Gives importance to areas of concern identified by the teacher.

AREA V: COMMITMENT TO GROWTH

During the conference, the principal:

47. Ensures that the teacher understands the importance of improvement.

48. Ensures that the teacher understands the skills in need of improvement.

49. Involves the teacher in the identification and development of a growth plan for improvement.

50. Solicits a commitment from the teacher to implement desired change as identified in the conference.

AREA VI: CLOSURE

Near the end of the conference, the principal:

51. Ensures that the most important issues of the conference are summarized.

52. Reinforces with the teacher the specific areas for growth as formulated during the conference.

53. Identifies a time to meet again if a specific growth plan is to be developed at a later date.

54. Checks for agreement and understanding of the issues and direction for growth.

55. Attempts to end the conference on a positive, but realistic, note.

56. Explains that all issues for improvement will be addressed in an appropriate time frame, but begins with a focus on one or two issues.

57. Asks the teacher to evaluate the conference when such an evaluation can be done objectively and can be useful in improving conferencing strategies.

AREA VII: INTERPERSONAL COMMUNICATION

During the conference, the principal:

58. Seeks to understand what the teacher is trying to communicate in the conference.

59. Behaves in a manner that builds the teacher's confidence and encourages trust.

60. Is receptive and willing to listen to the teacher's thoughts.

61. Deals constructively with conflict that might occur in the conference.

62. Demonstrates effective active listening skills (e.g., eye contact, positive facial expressions).

63. Probes effectively and appropriately for more information and insight.

64. Gives the teacher his or her undivided attention during the conference.

65. Demonstrates a genuine interest in the teacher.

Index